# STAGING *TIANXIA*

# STAGING *TIANXIA*

## *Dunhuang Expressive Arts and China's New Cosmopolitan Heritage*

Lanlan Kuang

INDIANA UNIVERSITY PRESS

This book is a publication of

Indiana University Press
Office of Scholarly Publishing
Herman B Wells Library 350
1320 East 10th Street
Bloomington, Indiana 47405 USA

iupress.org



First Printing 2024

Cataloging information is available from the Library of Congress.

ISBN 978-0-253-07089-0 (hardcover)
ISBN 978-0-253-07090-6 (paperback)
ISBN 978-0-253-07091-3 (e-book)

# CONTENTS

# ACKNOWLEDGMENTS

As a Chinese saying goes, "No words can express my gratitude" (大恩不言谢). I could write another two hundred pages to express my gratitude to those who have been mentoring me over the years, but I have decided to do it with simple words.

This monograph is based on my ongoing ethnomusicological research on the Dunhuang arts, performative memories, and aesthetics in general. It would not have been possible in anything remotely like the present form without my family, my mentors, and various sponsoring agencies and institutions. They have my deepest gratitude.

Research conducted for this monograph has been sponsored by (in chronological order) Indiana University Bloomington; China Arts Academy; Dunhuang Academy; the United States Fulbright Program; the International Institute for Education; Lanzhou University; Northwest Minzu University; Gansu Provincial Radio, Television, and Film Service (now GanSu Media Group); the China Television Artists Association Tourism Television Committee; Shanghai Jiaotong University; and my current home institute, the University of Central Florida.

I am fortunate to have continuous guidance from Professors (in alphabetical order) Jason Jackson, Roger Janelli, Jacob Wainwright Love, Portia Maultsby, Ruth Stone, and Sue Tuohy. These scholars have been mentoring me since I became a graduate student in the Folklore and Ethnomusicology Department at Indiana University Bloomington. They are giants who inspire students to do great things, yet they remain humble and generous.

I thank Professor Dong Xijiu 董锡玖 and Professor Gao Jinrong 高金荣 for their trust and teaching of the *Dunhuang bihua yuewu*. They are not just living treasures of China but also close family friends. I am honored to be entrusted with their lifelong learning and wisdom. Director Emeritus Fan Jinshi 樊锦诗 of the Dunhuang Academy granted me the invaluable opportunity to stay on-site at the academy and examine the restricted Mogao Grottoes. I thank Dunhuang Academy's past directors Wang Xudong 王旭東 and Zhao Shengliang 趙聲良, past vice director Zhang Xiantang 張先堂, current director Su Boming 蘇伯民, and vice director Zhang Yuanlin 張元林 for their continuous support of my on-site research. Sun Zhijun 孫志軍, senior researcher and vice director of Dunhuang Academy's Arts Department and committee member of the China Society of Cultural Relics Studies, has granted me a great amount of guidance and provided photographic images for this book. My fieldwork would not have been possible without support from Professor Zheng Binlin 郑炳林, director of the Institute of Dunhuang Studies of Lanzhou University; Professor Li Qi 李琦, dean of the Dance College of Northwest Minzu University; Professor Jin Liang 金亮 at Lanzhou University of Arts and Sciences; Professor Kong Peipei 孔培培, vice director of the Drama Institute of China Arts Academy; Professors Li Song 李松, Zhang Gang 张刚, and Wang Jing 王靜, directors of China's Center for Ethnic and Folk Literature and Art Development, Ministry of Culture and Tourism; Professor An Deming 安德明, senior research fellow and director of the Institute of Literature, Chinese Academy of Social Sciences; Professor Yang Lihui 楊利慧 at Beijing Normal University; Professor Piao Yongguang 朴永光 at China Central Minzu University; Professor Wang Ning 王寧, dean of Shanghai Jiaotong University; Professor Xie Bailiang 謝柏梁 at the National Academy of Chinese Theatre Arts; Yang Qian 楊乾, director of China Central Television Station; Professor Ma De 馬德 at Dunhuang Academy; Professor Zhang Duo 張多 at Yunnan University; Professor Liu Jian 劉建 at Beijing Dance Academy; and Researcher Zheng Yinan 鄭怡楠 at the Palace Museum.

Bai Chao 白超, Fan Xuesong 樊雪崧, Fu Hualin 付華林, Geng Dewen 耿德文, He Yanyun 贺燕云, Hu Haixu 胡海旭, Li Feng 李峰, Liu Cuiying 劉萃瑛, Na Gang 那剛, Qi Xiaoqing 祁曉慶, Shi Min 史敏, Song Yanpeng 宋焰朋, Wang Cun 王存, Wang Qiong 王瓊, Wei Yingchun 魏迎春, Wu Jiongjiong 吳炯炯, Yang Jing 楊靜, Yang Liwei 楊利偉, and Zhang Gang 張剛 (in alphabetical order) were generous in their support. For my documentary on the Dunhuang arts, I thank all the administrators, producers, directors, and editors who worked with me at the Gansu Provincial Radio, Television, and Film Service 甘肅省廣播電影電視總台集團 and the China Television Artists Association Tourism Television Committee 中國電視藝術家協會旅遊電視委員會.

I thank Dr. Stephen Bokenkamp 柏夷, now at Arizona State University, for encouraging my first attempt to write academically on Chinese music using historical references; Dr. Susan Nelson for introducing me to Dr. Wu Hung's scholarly writings on the Dunhuang arts; and Dr. Robert Eno at Indiana University's Department of East Asian Languages and Cultures for his support of the CIC-FLEP Fellowship that I received. I thank Dr. Gerson Yessin at the University of North Florida for years of mentoring with extraordinary music and character; Professor Arthur Bloomer for harpsichord lessons and Christmas parties; Dr. William Slaughter for Foucault and existentialism (I still have the William Barrett book you gave me); and Dr. Mark Workman for Faust, Proust, and folklore. I thank Janet Upton at the Fulbright-IIE Beijing office, Nathan Keltner at the Fulbright Hong Kong office, and Jonathan Akeley at the Fulbright-IIE New York office for their assistance. I also thank my colleagues at the University of Central Florida: Dean and Professor Emeritus José Fernández, Dean Jeff Moore, Dr. Rudy McDaniel, Dr. Bruce Janz, Dr. Geri Smith, Dr. Michael Strawser, Dr. Nancy Stanlick, Dr. Stella Sung, Dr. Consuelo Stebbins, Dr. Cyrus Zargar, and Director Mark Hartman at UCF Global. I thank Christy Lynn, Heather Gibson, and Matthew Dunn for their great friendship. Dr. Peggy Bulger, Dr. Chen Huaiyu 陳懷宇, Dr. Hilary V. Finchum-Sung, Dr. Annette B. Fromm, Dr. Jessica Anderson Turner, Dr. Zhang Wenxian 張文獻, and Dr. Emily Wilcox have my gratitude for their support of my academic career.

I thank my uncles for assisting me with international travel: Uncle Jiansheng 見生舅舅 for hosting me during my visits; Uncle Jianliang 見亮舅舅 for caring for me during my illness; Uncle Xiaocong 小聰舅舅 for engaging in enlightening discussions on traditional Chinese painting; and Uncle Xiaoming 小明舅舅 on Taiji. I thank my cousin Fei 菲 for creating the maps used in this monograph.

In addition to the individuals and institutions listed above, I am indebted to many others who have helped me in countless ways. I wish to convey my sincere gratitude to Indiana University Press for their exemplary professionalism, meticulous feedback, and invaluable guidance throughout this project. The editorial team at IUP has demonstrated outstanding dedication, providing comprehensive directions and insightful recommendations of the highest caliber. Their expertise has been instrumental in elevating the quality of this scholarly work. Confucius said: "In a group of three people, I can always find someone to teach me" (子曰: "三人行, 必有我師焉"). I consider all the aforementioned and countless others my teachers, in one way or another, and thank them for their kindness.

Everything I have learned and shared began with my parents and my family. My late father, Kuang Jianren 鄺健人, was a famous playwright and newspaper founder who gave me a Chinese copy of Italo Calvino's *Italian Folktales* as a birthday gift and took me to film-production sites and business meetings. My love for the arts and cultures was instilled in me during long and memorable family vacations around the country, first in China and then in the United States, after we moved to New York in the late 1980s. My mother, Yang Xiaoyuan 楊小苑, a Chinese-language teacher, single-handedly brought up my brother and me after Dad passed away, in 2013. In the early 1980s, she took me to weekly piano lessons while pursuing a graduate degree in Chinese literature. My decision to be an educator was inspired mostly by her. Jameson Ye Kuang 鄺野 shares with me the love and caring received from my parents. He has grown up to be an exceptional med-ped physician loved by his colleagues and patients, a brother who would take care of the family in every way he could. Still learning to be a sister—an important lesson to learn after being the only child for fourteen years—I am extremely fortunate always to have the trust and support of my family. They have my deepest love and gratitude.

# NOTES ON TRANSLATIONS, PRONUNCIATIONS, AND STYLE RULES

Readers unfamiliar with Chinese written characters may refer to this style overview when encountering unfamiliar key words and translations. The written scripts in this book are traditional Chinese characters for analyzing classical poems, scores, and calligraphy. Most Chinese characters are morphemes. Only a few characters cannot be used as a word independently. To simplify exposition, I use the terms *words, characters,* and *lexical entries* interchangeably. Translated key words are often clusters of words without tenses, punctuation, or even syntactical order and should be understood in correlation with the words around them. For instance, the name of the expressive art genre *Dunhuang bihua yuewu* 敦煌壁畫樂舞 is a combination of three words: *Dunhuang* 敦煌, *murals* 壁畫, and [the expressive art genre consisting of] *music and dance* 樂舞. The name of the staged Dunhuang arts is also a combination of three words: *Dunhuang* 敦煌, *staged/expressive* 表演, and *the arts* 藝術. Each of these words consists of two characters—compound ideograms that individually can yield several different meanings. For this reason, anaphora and acronyms are often employed throughout the book.

The forms of romanization in this book follow the standard usage of the pinyin system, especially for the translated field notes and interviews. The now increasingly obsolete Wade-Giles system of romanization appears only in citations when I follow the usage of the authors. For instance, *Dunhuang* is used throughout the book instead of *Tun-huang,* which appears in some citations and references.

Chinese texts that were written before 1949 are mostly cited and listed by title rather than by author. In some cases, a scroll number is also given, followed by a page number. Links to original texts from online electronic sources, such as the Chinese Text Project (http://ctext.org), the online open-access digital library compiled and edited by Donald Sturgeon (2011), are provided in the endnotes when scroll and page numbers are not given.

When discussing the tangible sources of the Dunhuang expressive arts, namely the United Nations Educational, Scientific, and Cultural

Organization (UNESCO) World Heritage Site for the Dunhuang Mogao Grottoes, *cave* and *grottoes* are used disparately. *Cave* is used when referring to a specific grotto that has been categorized or named by scholars. For instance, Mogao Cave No. 17 is one of the many grottoes, and it is known as the Dunhuang Library Cave. *Grottoes* is used to denote an entire cave complex or the ground of an archaeological site. For instance, the Mogao Grottoes, the Yulin Grottoes, and the Western Thousand-Buddha Grottoes are three cave complexes located in the city of Dunhuang.

Of several proposed categorizing systems for the Dunhuang grottoes, the best known are the one devised by French Sinologist Paul Pelliot (1878–1945) and the one created by Chinese painter Zhang Daqian (1899–1983). Unless otherwise specified, the cave-numbering system used in this book follows the Dunhuang Academy system, developed in 1964 from Zhang's system. For instance, Mogao Cave No. 85 and Yulin Cave No. 3 refer to two different caves labeled according to the Dunhuang Academy system. Cave numbers are used most frequently when discussing murals and sculptures.

The categorizing systems for the Dunhuang archival materials are different from those for the grottoes. This reflects the fact that Dunhuang murals, sculptures, and manuscripts were dispersed to institutions worldwide in the early 1900s. This book cites three categorizing systems: the Aurel Stein (1862–1943) system, used to categorize the collection containing S.5643, the original copy of Dunhuang dance notation, at the British Museum; the Paul Pelliot system, used to categorize the collection containing P.3808, the original copy of Dunhuang *pipa* score, at the National Library in France; and the Dunhuang Academy system, used to categorize the collection containing the *Nirvana Sutra* calligraphy copy dated to the Northern Wei dynasty (220–265).

# CAVE CHARTS

Dynasties, Periods/Phrases (of Tang Dynasty, 618–906), and Republics
Numbers of Caves from Each Period, Based on the Contents of the 492 Caves

| Dynastic Names and Dates | Dynasties, Periods/Phases, and Republics | Based on the 1996 Edition of *General Catalogue of the Contents of the Mogao Grottoes* (Number of Caves) |
| --- | --- | --- |
| Sixteen Kingdoms | 366–439 | Seven caves |
| Northern Wei | 439–534 | Ten caves in the early phase, ten caves in the later phase |
| Western Wei | 535–556 | |
| Northern Zhou | 557–580 | Fifteen caves |
| Sui | 581–618 | Seventy caves |
| Early Tang (the first years of the Tang dynasty; Emperor Taizong Li Shimin declared Heavenly Qaghan in 630; Xuanzang returns from India in 645; Tang conquers Paekche in 660 and Koguryo in 668; Empress Wu Zhao takes control of government in 664) | 618–704 | Forty-four caves |
| High Tang (the period that witnessed the high tide of the Tang imperial power; Tang dynasty restored; frontier formally divided into ten military commands; An Lushan takes command in the northeast in 742; he later rebels in 755) | 705–781 | Eighty caves |
| Middle Tang (the phase of decline of the Tang power after An Lushan rebellion ends in 763; also known as the Tubo period because Dunhuang was under Tibetan occupation) | 781–847 or 791–825 | Forty-four caves |
| Late Tang (the last phase of the Tang dynasty, during which Dunhuang returned to Chinese rule because of the military feat of a local general, Zhang Yichao; in 801, alliance with Nanzhao to defeat Tibet) | 848–907 | Sixty caves |
| Five Dynasties | 907–960 | Thirty-two caves |
| Song | 960–1036 | Forty-three caves |
| Western Xia | 1036–1227 | Eighty-two caves |

(*continued*)

| Dynastic Names and Dates | Dynasties, Periods/Phases, and Republics | Based on the 1996 Edition of *General Catalogue of the Contents of the Mogao Grottoes* (Number of Caves) |
|---|---|---|
| Yuan (Mongol) | 1227–1368 | Ten caves |
| Ming | 1368–1644 | |
| Qing | 1644–1911 | |
| Republic of China | 1912–1949 | |
| People's Republic of China | 1949– | |

Chart created by the author using the following references:
*Dunhuang Arts through the Eyes of Duan Wenjie* (Duan 1994) and *Dunhuang Mogaoku neirong zonglu* 敦煌莫高窟内容總錄 [General record of Dunhuang Mogao Grottoes contents] (Dunhuang Academy 1996)

Dynasties, Periods/Phrases (of Tang Dynasty, 618–906), and Republics
Caves Listed in the 1993 Edition *Dunhuang wudao* by Gao Jinrong
Model Caves (*dianxing dongku* 典型洞窟) for Creating *Dunhuang bihua yuewu*

| Names | Dynasties, Periods/Phases, and Republics | Based on the 1996 Edition of *General Catalogue of the Contents of the Mogao Grottoes* (Cave No.) |
|---|---|---|
| Sixteen Kingdoms | 366–439 | |
| Northern Wei | 439–534 | 248, 254 |
| Western Wei | 535–556 | 249, 285, 288 |
| Northern Zhou | 557–580 | 297, 428 |
| Sui | 581–618 | 304, 427, 420 |
| Early Tang (the first years of the Tang dynasty) | 618–704 | 205, 220, 321, 329, 331, 334, 335, 341 |
| High Tang (the period that witnessed the high tide of the Tang imperial power) | 705–781 | 23, 66, 126, 129, 148, 172, 180, 215, 217, 445 |
| Middle Tang (the phase of decline of the Tang power; also known as the Tubo period because Dunhuang was under Tibetan occupation) | 781–847 | 112, 154, 158, 197, 201, 236 |
| Late Tang (the last phase of the Tang dynasty, during which Dunhuang returned to Chinese rule because of the military feat of a local general, Zhang Yichao) | 848–907 | 12, 85, 138, 144, 156, 232 |

(*continued*)

| Names | Dynasties, Periods/Phases, and Republics | Based on the 1996 Edition of *General Catalogue of the Contents of the Mogao Grottoes* (Cave No.) |
|---|---|---|
| Five Dynasties | 907–960 | 98, 100 |
| Song | 960–1036 | 61 |
| Western Xia | 1036–1227 | |
| Yuan (Mongol) | 1227–1368 | 3, 95, 465 |
| Ming | 1368–1644 | |
| Qing | 1644–1911 | |
| Republic of China | 1912–1949 | |
| People's Republic of China | 1949– | |

Chart created by the author using the following references:
*Dunhuang wudao* 敦煌舞蹈 [Dunhuang dance] (Gao 1993), *Dunhuang Arts through the Eyes of Duan Wenjie* (Duan 1994), and *Dunhuang Mogaoku neirong zonglu* 敦煌莫高窟內容總錄 [General record of Dunhuang Mogao Grottoes contents] (Dunhuang Academy 1996)

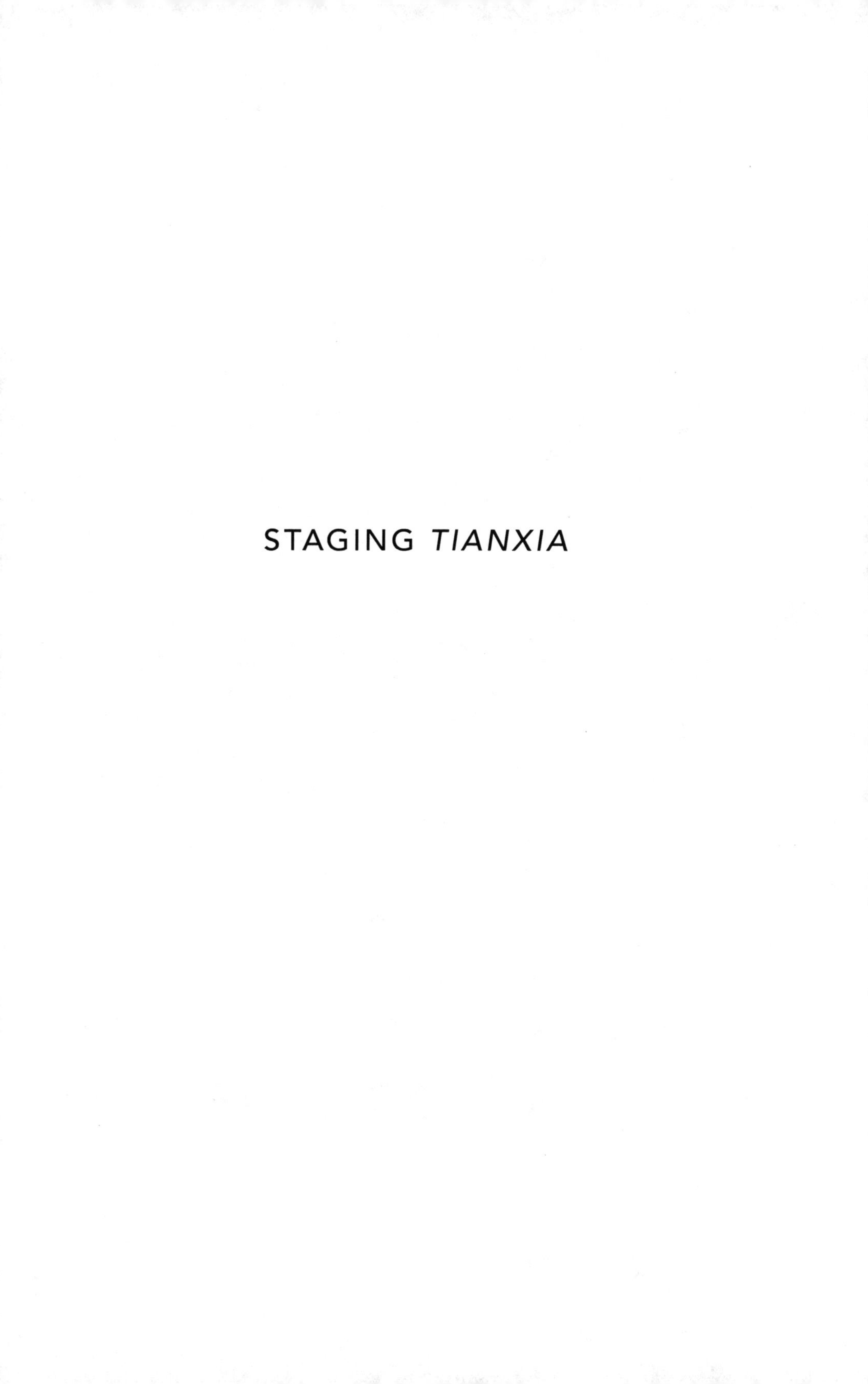

# STAGING *TIANXIA*

# 1

# INTRODUCTION

When music is perfect, there is no rancor; when rites are perfect,
there is no contention.
To bow and yield, yet govern the world (*tianxia*), is the true meaning
of rites and music.
樂至則無怨, 禮至則不爭。揖讓而治天下者, 禮樂之謂也。
*Great Preface*, the *Book of Song*
《禮記·樂記》

When Tianxia lacks the *Dao*, warhorses multiply in the suburbs.
天下无道, 戎馬生於郊。
**Chapter 46, *Laozi***
《老子》第四十六章

IT WAS A WINTER NIGHT IN NEW YORK City. Lights at the Lincoln Center for the Performing Arts were shining brightly.

The performance hall in the David H. Koch Theater was filled gradually by the howling of desert wind, creating the aural scape of a dry, desolate land far from the metropolis.

It was January 2020—120 years since the discovery of the Dunhuang Library Cave 敦煌藏經洞, one of the 735 numbered grottoes later excavated at Mogao 莫高 along the 1.6 kilometers of cliff face above the Daquan River. Located near the oasis city of Dunhuang on the edge of the Gobi Desert in northwest China, these caves are collectively known as the Dunhuang Mogao Grottoes 敦煌莫高窟.

The curtain rose.

Onto center stage, where a scenic construction of a mountain cliff and a desert landscape was dimly lighted, entered the character of Wang Yuanlu

王圆箓 (1849–1931), a Daoist priest. Dressed in a worn and dusty outfit of dark blue cotton characteristic of Daoist priests, the actor performing Wang Yuanlu began to sweep the floor. After a few moments, he discovered a hidden chamber sealed inside one of the rock sanctuaries carved into the cliff.

Signaled by a quick, crystalline, stirring wave of chimes, a melodious Chinese ocarina solo joined in slowly from the background. Astonished by the thousands of Buddhist sūtra scrolls, murals, and sculptures he had just accidentally discovered in the caves, Priest Wang set his broom aside and began to examine these treasures. Dawn had not yet arrived, and the desert sky was pitch black. Priest Wang held his oil lamp high, strode rhythmically in excitement, and finally sat cross-legged in a meditative pose. He unfolded a scroll. The sound of the ocarina became fuller and richer and the texture of the music more complex as several other instruments joined in.

This was the opening scene of *A Grand Dream of Dunhuang* (*Dameng Dunhuang*《大梦敦煌》), an award-winning dance drama staged in various places around the globe. The scene locates the audience at the Mogao Grottoes, in the rock sanctuaries that have long served as temples, sites for performative events, and archives of artifacts reflecting centuries of multicultural dialogues along the Silk Road. By employing the Chinese clay ocarina, one of the oldest Chinese instruments, excavated from caves in the Northwest and frequently used in court music and Buddhist and Confucian rituals, composer Zhang Qianyi 張千一 sonically enhanced the scenic construction, an attempt to stage the sense of place of Dunhuang.

Historically a frontier metropolis, Dunhuang is a strategic site, a crossroads of trade, and a locus for religious, cultural, and intellectual influences since the Han dynasty (206 BCE–220 CE). Artifacts excavated there and from the surrounding territories reveal an aesthetic ideal that exhibits the country's multiethnic and cosmopolitan past.

In 1987, when China was becoming one of the world's fastest-growing economies after adopting its so-called open-door policies, the Dunhuang Mogao Grottoes became one of the earliest United Nations Educational, Scientific, and Cultural Organization (UNESCO) World Heritage Sites designated in China.[1] In 2000, the discovery of the Dunhuang Library Cave inspired *A Grand Dream of Dunhuang* (*Dameng Dunhuang*《大梦敦煌》), a state-sponsored dance drama that has since being staged frequently around the globe. It tells of the journey of Mogao, a young pilgrim painter traveling from Chang'an, China's Tang dynasty capital, to an unfamiliar land in search of the arts that have inspired him. Far from his home, he ends his

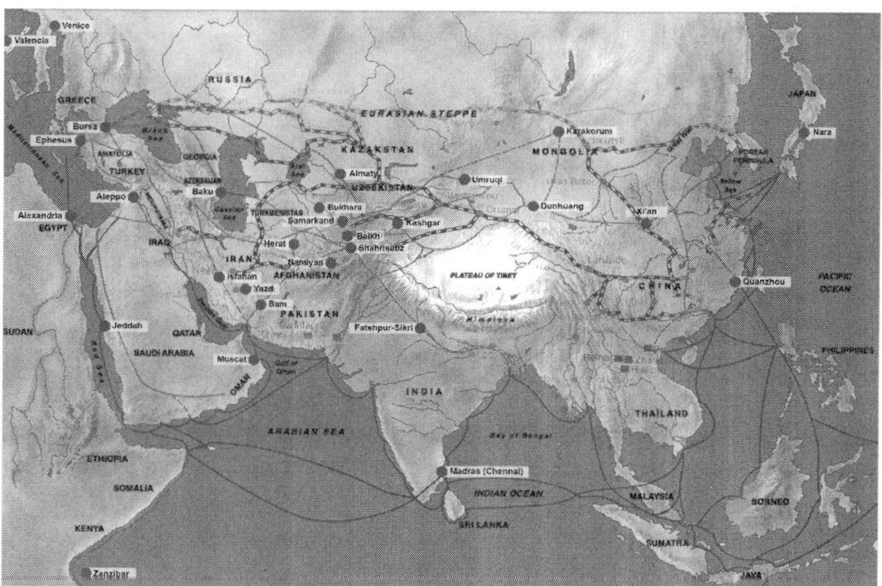



Figure 1.1. The new global infrastructure network. Fine lines show the ancient silk routes by land and sea; bold dotted lines show the railroads, ports, and pipelines built as part of China's Belt and Road Initiative. Map created with information from UNESCO and the Mercator Institute for China Studies. Artistic rendition courtesy of Fei Kwong, 2023.

journey in Dunhuang, historically considered the northwestern periphery of China, well beyond Yangguan 陽關 and Yumenguan 玉門關, the bordering passes that separate China from foreign lands. Arguably, the 2020 performance of this work at the New York City's Lincoln Center celebrated both the discovery of the Dunhuang Library Cave and the dance drama's own journey overseas as it marked its first appearance in a major North American theater.

Staged more than four hundred times since it premiered in Beijing in April 2000, *A Grand Dream of Dunhuang* is a leading example of Dunhuang expressive arts, featuring the *Dunhuang bihua yuewu* 敦煌壁畫樂舞, a rich and multifaceted genre of music and dance performances created in the twentieth century and based primarily on excavations near Dunhuang. The term *Dunhuang bihua yuewu* is a singular noun referring to an expressive art genre; it literally means "Dunhuang mural music and dance." It is also used as an adjective to describe individual programs that may be categorized within the genre. Some of the examples discussed in this book employ staging features other than music and dance inspired by the Dunhuang artifacts, such as theories and techniques for creating theatrical and film productions. In these cases I have decided to use *staged Dunhuang arts* instead of *Dunhuang bihua yuewu*. In contrast, *Dunhuang arts*, a more general term, is often used by scholars for discussing paintings, murals, and other static, nonperforming arts. I have abided by scholarly tradition and used *Dunhuang arts* when referring to such static objects. This book focuses on staging processes and the performing arts genre, however, and the term *staged Dunhuang arts* potentially highlights interaction and performativity better than *Dunhuang arts*.

The sources of the *Dunhuang bihua yuewu* genre consist mainly of images, narratives, and musical tunes depicted in the historical murals and documents discovered in the Dunhuang Mogao Grottoes. According to the creators of the genre, they tend to draw primarily from the artistic creations of the Sui (581–618 CE) and Tang (618–907 CE) dynasties. Artistic patterns established earlier, beginning in the Han dynasty, are also evident in folkloric motifs in contemporary popular narratives and vernacular literature with nonreligious themes.

In the final act of *A Grand Dream of Dunhuang*, after a steady crescendo and the entrance of full orchestral music, the stage lights brighten, revealing a scenic painting of two flying deities (*feitian* 飛天) waving long, colorful ribbons and sprinkling flowers from the heavenly realm.[2] *Feitian* in the Sinitic tradition of Buddhism are known as *apsaras* in early Gandhāran art and possibly as *Nike-apsaras* in Greco-Buddhist art.[3]

*A Grand Dream of Dunhuang* was created by China's Lanzhou Municipal Song and Dance Theatre (*Lanzhou gewu juyuan* 蘭州歌舞劇院) in 2000. It is one of the most successful staged Dunhuang arts programs ever produced. With revenue of more than thirty million renminbi (RMB),[4] it ranks as the most expensive theatrical dance drama produced in China, with a preproduction cost of six million RMB.[5] It receives financial support from the Gansu provincial government and China's Ministry of Culture for its "distinctive ethnic features" and its "aim to promote traditional Chinese culture," according to Xu Rong, an official in the Cultural Industry Department of the Ministry.[6] Labeled a dance-drama of the Chinese nation, it presents domestic and international audiences with a vision of China as a historically multifaceted and cosmopolitan nation. Its production company has been on tour in selected cities throughout China and in countries

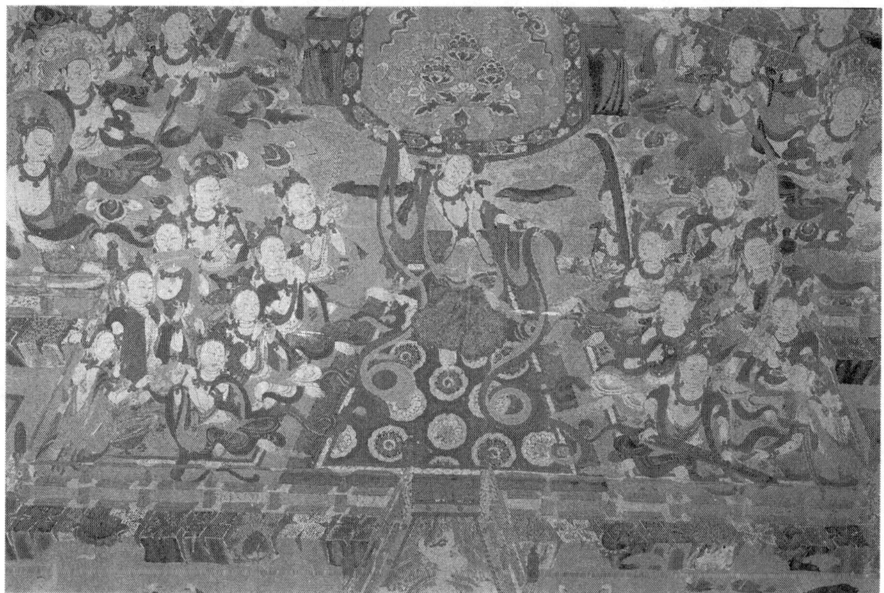

Figure 1.2. Dancer featured in Mogao Cave 85's southern-wall mural of the *Great Skillful Means Sūtra on the Buddha's Repayment of Kindness* (大方便佛報恩經). Permission to use image granted by Dunhuang Academy.

abroad, including Austria, Spain, and France; eventually, it became one of the top ten titles in China's National Stage Project.

As an expressive art form, the staged Dunhuang arts genre has been thriving since the late 1970s, long before *A Grand Dream of Dunhuang* achieved its domestic and international fame. For instance, in 2004, *The Thousand-Handed and Thousand-Eyed Avalokiteśvara* (*Qianshou qianyan Guanyin* 千手千眼觀音)—one of the most representative staged Dunhuang arts programs—was performed as part of the cultural program during the Paralympic Games in Athens, Greece. In 2008, at the Summer Olympic Games in Beijing, a group of twenty-one staged Dunhuang dancers with long ribbons were featured in the opening ceremony and artistic presentation.[7] In 2009, during an interview concerning the Ministry of Culture and Tourism's endorsement of large bank loans (of which *A Grand Dream of Dunhuang* was one of the first fifteen recipients) to support China's cultural industry, Cai Wu 蔡武, minister of culture and tourism, stated, "Efforts should be made to build competitive international cultural brands and promote the influence of Chinese culture."[8]

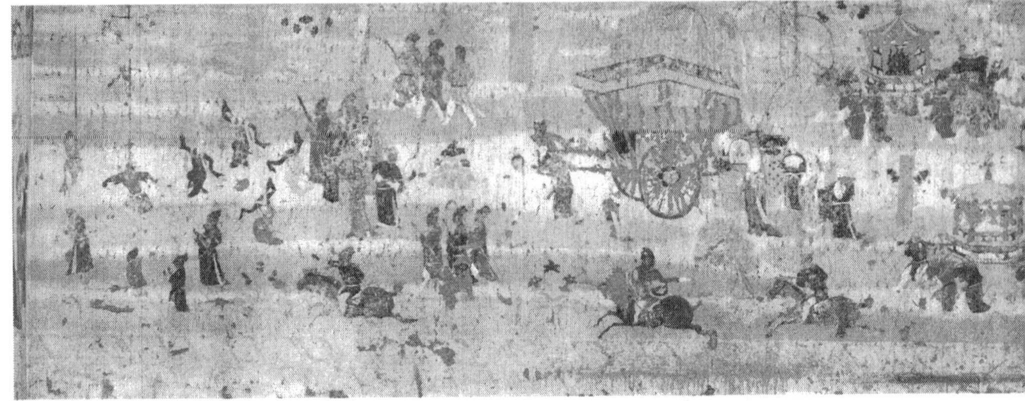

Figure 1.3. Mogao Cave 156, lower west side of northern wall, mural of the excursion of Lady Song of Henei Prefecture in the state of Song (宋國河內郡夫人宋氏出行圖). Permission to use image granted by Dunhuang Academy.

## Scope and Issues

Within the contemporary context of global interdependencies, performative arts have been used as strategic devices for social mobilization and the representation and performance of modern national histories. In highlighting the *Dunhuang bihua yuewu* genre, this book presents the first major English-language study of the staging processes of Dunhuang arts as a phenomenon performative of what I call a staged Chinascape (*Zhongguo jingguan* 中國景觀), a fluid and open conceptual landscape that emerged from the recently revived concept of *tianxia* 天下 (all under heaven), the ancient Chinese vision of world order, repurposed to become China's new cosmopolitan heritage. By "recently revived," I hint at the classical root of the *tianxia* concept, which can be traced to China's Shang and Zhou dynasties (1600–256 BCE) and which became an archaic idea in Confucian ethics and Daoist teachings. The introduction and chapter 2 introduce this ancient concept and the *tianxia* system proposed by Zhao Tingyang 赵汀阳 in 2005, reflecting his interpretation of selected classical canons and including a survey of scholarship both supporting and challenging his system. Nevertheless, while the use of *tianxia* explains certain sociocultural and political-economical phenomena in contemporary China, as in the works of Zhao Tingyang and other scholars, I have come to realize during the course of my research for this book that *tianxia*'s ancient/classic origin could be a double-edged sword. Its origin in the Chinese classics indeed implies that

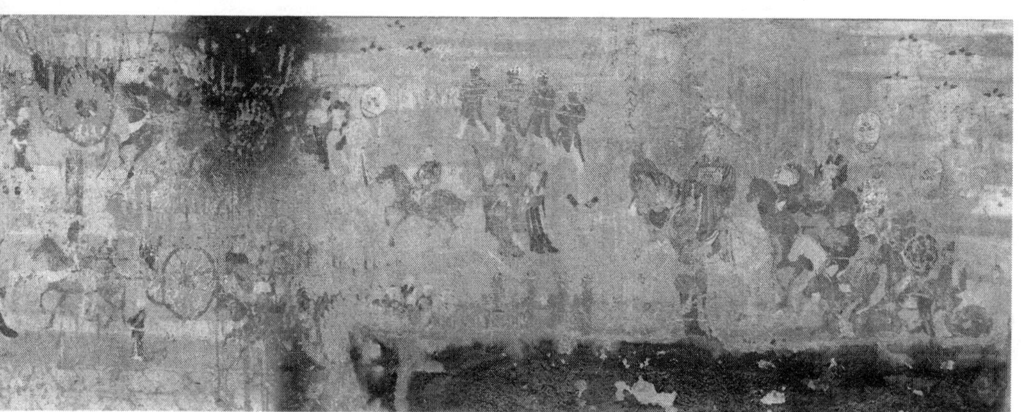

it emerged from a rich indigenous past, and I use *tianxia* in the book's title for this exact reason: to highlight the continuous effects of the ancient on the country's present. Employing the term *Chinascape* might help scholars, policymakers, and general readers understand that *tianxia* may not always be the most appropriate approach for reading modern and contemporary Chinese political philosophy and administrative styles.

Chinese scholars categorize the *Dunhuang bihua yuewu* as a genre of Chinese classical dance dating from the 1970s. Based primarily on excavations from China's northwestern frontier metropolis, it embodies the historically multifaceted cultural exchanges that occurred along the ancient Silk Road and the effects these exchanges have had on Chinese culture.

As a site of religious, cultural, and intellectual influences on the Silk Road since about 200 BCE, Dunhuang experienced frequent conflicts between Chinese sovereigns and nomadic peoples, but even as a frontier metropolis, it was imbued with the customs and institutions of central China. Artifacts excavated from its Mogao Grottoes reveal a distinctive aesthetic ideal. History, the core of the nation and one of the main conceptualizing elements in staging the *Dunhuang bihua yuewu*, was made by social actors through the interplay of languages, symbols, and movements, as dynamic relations of power(s), rather than static sets of meanings. I approach its staging as a performative process, intended by social actors to contribute to the creation of a new national heritage.

In a poetic sense, Dunhuang in the Chinese cultural imagination has long been a symbol of the frontier and of interactions with the foreign.

Approaching it as a constellation of contemporary meanings and relationships that come into existence through the activities of social actors in live performances, I reconceptualize it from a collection of static historical objects to a field of contemporary cultural production in which artists, scholars, performers, and audiences collaboratively construct and project new visions of a multicultural China into domestic and international media and performance spheres. The performative processes of creating these Chinascapes embodied in the Dunhuang expressive arts provide insights into China's changing approach to manifesting *tianxia* by restaging its cosmopolitan heritage.

The rise of hermeneutics, especially that of Martin Heidegger, Paul Ricoeur, and Julia Kristeva, and the "spatial turn" in the humanities pioneered by Henri Lefebvre and Tuan Yi-fu 段義孚 provide an alternative approach to understanding the emergence of Chinascape as a conceptual landscape suggestive of the *tianxia* notion, especially in the case of staged Dunhuang arts. Instead of viewing *tianxia* as a pragmatic system, which is contested by diplomats and political theorists instrumental in rebuilding a China-centered global order, *tianxia* unfolds in this study like a staged Chinese worldscape through the staged Dunhuang expressive arts—essentially, an aesthetic understanding of a potential being-in-this-world within Chinese hermeneutic contexts.[9] The staged Dunhuang arts are approached as a set of ideas, values, and relationships that come into existence through social actors and institutions in public performances.

## Questions and Methodologies

Musicians, choreographers, and playwrights often use historical materials in their performances to connect the past and the present (Bohlman 2002b; Herzfeld 1985; Lam 1998; Rees 2000; Shelemay 1980; Tuohy 2001; Wade 1998; Yung, Rawski, and Watson 1996). The staged Dunhuang arts are a sociocultural phenomenon that emerges through interactions and negotiations among multiple actors and institutions. Focusing on issues of power, identity, and representation through an interdisciplinary perspective that integrates artistic, political, and cultural theories, this book explores how this phenomenon is involved in recreating the historical memory and identity of China in contemporary moments of contestation and transformation.

Why was Dunhuang chosen as the basis for a new art form? It was certainly not because of the historical authenticity of the theatrical reenactment of events. As portrayed in the opening scene of *A Grand Dream of Dunhuang*, Wang Yuanlu's discovery at the Mogao Grottoes, near the end of the reign of Qing Emperor Guangxu (光緒 1875–1908), had little to do with the main plot of the dance drama, and this love story between a young and talented artist from the Central Plateau (also known as Zhongyuan 中原) and a passionate warrior-princess from the multiethnic northwestern borderland had little to do with the religious content of the scrolls discovered in the caves. Performances of *Dunhuang bihua yuewu* are not intended as the reenactment of historic events; instead, they serve as a contemporarily designed forum to stage an imaginative geography of the Chinese nation, rooted in an ancient cosmopolitan past.

Why was a contemporarily created *Dunhuang bihua yuewu* program called a theatrical dance drama of the Chinese nation and an artistic form with distinctive ethnic features? When performing in different contexts or for different audiences, what stylistic choices do musicians and choreographers make and why? What archaeological materials from the past do they choose, according to specific aesthetic principles or laws, in the process of staging? What aspects of music and dance traditions do performers, scholars, and government officials promote, in what contexts, and why? Do the cultural agents of today's China, in discourse or in practice, model themselves on the successes of artists from the Han, Sui, and Tang dynasties, when the arts were integrated into the imperial state policies for governing its ethnic populations? How do these performances and the multiple actors involved in creating and performing *Dunhuang bihua yuewu* become implicated in the performance of concepts of Chineseness and the creation of Chinascapes? Finally, how does my research affect the subject of my investigation? These are among the questions I seek to answer in this book.

## History, Archaeology, and Ethnography

This research builds first on recent theories about processes of nationalism, globalization, and the construction and representation of identities (Appadurai 2003; Jameson 1998; Karp et al. 2006). By combining methodologies of performance studies and ethnographic research, this study explores how ideas about the Chinese past are enlisted in the service of staging and representing the modern nation through the staged Dunhuang arts. Additionally, it identifies historic moments where the creation and representation of Chinese music and dance undergo continuous transformations within this genre. I analyze these processes within the current context of global interdependencies, focusing on performance and the enactment of power through the expressive arts. I show how performative arts, and in particular the staged Dunhuang arts, function as strategic devices for social mobilization and how they are associated with the configuration of a modern Chinese national history (Davis 2005; Rees 2000; Tian 1994; Tuohy 2001; D. Wong 1991; D. Wu 2004).

Combining historical and ethnographic research methods, including archival and textual research, interviews, and participant observation of rehearsals and performances, I explore how the staging of productions in this genre affects the nature and development of performances in public venues. I analyze the ways that these performances, staged in different times and spaces, represent the goals and expectations of different kinds of political, artistic, and commercial institutions. By documenting, describing, analyzing, and representing these efforts to stage China as a modern geopolitical entity with a unified multicultural and cosmopolitan past and a single, autonomous embodiment of public memories at various events and in different contexts, I highlight the actors and institutions—and the relations between them—that serve as the constitutive forces that performatively represent Chineseness today.[10]

Scholars who have explored historical constructions of Chineseness have pointed out the complexity involved in conceptualizing the term. Some have stated that China should be "conceived as a set of many Chinas," and some have argued that Chineseness should not be held as a monolithic entity attached to a particular place—"the mythic homeland," the imaginary root, or a traceable origin—but should be approached in terms of an ongoing history of dispersal and as a provisional, "open signifier" (Blum and Jensen 2002; Chow 1998). Wu Xiaoming, elaborating on Feng Yulan's philosophical writings, has argued that Chineseness is essentially defined by suggestiveness: "Once translated, the Chineseness is lost, but one does not consequently get a universal 'philosophy' purified of 'Chineseness.' On the contrary, one loses the whole [of] Chinese philosophy" (1998: 436). Suggestiveness is an essential concept in Chinese aesthetics and a norm that guides the staging of the *Dunhuang bihua yuewu*. It is associated with self-referentiality in the meta-elements that constitute the Chinascape.

After establishing the notion of an invented Chinese philosophy by discussing suggestiveness, Wu Xiaoming argues that the whole discourse of Chinese philosophy is "condemned to ambiguities and 'contradictions'" because the invention of "Chinese philosophy" attests to "the desire for the assertion of a national and cultural self-identity," which can "only be constituted by and through the other" (1998: 436). Similarly, as a process of aesthetic politicization, the staging of the *Dunhuang bihua yuewu* is constituted by and through the other. In a study of folk dance, Anthony Shay points out that choreographic strategies of representation are "a form of power of describing others. [They] foreground some of the most deeply felt and unspoken aspects of national discourses" (2002: 224). In *Dunhuang bihua yuewu*, the staging of the self as a constituent of others foregrounds the multiethnicity and multifaceted nature of modern China. Unlike the staging of expressive art forms of ethnic minority groups, which in China emphasizes a process of describing others (as seen, for instance, in Carole Pegg's [2001] studies of the music and dance of Mongolians and in Helen Rees's [2000] studies of the Naxi ethnic groups), the staging of *Dunhuang bihua yuewu* brings forth a construction of "a self of others." At the same time, the historical authenticity of this staged Chineseness is contested and challenged by the very act of staging—a process discussed in this book.

### Ethnographic Archaeology

One of the main challenges of this study is to visualize the processes of reinventing the *Dunhuang bihua yuewu* by combining what I learned through participant observation, interviews, ethnographic archaeology, archival research, and ethnomusicological documentary filming. I have been fortunate as an ethnographer in that I have been able to work both on-site at the Dunhuang Mogao Grottoes and in northwestern China more broadly during multiple visits to the region.

It was in October 2002, during the national holiday (*guoqingjie* 國慶節) for celebrating the founding of the People's Republic of China, when, for the first time, I stood outside the Dunhuang Mogao Grottoes. With nearly forty-five thousand square meters of murals and more than 2,400 polychrome sculptures, these caves encompass the largest known depository of historic artifacts along the Silk Road; their discovery was hailed as one of the great archaeological finds of the twentieth century. They—along with four other cave complexes in the Dunhuang region, including the Western Thousand Buddha Grottoes, the Five Temple Grottoes, the Yulin Grottoes, and the Eastern Thousand Buddha Grottoes—bear witness to the sociocultural, religious, political, and commercial activities that occurred in Dunhuang across the first millennium. The Library Cave, known to scholars as Mogao Cave No. 17 and seen in *A Grand Dream of Dunhuang*, contains documents in at least seventeen languages and twenty-four scripts, many of which have been extinct for centuries or are known from only a few examples. These documents, which include music and dance scores, mirror the diversity of Dunhuang itself, where Buddhists dwelled alongside Manicheans, Zoroastrians, Christians, and Jews; Chinese transcribers have even recorded Tibetan prayers that were translated from Sanskrit by Indian monks working for Turkish khans. These materials embody a history of negotiation and contestation among monolithic and pluralistic value systems in China, a process that continues to this day.[11]

When I first arrived in Dunhuang, the Mogao Grottoes—one of the earliest UNESCO World Heritage Sites designated in China (in 1998)—had already become a tourist site. It was being heavily guarded by the Dunhuang Academy's security unit 文物保護所, which specializes in protecting cultural relics.[12]

I stayed in a hotel at least one hundred miles away. Accompanied by two local tour guides specially trained by the Dunhuang Academy, I took a taxi to the caves early enough one morning to benefit from the natural daylight that would illuminate the grottoes. I stood outside the main entrance with an admission ticket in my hand. The ticket was a gift from my friends, natives of Gansu Province, who had been accompanying me since I had arrived in Lanzhou. We arrived at Xiahe 夏河, in the Gannan Tibetan Autonomous Prefecture, and our Jeep made clouds of dust as it went on to Dunhuang. The trees had emerald-colored leaves, and the desert wind was howling. Dunhuang is an oasis at the confluence of the Sule 疏勒 and Danghe 黨河 Rivers. The brilliantly clear blue sky stretched far beyond the nearby mountains, merging with a landscape completely new to me.

I felt the self-consciousness of being a tourist who had grown up far away, as a child in southern China and, in the 1990s, as a teenager in New York City. During the Tang dynasty (618–907 CE), and even today, I would be considered an inhabitant of the Central Plateau (*Zhongyuan renshi* 中原人士), where Buddhism eventually arrived by land and sea during the Eastern Han dynasty (25–220 CE). Yet even before the Sea Silk Route had become a dominant portal for foreign goods, Buddhism had conquered the northwestern borderland of China and had begun to assimilate, as well as be assimilated by, the local cultures and folk religions it encountered, especially those of the Tibetans. Labrang Monastery (*Labuleng si* 拉卜楞寺), a prominent

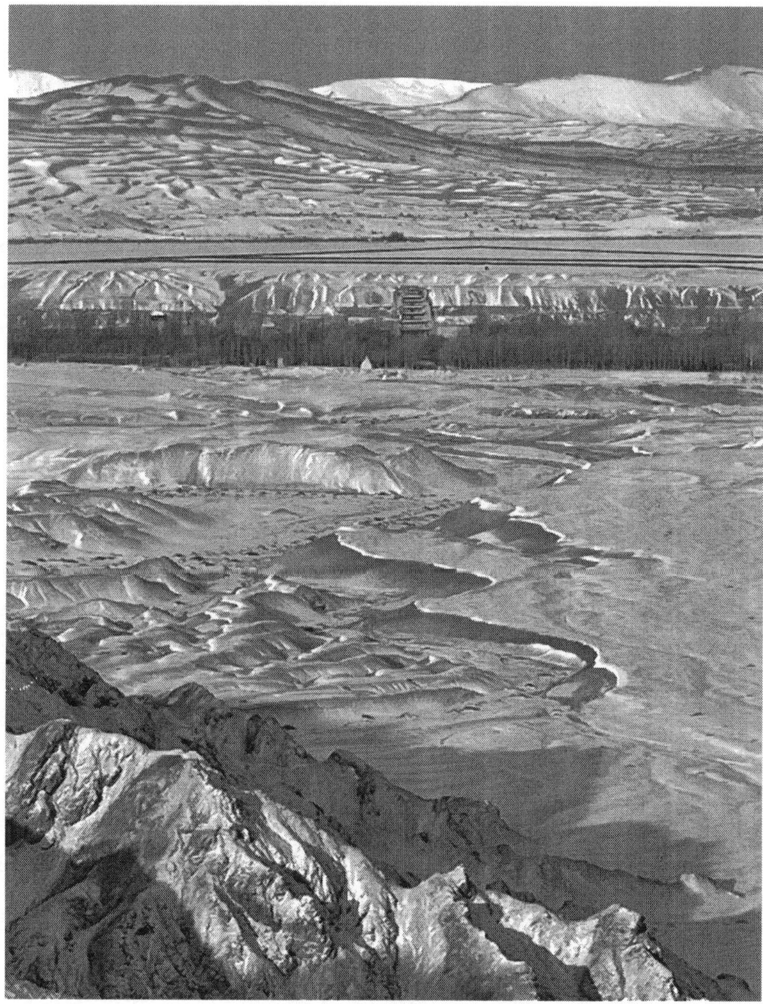

Figure 1.4. A photograph of the present-day Dunhuang Mogao Grottoes. Spring 2022. Courtesy of Sun Zhijun 孫志軍, Dunhuang Academy.

center of Tibetan Gelugpa Buddhism, was built in the same province as the city of Dunhuang, in Xiahe, in 1709 during the Qing dynasty and the reign of Emperor Kangxi 康熙 (1661–1722). The murals in the Dunhuang Mogao Grottoes, nevertheless, reflect the transmission of Tibetan Buddhism during the Mongol Yuan dynasty (1271–1368), much earlier.

Mr. Qin, a seasoned tour guide in his early forties, tall, with thick eyebrows, braved the exceptionally large groups of holiday tourists swarming in front of the archway and made his way to the gate area. There he entered a small office hidden behind the security stand without the slightest hesitation—it is a characteristic of northwesterners to be direct, I was told. I was instructed to wait for him at the entrance, since he was to get the keys and take me into the special caves (*teku* 特窟), opened only with permission from the Dunhuang Academy. The 492 cave temples cut into a mile-long cliff at the site of Mogao left an impression—just deep enough to be on my been-there list.

My next encounter, in 2005, with dance scholar Gao Jinrong and the *Dunhuang bihua yuewu* was unexpected. In the summer of that year, I returned to Dunhuang to conduct preliminary research. By then, I had met some Dunhuang specialists. Eventually, I gained support from the China Arts Research Academy (*Zhongguo yishu yanjiu yuan* 中國藝術研究院) and the China Dunhuang and Turpan Academic Society (*Dunhuang Tulufan xiehui* 中國敦煌吐魯番學會) for preliminary work at Dunhuang. Major interventions had occurred in the oasis city since my 2002 visit. On the ground of the Mogao Grottoes complex, small shops nearby had been demolished, shops selling touristic souvenirs had been built in abundance, and the area in front of the Nine-Story Building 九層樓, the landmark structure of the Mogao Grottoes, had been renovated. The Nine-Story Building houses the 35.5-meter-high Maitreya Buddha statue in Cave No. 96, which was constructed in 695 under the edicts from Tang Empress Wu Zhao 武曌 (624–705).

I spent an entire summer on-site. Fan Jinshi 樊錦詩, a renowned Dunhuangologist and director of the Dunhuang Academy, was a colleague of the late professor emeritus Dong Xijiu 董錫玖, one of the principal interviewees for this study. Professor Dong had written a letter to Director Fan, asking her to assist me with my research. I thereby gained permission to stay at the small lodge open only to guests with an internal affiliation (*neibuzhaodaisuo* 內部招待所), such as certified academicians and government officials. The lodge is located at the back of the main entrance to the caves, facing the northern caves.

In the summer of 2019, I returned to Dunhuang as a visiting scholar of the Dunhuang Academy, which by then had developed significantly as a state-sponsored research institution. It had been collaborating with major research institutions around the globe, such as the British Museum and the Getty Conservation Institute, to develop and implement conservation and preservation projects. The grottoes had been fully digitalized by a team of experts under photographers Sun Zhijun 孫志軍 and Wu Jian 吳健 from the Dunhuang Academy's Center for Digitalization. A new website for providing open resources from the Dunhuang Academy, called "Digital Dunhuang," was still in its developmental stage. This website is now accessible with support from Tencent Holdings 腾讯, a Chinese multinational technology and entertainment conglomerate and holding company headquartered in Shenzhen.[13] Founded in 1998, Tencent is one of the highest-grossing multimedia companies in the world and a strategic partner of the Dunhuang Academy. Tencent has incorporated what I have identified as Dunhuang meta-elements in the multiplayer online battle arena (MOBA) strategy video games for which it is known, such as *Honor of Kings* 王者榮耀. Tourism, which has benefited from the Dunhuang Academy's archaeological heritage management team, breaks national records almost annually in terms of visitor numbers and best-service rankings. Even the hotel open only to guests with an internal affiliation has undergone substantial renovations.

### Archival Research

Artifacts found in excavations in the Dunhuang region are scattered across many countries today. Joint efforts have been made to secure the release of both original and reproductions of artifacts for research over recent decades, but a full collection of the published documents requires substantial financial investment, which individuals and even medium-sized libraries cannot afford. In addition, the documents are published under uncoordinated serial numbers by institutes that catalog them in their own customized microfilm inventories, raising yet another barrier for those seeking to locate information. With permission from Fan Jinshi, I gained access to the Dunhuang Academy's library for archival research and to some of the most restricted caves for on-site research. The library houses one of the most comprehensive collections of scholarly works of Dunhuangology. Some earlier Dunhuangological publications, especially data on music and dance images in the caves, are out of print, but I found them in the archive with the help of the research scholars there.

Culture, produced historically and actively contested, can be considered to be "nothing but historical processes constructed and transported through time, which meet, clash and partly fuse with other cultures and other traditions, thus giving rise to cultural 'whole' traditions or half-caste cultures" (Ferrarotti 2002: 24). It is temporal and emergent, "not a unified corpus of symbols and meanings that can be definitively interpreted"

(Clifford and Marcus 1986: 18). In this kind of historical account, we rely eventually on intertextual and shared references to communicate and interact in a series of historical processes. Intertextuality lets us examine how social arrangements affect the nature and contents of cultural expressions such as music; it lets us access cultural literacy, by which we achieve a certain irreducible historicity—the view that we humans are historical in our being, through a temporal understanding of the world.

Although I emphasize ethnographic research, the historical approach remains an important part of my research methodology since it allows me to examine the ways that ideas about the classical, multicultural, and cosmopolitan past are enlisted in the service of representing the modern nation, as well as to identify and analyze the moments in which encounters with foreign sources challenge and provide opportunities for creating and representing music. Particular historical moments create the conditions for mediating and problematizing the distance between self and other through musical practices (Bohlman 2002a and 2002b). My research and this monograph further that argument and help us gain a better understanding of the constitutive process of Chineseness and Chinascape.

My archival research on the *Dunhuang bihua yuewu* partly consisted of examining the ancient texts that contain narrations of music and dance from along the Silk Road. I paid special attention to historical records on rituals and court performances. I studied poems from the Han and Tang dynasties and used poems from the latter dynasty as historical references for the music and dance scholars of contemporary China. For instance, in the *Complete Collection of Tang Dynasty Poetry* (*Quan Tang shi* 全唐詩), many poems describe events that consisted of performances of music and dance. Some of these poems were written for religious rituals, some for warfare, and some for courtly entertainment. They portray not only the sounds and movements of the performers, the instruments, and the costumes the performers were wearing but also the contexts within which these performances were staged.

Archival research focusing on historical records and classical canons of the expressive arts provided a deeper understanding of the roles that artistic productions have played in the formation of identity in China. By associating the historical records and classical canons of the expressive arts with the *Dunhuang bihua yuewu*, I could interpret the staged metaelements in rich, layered context. The archival materials were essential to my understanding of the *Dunhuang bihua yuewu*'s intertextuality, which, in association with the historical references and classical canons, ultimately granted the genre its aesthetic suggestiveness and self-referentiality, decisive concepts in Chinese aesthetics and philosophies. My research may thus serve a similar function for future audiences and scholars who wish to have a better understanding of the construction and staging of Chinascapes.

## *Ethnoarchaeology*

Ethnomusicologists not uncommonly examine archaeological materials as a part of their work. Bonnie Wade (1998), for instance, studied the musical, social, and political culture of Mughal India through historic paintings; her analysis provided the archaeological information and historical context of the paintings. Nevertheless, her focus was on the historic events portrayed in the paintings, not on the modern interpretations of these historic events. As a subfield of the interdisciplinary ethnomusicology, music archaeology has grown significantly since the 1970s. The International Council for Traditional Music Study Group on Music Archaeology, founded in 1981, and the International Study Group on Music Archaeology (ISGMA), founded in 1998, are two of the most active scholarly associations dedicated to supporting research joining the two distinct disciplines of musicology and archaeology.

Previous research on the *Dunhuang bihua yuewu* involved primarily on-site archaeological investigations of the early materials, such as the murals and related documents, including tablature, a notation that requires careful decoding, especially in the absence of information about the temperaments in use during its production.[14] Archaeology has been the prominent research method in Dunhuangology, but few have conducted ethnographic studies at Dunhuang.

Sarah Fraser, an art historian who participated in renovating, preserving, and reproducing the murals at the Mogao Grottoes, collected data on long-vanished artistic behavior; nevertheless, she defined ethnoarchaeology as using "the present to reconstruct the past" (2004: 8). In contrast, I used methodologies from ethnoarchaeology for my ethnomusicological research and investigated the processes of artistic creations in both the past and the present. To borrow Victor Buchli and Gavin Lucas's statement on ethnoarchaeology and modern material culture studies: "Two main strands of modern material culture studies in archaeology may be identified: first are those that are explicitly ethno-archaeological and concern themselves with more general issues of material culture which are supposed to feed back into research in traditional archaeological periods. Second though, are those that deal explicitly with the present as an archaeology of us, sometimes enfolding their study within a longer-term, historical perspective" (2001: 4). My research falls into the second category, although it goes beyond archaeology and material culture studies.

Ethnoarchaeology may be traced back to the early seventeenth century and has been defined differently by scholars. Richard A. Gould termed it "living archaeology":

> As I would define it here, living archaeology is the actual effort made by an archaeologist or ethnographer to do fieldwork in living human societies, with special reference to the "archaeological" patterning of the behavior in those societies. Ethnoarchaeology, as I see it, refers to a much broader general framework for comparing ethnographic and archaeological patterning. In this latter case, the archaeologist may rely entirely upon published and archival sources or upon experimental results . . . for his comparisons without having to do the actual fieldwork himself. Thus ethnoarchaeology may include studies of "living archaeology" along with other approaches. (1974: 29, quoted in Stiles 1977: 88)

The same article lists some of the ethnoarchaeological methods I used for my research. These include certain methods of obtaining information: the literature of normal ethnographic studies, early travelers' published accounts, museum collections of material culture, experimental studies, and explicit archaeological ethnographic studies (Stiles 1977: 91).

Not only did I spend years examining museum and on-site collections of Dunhuang materials but I also collected extensive archival material from scholarly publications on topics related to the *Dunhuang bihua yuewu*. These publications include Dunhuangological studies that focus on archaeological findings along the Silk Road. Since there were neither previous ethnographic writings on the *Dunhuang bihua yuewu* nor experimental studies on the subject, I had to review ethnographic notes and recorded video clips produced through participation-observation and interviews.

By adopting some of the ethnoarchaeological methods mentioned above, I examined the creative processes and artistic behaviors involved in constructing the *Dunhuang bihua yuewu* in the present. I studied the staging processes that utilized archaeological materials from the grottoes, such as body movements described in Dunhuang dance notation, painted on the cave walls, selected and collected by artists and state-appointed dance scholars in the late 1970s, selected and choreographed by state-appointed dance educators, and staged in public venues as *Dunhuang bihua yuewu* performances.

I interviewed producers, choreographers, and government officials who were responsible for creating staged Dunhuang arts performances. I followed each of them extensively, participated in some of the planning and directing processes, and performed as a dancer while conducting research. The most challenging and yet rewarding part of my ethnoarchaeological research on this genre has been the fact that the discovered dance notations were transcribed in textual narrative form. These notations are formally known as Dunhuang dance notation (*Dunhuang wupu* 敦煌舞譜) from the Tang dynasty (618–907). Dance historians, including Dong Xijiu, have tried to decode and interpret them in literary context encoded in historical documentation; however, since no multimedia records, such as sound or audio clips from the past, are available to allow us accurately to determine whether these text narratives have been decoded correctly, the murals inside the grottoes remain the closest thing we have to an iconographic interpretation of the archaeological materials.

The *Dunhuang bihua yuewu*, though a contemporary genre of expressive arts, is rooted in the archaeological materials from Dunhuang's Mogao Grottoes. To understand the changes that have been applied to the archaeological sources from which it derived, I needed to become familiar with the historical references associated with these materials before I could start interpreting them. In 2002, 2005, and 2008, I spent an extensive amount of time working on-site at the grottoes. Granted special permission, I entered some of the restricted caves, especially the ones containing some of the best-preserved murals, those that have been selected for the collections of images from which Gao Jinrong created the *Dunhuang bihua yuewu*.

My visits to the grottoes were often accompanied by a guide trained by the Dunhuang Academy or by a scholar specializing in Dunhuang arts. I also freely explored the caves alone and spent hours examining the murals for their historical and artistic characteristics. I learned to identify the aesthetic styles associated with the sculptures and murals by determining the material used and the mineral colors applied to these artifacts. Furthermore, by living for many months in northwest China and traveling along the Hexi Corridor 河西走廊, visiting the key archaeological sites along the ancient Silk Road (such as Zhangye 張掖, Jiuquan 酒泉, and Jiayuguan 嘉峪關), I learned to contextualize the *Dunhuang bihua yuewu* in local historical settings and compare those to contemporarily staged visions in present-day

Gansu, Beijing, and Guangdong. Discussions of the murals, as both archaeological objects and artistic creations, with scholars and researchers from the Dunhuang Academy and the Dunhuang Institute at Lanzhou University expanded my knowledge and helped with my research.[15]

## Ethnographic Research on Contemporary Processes

In 2008 and 2009, I undertook research in China as a Fulbright-IIE (Institute of International Education) scholar. Before then, I had been affiliated with the China Arts Academy 中國藝術研究院 (in Beijing) and the China Dunhuang and Turpan Academic Society 中國敦煌吐魯番學會. The China Dunhuang and Turpan Academic Society is a scholarly association dedicated to Silk Road studies and Dunhuangology 敦煌學 established in Beijing in 1983. The Dunhuang Academy 敦煌研究院 is in Dunhuang, a county-level city 縣級 市 administered by the city of Jiuquan 酒泉,[16] and the Lanzhou University Dunhuang Research Institute is in Lanzhou 蘭州. Before I traveled to these cities to conduct ethnographic research, I set up appointments with administrative personnel and faculty members to discuss my research plans and initiate relationships with additional collaborators.

The state's involvement in ethnographic research on the expressive art forms in China has a long history. The practices of *caifeng* 采風 (reporting local customs) and *guanfeng* 觀風 (observing local customs)—both ethnographic in nature—have been important traditions of learning classical Chinese poetry since the Zhou dynasty or before. According to the *Book of Rites* 禮記, "The Son of Heaven would send officials out every five years to collect songs (*shi* 詩) in order to observe the customs of the people."[17] In the *Analects*, Confucius urges his disciples to study the *Shijing*, maintaining that one of the functions of poetry is to serve as a basis of observation (*guan* 觀).[18] This idea is strengthened by Ban Gu 班固 (32–92) in his *Han shu* 漢書 (*History of the Han*), in which he stresses that the ancient practice of collecting folk songs provided a means for the sovereigns to "observe social mores." The collecting of folk ballads (*yuefu* 樂府) in the Han dynasty served a similar purpose.[19]

My approach to conducting participant observation draws from the theories and methods of performance studies and phenomenology, in which analyzing interactions among cultural actors is a central focus, attending to multiple meanings and values that emerge through interactions and negotiations in specific contexts. These methods help us understand how individual and collective identities are created and recreated in situated contexts.

*Participant observation* is a term often used to describe the basic research method used by ethnographers. It entails deep immersion in a social setting, in which the researcher engages with the people involved in their daily routines. While developing ongoing relationships in the community, the researcher records observed details in notes (Emerson et al. 1995: 18–19, 26–30). Additionally, ethnomusicological research usually employs technological devices such as sound recorders and video recorders to capture the aural and visual elements of an expressive art and enhance researchers' abilities to reconstruct and analyze events.

Digitized data lets researchers review and analyze details in a nonlinear fashion using appropriate software. Therefore, for my research, in addition to the traditional methodology of writing research notes, I employed technological video cameras to capture the movements and facial expressions of the interviewees, dancers, and other persons at each setting. A production team consisting of a seasoned program producer, a professional cinematographer, and a trained lighting and camera operator from the Gansu Provincial Radio, Television, and Film Service (Gansusheng guangbo dianying dianshitai jituan 甘肅省廣播電影電視總台集團; GPRTFS), also known as GanSu Media Group (GSMG), traveled with me to the dance studios at Northwestern Minzu University for location shootings. I set up several interview sessions at the recording studios at the GPRTFS.

In 2023, during my most recent research trip to China, I interviewed Yang Qian 楊乾, whom I had met during my 2019 fieldwork in Lanzhou. Yang had directed the forty-minute "Episode on Dunhuang" for China Central Television Station's grand ongoing documentary series project, *The Local Records of China*. He and I met on-site at Northwestern Minzu University's Dance College when he was filming the staging processes of Dunhuang dance for the episode. I was immediately intrigued, wanting to learn and compare our approaches on documenting the staged Dunhuang arts. Our 2023 meetings were highly rewarding. I joined him for a documentary project on-site in Changsha and obtained materials for discussing the processes of producing documentaries. By examining and comparing our filming scripts and our pre- and postproduction editing notes, I gained a better understanding of the intertextual processes of producing an ethnomusicological documentary on staged Dunhuang arts, and I present my interpretations in the chapters that follow.

## Chapter Summaries

Music and dance have long been at the heart of the sociopolitical and cosmic order in China. In chapters 2 and 3, I lay out the basic structure of the study by identifying the primary ideas and questions concerning the nature of staging and the concept of *tianxia* within Chinese hermeneutic contexts of aesthetic experiences. Together, these chapters present the theoretical, political, and philosophical implications of the performativity of staging an alternative world order that is universally valid through the Silk Road expressive arts. As an intangible culture embodied and emergent in time-space, these arts come into being in an ephemeral space through staged performative processes.

Chapter 2 follows this introduction by laying out an alternative, ethnopoetics-centered framework for approaching the staging of Dunhuang expressive arts and the changing concept of *tianxia* as discursive formations of Chinascapes in contemporary global contexts. To allow an open-ended assessment of the *tianxia*'s application beyond the norm, chapter 2 explores both the ancient concept and the modern *tianxia* system proposed by Zhao Tingyang 趙汀陽 in 2005. It includes a survey of scholarship both supporting and challenging his system and provides a theoretical framework for interpreting the contents and case studies in the next three parts of the book.

Chapters 3 and 4 situate Dunhuang geographically and conceptually as a historic frontier metropolis on the Silk Road. Chapter 3 studies Dunhuang's strategic location in China's northwestern periphery by analyzing the state's policies for developing the region. It lays a literary and artistic foundation for modern stagings of Dunhuang expressive art forms. Literary references and pictorial analysis of historical and contemporary references highlight the negotiation between the periphery and the center and indicate a textual space within which a groundwork has been established for modern productions. I present the imagined landscape of Dunhuang through narratives embedded within frontier poetry, a genre that emerged from sociopolitical interactions and cultural integrations after China's Han and Tang periods. Via ethnopoetic methods, I introduce and investigate poetic narratives from today. This chapter ends with an analysis of the sociocultural spatialization of selected Mogao Grotto artworks and an introduction of the religious elements that have been incorporated in modern staging processes. Chapter 4 focuses on the interplay between institutions and agents as they have embodied the historical processes through which the Dunhuang expressive arts have been incorporated as a cultural device in state building. Comparisons of the music suites in this chapter offer a forum for teasing out similarities and differences in the administration of multiethnic groups and their cultural heritage in both the past and the present.

Chapter 5 provides a deeper explanation of some of the key concepts and terms for understanding the pertinent staging processes. Chapter 6 places the genre within its sociohistorical and geopolitical contexts, providing insight into its creators and audiences. It offers a guide to the presence of different agencies and their roles in case studies of the three most representative programs: *The Thousand-Handed and Thousand-Eyed Avalokiteśvara* (*Qianshou qianyan Guanyin* 千手千眼觀音), *Lotus Aloft* (*Bubu shenglian* 步步生蓮), and *The Flying Apsaras* (*Feitian* 飛天).

Chapter 7 turns to the issues of ethnomusicological transcription, research documentation, and exhibition. It draws on methods from preexisting multimedia forms to reveal the intertextuality of staged Dunhuang expressive arts through the process of recollecting, recontextualizing, representing, and reflecting on the staging process. It investigates the nature of the staging process in relation to my research by introducing Martin Heidegger's theory of *Dasein* (emphasizing temporality and representation) and Julia Kristeva's theory of intertextuality. It introduces my long-term research as an integral part of the staging process. *Being-in-the-field* means my engagement and immersion.

In the arts, cosmopolitanism can be said to embody an aesthetic and poetic attempt to transcend the localisms and particularisms constituted by a modern nation. The previous chapters examine this hypothesis through the staging of Dunhuang-themed dance dramas, but chapter 8 investigates this phenomenon by focusing on the modern-day development of the Dunhuang metasystem in China and around the globe through academic and creative collaborations. It analyzes "Dunhuang, Silk Road, and Multinationality" (a slogan advanced by local artists in Gansu Province), citing four cases, each showing the strategies used for balancing the power between central and peripheral, old and new: two new versions of *Along the Silk Road* (*Silu huayu* 絲路花雨) the theatrical dance drama, a Dunhuang-themed Peking opera 京劇 highlighting the history of the Dunhuang Academy and the generations of researchers in the grand backdrop of the founding of the modern Chinese nation in 1949, and a 2023 Dunhuang-themed production adopted from an award-winning Japanese novel and staged in the form of

Long opera 隴劇, which is a regional folk drama found in China's Gansu and Shanxi Provinces. These works demonstrate China's promotion of the Dunhuang metaculture to serve in its state-building strategies. Reconceptualizing the *tianxia* notion with China's Belt and Road Initiative and the *tianxia* worldview's recent revival as a key theoretical construct that has reemerged in the last two decades, the book concludes with questions and inquiries into the historical, performative, and rhetorical processes by which the expressive arts and cultural heritages inform a vision of China as a historically multiethnic and cosmopolitan nation.

## Resituating the Study

Live, staged performances are most commonly understood as the "art of the present" because of their ephemerality. Ethnomusicologists, however, often travel between the invisible boundaries set by the concepts of a beginning and an end. In a similar sense, this monograph contains resituated materials and case studies from my ongoing ethnographic field work spanning more than two decades. The lack of permanency and the focus on the present invites the resituating (if not reappropriating) of live, staged performances that are still and always emerging and *becoming* something else, in a different time and space. Nevertheless, this new book distinguishes itself from my previous publications by spotlighting the recent development of the Chinascape and *tianxia* concepts in association with the staging process. Recent examples of staged Dunhuang arts serve as case studies in the later chapters, which look to show the changes in China's nation-building strategies by underlining the attention that the state increasingly pays to heritage management, promotion, and education.

## Notes

1. On China's open-door policy and the country's economic growth in the 1980s, see Wei 1995: 73.

2. Visit Lanzhou Grand Theater's official website (http://www.lzyyjt.com) for photos of the dance drama.

3. Further discussion of the sinicized *feitian* 飛天 appears in chapter 6 as part of a case study. See Yang 2019: 234.

4. The renminbi is the basis of Chinese currency; at the time of writing, seven million RMB were worth approximately one million US dollars. For the current ratio of RMB and the dollar, please see Federal Reserve Bank of St. Louis, "FRED Economic Data," https://fred .stlouisfed.org/series/EXCHUS.

5.  RMB stands for the currency system in China, renminbi 人民幣. The base unit of the renminbi is *yuan* 元, which can be written as CNY.

6.  "Chinese Cultural Industry Keeps Growth via Loans," Xinhua for *China Daily*, August 5, 2009; original source removed from http://www2.chinadaily.com.cn/business/2009-08/05/content_8526925.htm, copy found at http://webcache.googleusercontent.com/search?q=cache:http://www2.chinadaily.com.cn/business/2009-08/05/content_8526925.htm. Last accessed April 4, 2012.

7.  Multimedia components for *Staging* Tianxia, such as active maps, working color metagraphs, audiovisual files, and documentary film clips, can be found at https://lanlankuangofficial.pub/.

8.  A complete transcript of this interview for Phoenix Infonews Channel's "Mainland Q & A" program hosted by Feng Xiaoli, titled "Minister of Culture and Tourism Cai Wu: 'The Road to Renaissance' does not avoid the Cultural Revolution," can be found on Phoenix New Media's official website: https://phtv.ifeng.com/program/wdsz/detail_2009_09/12/1080587_0.shtml.

9.  Kuang (2012, 2016a) has addressed the staging processes of *tianxia* and Chinascape as aesthetic politicization in connection to cosmopolitanism. Ban Wang (2017) has cited Kant and Kang Youwei on how moral and aesthetic experience can build bridges among peoples and nations.

10.  Multiple versions of public memory occur at local, provincial, and regional levels. The staging processes studied show how versions of individual and public memory are organized and represented as a national one.

11.  See especially Fraser 2004.

12.  Unlike the Mogao Police Station 莫高窟派出所, which was established on the ground in 2018 to oversee the neighborhood's public security and which reports to the Dunhuang Municipal Public Security Department 敦煌市公安局, the cultural-relic security unit reports to the Dunhuang Academy, administrated by the National Cultural Heritage Administration 國家文物局, an administered agency subordinate to China's Ministry of Culture and Tourism. The police station is arguably a byproduct of increasingly vigorous tourism in Dunhuang and its surrounding region. The coexistence of the two units should be seen as a development in relic management in China.

13.  The "Digital Library Caves" project is accessible through https://dlc.e-dunhuang.com.

14.  Dance notations prominent in the Tang dynasty (618–907) are collectively known as Dunhuang dance notation (*Dunhuang wupu* 敦煌舞譜).

15.  Multimedia components for *Staging Tianxia*, such as active maps, working color metagraphs, audiovisual files, and documentary film clips, can be found at https://lanlankuangofficial.pub/.

16.  A county-level municipality or county-level city, formerly known as a prefecture-controlled city, is a county-level administrative division of the People's Republic of China.

17.  Cited in Yang 1981: 1:190.

18.  See Yang 1984: 185.

19.  Ban Gu 1962: 6: 1708, 1756. For a brief discussion of the concept of *guan*, see Zhang 2005: 66–68.

# 2

## *TIANXIA*, CHINASCAPES, AND DUNHUANG

Everything is the king's business [and should be a responsibility shared by all],
yet I [alone] labor here virtuously.
此莫非王事。我獨賢勞也。

Mencius's response to an inquiry regarding a king's responsibility
to *tianxia* based on a poem in the *Book of Songs*:
Of all that is under Heaven,
No place is not the king's land;
And to the farthest shores of all the land,
No man is not the king's subject.

*Mencius* V.A. 4.ii
《禮記·樂記》

IN 2008, AUDIENCES AROUND THE GLOBE WITNESSED THE rise of the Olympic symbol into the night sky above the Bird's Nest Stadium in Beijing, China's capital city, through the cinematic lens of the American National Broadcasting Company (NBC).[1] The Olympic symbol, consisting of five interlocking rings, was framed by several apsaras in midair. Through the voice of Joshua Cooper Ramo, NBC's then on-air China expert and author of *The Beijing Consensus*, audiences learned the supposed meaning of these figures: they were deities that decorate the wall paintings at the Mogao Grottoes in China's northwestern Gansu Province, a region through which the ancient Silk Road passed.

In January 2022, the apsaras from the Mogao Grottoes, with their flowing ribbons, were staged as so-called inspirations for various Beijing Winter

Olympics designs.[2] The Dunhuang meta-elements (as I call them) made center stage as the sky over the stadium was lit up with fireworks showing "One World One Family"—in Chinese characters, 天下一家 *tianxia yijia*.[3] Citing China specialists such as Joshua Cooper Ramo and Joshua Kurlantzick, American policy scholar Jacques deLisle (2022) points out that "staging the Olympics is often—and is for China—a normative pursuit" since the games provided an occasion for China to exhibit its cultural immensity and soft power.

China's foreign policies in the last two decades, especially the Belt and Road Initiative (BRI) from 2013 and the Global Development Initiative from 2021, are arguably reminiscent of the ancient Silk Road and the *tianxia* system, respectively.[4] Chinese president Xi Jinping 习近平 often cites *tianxia* and has highlighted the harmoniousness of the historical Silk Road in the public diplomacy narratives of the BRI. Frequently in his speeches, he reinforces the BRI as an open and inclusive globalization platform (Jiang 2022). The staging of Dunhuang arts from along the Silk Road consequently points to changing approaches in contemporary China's view on the style of governing domestically and globally. Recent state policies are venues for the performative phenomena within which the Chinascapes being enacted through staged Dunhuang arts emerge worldwide, revealing the true meaning of rites and music.

Music, dance, and other expressive arts staged as a part of rituals have always been at the core of state building and elite education in China and other East Asian countries, especially Japan and Korea (Provine, Tokumaru, and Witzleben 2001). Scholars such as Rulan Chao Pian (1967), Joseph Lam (1994, 1998), and Bell Yung (1996) have published extensively on music and ritual in ancient Chinese civilization. In *Harmony and Counterpoint: Ritual Music in Chinese Context* (1996), an edited collection dedicated to studying ritual music in China from an ethnomusicological perspective, Bell Yung, Evelyn S. Rawski, and Rubie S. Watson presented nine important studies on the context, content, and form of ritual music, including those of the non-Han ethnic groups, such as an essay by Helen Rees on the Naxi Music Association and an essay by Robert Provine on state ritual and Korean identity. Lawrence Witzleben's article "Music in the Hong Kong Handover Ceremonies: A Community Re-imagines Itself" highlights the continuity of this sophisticated cultural practice in modern China's state-building processes and its foreign-relation-shaping processes (2002: 120–133). From the majestic bronze bell performances staged during important state rituals

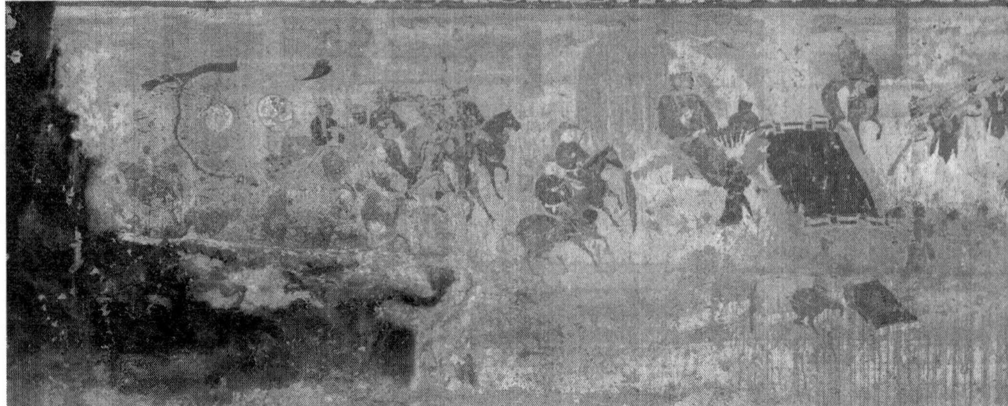

Figure 2.1. Mogao Cave 156, lower west side of southern wall, mural of Zhang Yichao leading the Return to Allegiance Army Parade (張議潮統歸義軍出行圖). Permission to use image granted by Dunhuang Academy.

for legitimizing an emperor as the Son of Heaven 天子to the playing of the seven-stringed *qin* zither in private settings as a way of cultivating sage-hood in the Confucian and Daoist traditions, staged ritual music, dance, and other expressive art forms are fundamental to our understanding of the emergence of *tianxia* and Chinascapes through staged Dunhuang arts and the Dunhuang metasystem, broadly speaking.

In the mural from the lower west side of the southern wall in Mogao Cave 156 (fig. 2.1.), Zhang Yichao 張議潮 (799–872), who seized control of the Hexi Corridor after years of the Tibetan 吐蕃 occupation (786–848) in the region, and his troops are highlighted in the center of a welcoming parade. In the mural we see a group of dancers, whose outfits and bodily movements suggest Tibetan influence. Residents of the Dunhuang region would have been born during the occupation period and thus would have been exposed to Tibetan culture and Buddhist practices and would have been fluently bilingual (Wang 2018). This mural embodies the historic moment that marks the return of Chinese Buddhist motifs to Dunhuang and the recovery of the Hexi Corridor from Tibetan occupation. Zhang's victory announced the beginning of the Guiyi Jun 歸義軍 period (Return to Allegiance Army, 848–1036) in China's Tang dynastic timeline (610–906). From a contextual-emergence point of view, the recovery of the Hexi Corridor changed the trajectory, *shi* 勢, of institutional consistency in multiple fields on various levels: the Dunhuang meta-elements that would become the main source

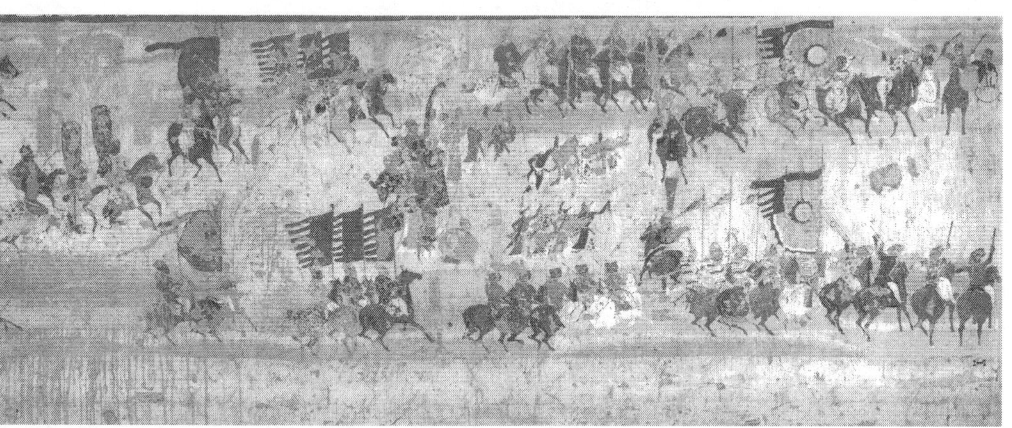

for the contemporarily staged Dunhuang expressive arts are predominantly in artistic styles aligned with the Tang court and the Central Plain 中原. In other words, the transformation of the Dunhuang meta-elements decisively changed the staging and institutionalization processes of the contemporarily created Dunhuang arts.

In the next few chapters, through historic references and ethnographic interviews, I bring forth more apparently the state's trajectory concealed in the country's artistic transformations and institutionalizations. While a stylistic choice made during the staging processes is certainly also under the influence of other critical factors, such as choreographers' personal tastes and beliefs or the changing state policies on cultural content, this could be understood as resulting from the esoteric Buddhism's decline in Dunhuang and the Northwest.[5]

President Xi, visiting the Mogao Grottoes in August 2019, called for greater efforts to preserve the quintessence of Chinese culture: "We ought to support the inheritance and promotion of fine traditional culture," he said.[6] Zhao Shengliang 趙聲良, Communist Party director of the Dunhuang Academy, a state-run research institution designated for administering the UNESCO Mogao Grottoes and the five other archaeological heritage sites in Gansu Province, responded to Xi's call in an interview during the twentieth Communist Party of China National Congress by stating: "In the past ten years, due to the party and the country paying more attention to us, Dunhuang culture has spread very fast. . . . Many people are very excited after seeing the artwork in Dunhuang and feel a sense of cultural confidence when they visit."[7]

In the twentieth century, when China was no longer an empire but had become what the early twentieth-century reformer Liang Qichao (梁启超, 1873–1929) called "a nation among nations," Dunhuang became instrumental in the formation of a modern Chinese nation of unified diversity rooted in an ancient cosmopolitan past. The Dunhuang expressive arts participate in this formation by aestheticizing Chinese history and geography. The staging of productions in the Dunhuang mural music and dance genre points to changing attitudes in present-day China's views on the style of governing, domestically and internationally.

Some creators of the Dunhuang expressive arts featuring Dunhuang music and dance have attempted to go beyond nationalistic rhetoric by invoking aesthetics and religious and other transcendental philosophies and ideologies, such as Buddhism and cosmopolitanism. In the arts, cosmopolitanism can be said to embody an aesthetic and poetic attempt to transcend the localisms and particularisms comprehended in a modern nation. Once aestheticized through embodied, staged performances, the historical and topological landscape of Dunhuang becomes a conceptual landscape that constitutes Dunhuang meta-elements. This conceptual landscape, composed of Dunhuang meta-elements, symbolizes the emergence of China-scapes. It is intricately linked to the intertextual staging process within Dunhuang arts and contributes to the ongoing discourse surrounding the widely adopted concept of Chineseness.

Nationalism and cosmopolitanism are ideals that often align with the practices of economic and cultural integration in the theoretical frameworks of modern nations. They have become central concerns of research in ethnomusicology, anthropology, and other disciplines. The staging of a much-contested "Chinese civilization" thus becomes a way to reconceptualize modern China as a coherent nation and to reaffirm or reconstruct an identity in a country that experienced multiple wars, revolutions, and transformations throughout the twentieth century.

The paradigmatic self-other dichotomy quickly shifted to an apposition between the purported identifying distinctiveness of the Chinese nation and a panoply of influences from the West. According to Prasenjit Duara:

> This split in the time of the nation is sometimes presented in terms of the dichotomy between the particular and universal or, in Asian studies, as the dualism between East and West. Thus Chinese "ti-yong" thinking (Chinese learning for essential principles, Western learning for practical use) and Indian dichotomies of (Vedantic) spirituality versus Western materialism have

been interpreted as East versus West binary thought designed to address the identity crises of Westernized intellectuals who have given up their own culture for Western modernity. The need to speak of a separate but superior or equivalent traditional culture or history is psychologically comforting for non-Western intellectuals. (1996: 30)

## Staged Performances as Enactments of Power, Identity, and Cosmopolitanism

As seen in the staged Dunhuang arts, the performative processes of staging and representing—the living, changeable, and seemly repetitive enactments of what is being imagined as and of China, to paraphrase Benedict Anderson's (1993) words—are constantly negotiated and appropriated according to a particular past or tradition as conceived by those in power. While history generates a variety of social formations—such as families, clans, tribes, estates, social orders, classes, religious organizations, political parties, and finally nations and states—to fulfill the basic human need to belong to an identifiable group (Berlin 1979), history in the modern age commits itself to the dissociation of identity as an essential phenomenon to unmask the plurality of identities and to reveal all the discontinuities that cross us (Foucault 1977: 161). The emergence of diverse historical directions and, with it, the ambiguity of futurity characteristic of the modern age leads to skepticism of fixed and singular identities. One might locate one's identity only within its dispersal.

Scholars from a wide variety of disciplines and theoretical perspectives have problematized the plurality of identity in different ways. For instance, Stuart Hall (1996) advocates understanding identity as produced in specific historical and institutional sites and within specific discursive formations and practices. Wendy Brown (1995: 55) argues that identity unravels as rapidly as it is produced. Judith Butler (1993) suggests establishing a transhistorical commonality by looking at the fixity of gender identification and cultural invariance. My study of the staged Dunhuang arts approaches identity in a fashion resembling that of Hall. I look at the staged vision of a historically multifaceted Chinese identity within specific, performative contexts.

In ethnomusicology, Sue Tuohy (2001) has examined the ways that, while reconstructing and authenticating a coherent Chinese national identity, aspiring nationalists and the modern Chinese state government reconstructed and reinterpreted a Chinese music history for contemporary uses.

This is what Tuohy called a practice of constructing "models from the past" to convey contemporary conceptions of identity (110). Intellectuals and political leaders, in their formations of a Chinese musical past, would claim that "the musical-political connection is a continuation or revival of earlier Chinese philosophers" and that "our legacy of national music is the product of two- or three-thousand years of class society. . . . Some represent the reactionary music culture of oppressing classes; some represent the progressive music culture of the oppressed classes" (111).

During the first four decades of the twentieth century, ideas originated from a non-China-centered scheme (or, put simply, a Western scheme of world history) that had arrived in the newly established modern Chinese nation. Whether they realized or admitted it, people of both schemes experienced a renegotiation or at least an involuntary intellectual challenge; this applies especially to those in China. This phenomenon continues to the present day, as groups within the country continue to work to reposition China in the world. Rey Chow notes, "This collective habit of supplementing every major world trend with the notion of 'Chinese' is the result of an overdetermined series of historical factors, the most crucial of which is the lingering, pervasive hegemony of Western culture" (1998: 2).

The plurality and complexity of China's past, present, and future confront the ways the geopolitical boundaries of a nation are imagined as people become aware of the power and nature of visions.

## Nationalism, Modernity, and the Concept of *Tianxia* (天下)

Nationalism has become one of strongest forces within the global political system over the last two hundred years. It is embedded in our world views (Anderson 1993; Calhoun 2007). Contemporary China, howsoever it is envisioned, exists within a world system composed of nations and states. To explore the ways that concepts of nationalism and cosmopolitanism are understood and enacted within performance, this study examines the concept of *tianxia*, a term that may be translated as "all under heaven." It is a mainstream Chinese vision of world order originated in the Zhou dynasty (eleventh century BCE–256 BCE). The concept of *tianxia* has pervaded Chinese history and emerged as a fundamental element in Chinese political thought concerning inter-state relations.

In the twentieth century, China's worldview was manifest in its diplomatic stances, its regional economic and social alliances with other nations, its insistence on independence and sovereignty, and its campaigns for international recognition. Varied discourses indebted to *tianxia* have resurfaced in modern China, and these have led to a reexamination of the ways that artists and scholars envision China's place in world history. William Callahan says, "Tianxia is interesting both because it was key to the governance and self-understanding of three millennia of Chinese empire, and also because discussion of *tianxia* is becoming popular again in the twenty-first century as an alternative world order that is universally valid" (2007: 2).

Zhao Tingyang, a Chinese scholar who promotes *tianxia* in China today, explains that *tianxia* was conceptualized as a world political system during the Zhou dynasty and posits the Tianxia system as an encompassing world order promoting co-existence. According to his interpretation, the Zhou dynasty *tianxia* system aims to solve the challenge posed by a small state ruling over numerous larger ones. The solution lay in integration, emphasizing relational rationality rather than individual interests. This approach aimed to resolve conflicts arising from diverse interests (2011, 2016, 2019; Zhao and Harroff 2021).

Some scholars nevertheless believe that Zhao's reading of the ancient idea represents "a hierarchical worldview that prioritizes order over freedom, elite governance over democracy, and the superior political institution over the lower level" (Jiang 2022). They say that such an interpretation of *tianxia* works in contradistinction to the Western conception of sovereignty, which stresses autonomy and boundaries. Zhao's reading encounters limitations in elucidating the dynamics of power competition within global politics. Therefore, scholars such as William Callahan point out that the discussion of *tianxia* could be "in ways that go against China's official policy of peacefully rising within the international system" (2008: 749): "The *tianxia* system became popular in China because it caught a wave of interest in Chinese-style solutions to world problems, and especially an interest in how the traditional concept of Tianxia combines the seemingly contradictory discourses of nationalism and cosmopolitanism" (750).

It is crucial that we see the possible conflict and contradistinction as results of the intellectual tradition of separating the design and working of the ancient East Asian state from that of the contemporary government. Wang Zhengxu (2022) remarks that, until recently, "international relations scholars [have been] prone to limiting their inquiry to the working of the so-called 'tributary system' and [have been] often quick to dismiss 'Tianxia' as a viable idea for the making of a global community" (252). However,

Wang also believes that in "a growing body of works produced by political philosophers, sociologists, [and] international relations and political science scholars, some may come to realize that we have quite a bit to learn about the pre-modern East Asian society and state" (2022).

Danah Zohar states that *tianxia* was not only "the origin of China's long preference for win/win solutions, and of Xi Jin Ping's own multilateralism. It is also the earliest known precursor of what I call a quantum global order" (2022: 246).

Like many scholars, Zohar recognizes the connection between the *tianxia* concept and the BRI and furthers the discussion by comparing them to the European Union: "The Tianxia governance model and philosophy underpins the development of China's ambitious, international Belt and Road infrastructure project, and something very similar is the model of governance used in founding the European Union. Both are precursors of a Quantum Global Order implemented by a RenDanHeyi management model. Just as in Haier's RenDanHeyi implementation of Quantum Management for companies, in both Belt and Road and the European Union, each participating nation retains its national sovereignty, governing itself in its own self-organizing way according to its own governing model, while cooperating with all others in the collective ecosystem" (2022: 246).[8]

In my view, focusing on the processes and means of artistic creation and representation, *tianxia* is best approached as a conceptual landscape—a world of ideas, manifested through performative meta-elements such as the staged Dunhuang arts and achieved through staging processes as a vision (*yixiang* 意象).[9] Arjun Appadurai (1990, 2002, 2003) and later scholars, such as Kay Shelemay (2001), have identified multiple scapes, including ethnoscapes, mediascapes, technoscapes, ideoscapes, finanscapes, and soundscapes. I argue that these concepts are architecturally interconnected and fundamental to the conceptual visualization of a Chinascape, the notion I associate with *tianxia*. For Appadurai, "the suffix -scape allows us to point to the fluid, irregular shapes of these landscapes" and "indicate that these are not objectively given relations which look the same from every angle of vision, but rather that they are deeply perspectival constructs, inflected by the historical, linguistic, and political situatedness of different sorts of actors" (2003: 33, 46, 37–8, 296). I approach these deep constructs as what Chinese philosophers Feng Youlan (1983) and Gu Mingdong (2003) call "aesthetic suggestiveness"—a poetic technique often discussed in classical Chinese philosophy and art theory.

The concept of *tianxia* is a theoretical implication of the traditional Chinese vision of world order; it often embodies a public perspective said to be rooted in Confucian moral and political thinking. Confucian notions of heaven are irreducibly process oriented and temporal. The Chinese term *tian* (天) is commonly translated as "Heaven" and "heavenly," encapsulating different meanings. Heaven (*tian* 天) permeates "ten thousand things" (*wanwu* 萬物), attaining self-realization with creativity. Whereas heaven or God in the West is a transcendental reality independent of space and time, *tian* is not transcendental in this sense. It generates "ten thousand things" and transmits its creativity to the self-realizing of these things, but there is no significant chasm between *tian* and *wanwu*. All events and all things, including *tian* and *wanwu*, are continuous and therefore processual: the creator and the created, the one and the many, mutually entail each other. This may be one reason why the Confucian tradition commonly uses compound terms such as heaven-earth (*tiandi* 天地) and cosmos (*qiankun* 乾坤) when emphasizing interdependence or correlativity.

*Tian* serves primarily as a holistic designation for all entities, encompassing heaven, earth, humans, animals, and various other elements—essentially embodying the entirety of existence. It also denotes the concept of "heavenly command" (*tian ming* 天命), conferring an ontological role or nature upon all beings. In addition, it signifies an explanatory source for events beyond human agency—incidents that unfold without any intentional cause. This third meaning is often associated with the term *ming* (命), translated as "destiny" or "luck." Together, these distinct meanings contribute to the comprehension of the celestial domain in the Chinese culture.

## Embodiment of Chineseness as Seen in Staged Dunhuang Arts

The human body came to the fore in Chinese thought in the fourth century BCE, when it became a shared topic of discourse through which different traditions articulated their values. The theme was established as central by the Daoist tradition, which made the proper valuing of the self the premise of its argument (Lewis 2005). The body as depicted in Chinese art was almost invariably a clothed body. As several scholars have noted, this representation reflects the fact that the body in early China, and indeed throughout Chinese history, was a social object. Its truth was not revealed in stripping away the costume to reveal the naked body beneath, for the naked body was not the true nature of man. Nudity demonstrated the unaccommodated condition in which humans once lived as animals, and the return to this state was a sign of social collapse, in which people ceased to be human. As part of a society, a necessary condition of being human, one had to be clothed, for clothes generated or marked the roles that made up the social order. Only in suitable attire marking social position or status, distinguished even by categories of mourning garments, did isolated people find their humanity within the broader order formed by the family and the state (Lewis 2005: 78). From the conceptual content embodied in performative, self-referential images (*xiang*) emerged the conceptual landscape or world of ideas (*yijing* 意境).

I am analyzing here both historical sources and contemporary staged Dunhuang arts to understand the ways that the laws—or the aesthetic principles—by which the images, forms, tropes, perceptions, and sensibilities of a transcendental cosmopolitanism developed and crystallized in the staged performances. Staged performances of the Dunhuang arts go beyond static images to add sounds and movements to the process of staging and enacting a multicultural and cosmopolitan vision of Chinese history.

I invite reflection on and study of the change in attitudes during China's major dynastic transitions, such as the much-studied Tang–Song transition, when politics caused tension and anxiety possibly similar to the tension and anxiety seen in the world today. Perhaps it brings us some ease to recall how Tang–Song tension led to remarkable sociocultural advancements (Bol 1994; Yang 2003. In 2022, "Poetic Dance: The Journey of a Legendary Landscape Painting," a dance program inspired by one of the most famous Chinese landscape paintings, *A Panorama of Mountains and Rivers* by Wang Ximeng (1096–1119) of the Northern Song dynasty (960–1279), became an instant hit in China after it premiered at the state-sponsored Lunar New Year Gala through China's Central Television Channel (CCTV). Cultural elements from the Song before the Mongol Yuan dynasty (1271–1368) have become more visible in China, inspiring more expressive art productions. After the war-torn Five Dynasties period (907–960) that followed the fall of Tang, rather than focusing on military prowess and strategic innovation, the Song favored realpolitik and a peace agreement with militant neighbors. Society was marked by the spectacular growth of the economy, the population, and urbanization, and the people were governed by highly educated scholar-officials chosen through a civil-service examination, who implemented Confucian ideology as political orthodoxy. Scholars often consider the Song dynasty one of the most humane, cultured, and intellectual periods in Chinese imperial history. From the mid-Tang period to the early Song, the Buddhist community in Dunhuang started promoting the practice of journeying to Mount Wutai, located in China's Central Plateau, rather than journeying abroad to central Eurasia. In the Southern Song (1127–1279), warfare in the Dunhuang region became more frequent, and commerce gradually shifted from land to sea routes. Accordingly, Dunhuang lost its stature as the economic gateway to the Western Regions. During the Yuan dynasty, one of the most famous staged Dunhuang art pieces, *The Thousand-Handed and Thousand-Eyed Avalokiteśvara* (*Qianshou qianyan Guanyin* 千手千眼觀音), was inspired by the Avalokiteśvara painted in cave murals. During and after the Ming dynasty (1368–1644), nomadic Mongolian tribes occupied the region, and no new caves were created.

Performatively, Dunhuang expressive arts bring forth the propensity (*shi* 勢) of the staged *tianxia* worldview through suggestiveness. *Shi* are trends hidden in the trajectories of power. The execution—the physical movement trajectories of the tangible—are core elements found in the staged Dunhuang expressive arts in space, but time, as the essence of all expressive art performances, directs our attention to the propensity of the staged *tianxia* worldview. The developments of the Dunhuang expressive arts as an integral part of contemporary China's advancement are arguably a concealed trajectory of power to be examined closely.

Perhaps most importantly, the staging process of these arts enables the emergence of the poetic and the specifics in time-space. The stage is a fluid performative metaphor, with boundaries that shift to redefine the center and the periphery, the civilized and the alienated, the settled and the frontier. Through staged performances, these arts bring into being a hermeneutical openness in aesthetic sensibilities and embody the past and present relations and the discursive formation of *tianxia* and its heritage. Allegorically, within the confines of performative metaphors, these arts serve as an embodied aesthetic metaphor of *tianxia*.

History, the core of all modern nations and one of the main conceptualizing elements in the Dunhuang expressive arts, is enacted by social actors through the interplay of languages, symbols, and movements, as dynamic relations of power rather than static sets of meanings. The performative processes of initiating the Chinascapes embodied in these arts offer glimpses of China's changing approach to manifesting *tianxia* by reinventing its heritage.

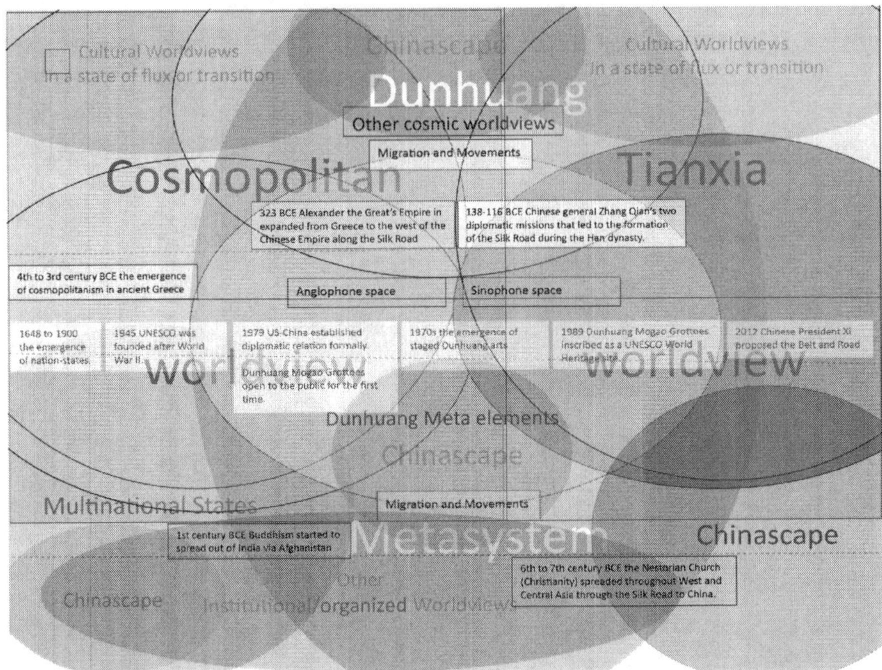



Figure 2.2. A working metagraph of the Dunhuang expressive arts in relation to the Chinascape and *tianxia* concepts. Please visit https://lanlankuangofficial.pub/ for a colorized version and other multimedia components for *Staging* Tianxia. © Lanlan Kuang, 2024.

Instead of a conventional timeline, the metagraph in figure 2.2 presents the ancient but exceedingly institutionalized *tianxia* worldview in the Sinophone space and highlights its presence and subtle—but debatably continuous—emergence through linguistic and sociocultural means. The Chinascape as a modern conceptual landscape comes into being with the classical *tianxia* worldview in the backdrop. Unlike *tianxia*, which has deeper roots and greater influence in the Sinophone space (making its cross-cultural transmission difficult), the Chinascape as a contemporarily traceable phenomenon banks on the modern nation-state and multinational state systems. The Chinascape therefore could be staged through elements such as those from the Dunhuang metasystem more easily in the Anglophone space, where the cosmopolitan worldview still exists as a cultural or academic ideal, even if it might no longer be an effective political world order. By using this graphic, of course, I do not mean to ignore other important factors in the shaping of a conceptualized cosmic worldview, such as military means and economic instruments: I focus instead on what Joseph Nye (2004a–d) called soft power, especially elements constituting the Dunhuang metasystem.

Frequently staged through projects produced by China's Bureau of Commerce, Office of State Propaganda, and Office of State Archival Research, the Dunhuang arts, as early as the 1990s, were developed and produced as a part of China's demonstration of soft power, defined as "the ability to get what you want through attraction rather than through coercion" (Nye 2004d: 256). For instance, in "A 30-Year History: Exhibition on China's Opening Up," a 2008 web exhibition set up by the Chinese government to celebrate China's thirty-year anniversary of its adoption of the open-door policy and liberal economic reforms in 1978,[10] displayed multiple versions of *Dunhuang bihua yuewu* programs. These were presented as examples of cultural development achievements submitted by Gansu Province.

According to Nye (2004c), "Soft power grows out of a country's culture; it grows out of our values—democracy and human rights, when we live up to them; it grows out of our policies." This power "could be cultivated through relations with allies, economic assistance, and cultural exchanges" (2004a, 2004b). The concept has been further developed in scholarly publications about China's growing prominence in the contemporary world. These works—such as Joshua Kurlantzick's publications in 2007 and the articles collected under the title of *Chinese Soft Power and Its Implications for the United States*, assembled by the Center for Strategic and International Studies (McGiffert 2009)—investigated China's soft power, in addition to its conventional military and economic power. Although my study on the staged Dunhuang arts does not focus on China's soft power per se, my look into the staging processes of the Dunhuang arts, especially the *Dunhuang bihua yuewu* genre, was conducted in the light and context of the contemporary discourse on soft power.

Art may embody a full ensemble of intellectual, aesthetic, and moral values, but these values are shaped by and represent power. As seen in *Dunhuang bihua yuewu*, music, dance, theatrical drama, and other forms of expressive arts are a means through which the moving force of these archaeological materials reveals the shapes and movements of power as it emerges, using rhetorical gestures—such as naming, discussing, and negotiating—to create a genre. In *Dunhuang bihua yuewu*, the movements of power that emerge through performance become associated with a nation and the representations of its history.

It is through performance and enactment that we can see the intersection of the past and the future and the politicization of aesthetics. It is through the embodiments of artistic time and space within layers of performances that history and geography acquire what Bakhtin called "a unique center of value" (1995: 208). Embodiments serve as the grounding for conceptual metaphors in art and culture, especially for the poetic language that metaphorically and intertextually "stages," or they evoke physiopsychologically sensuous imagery from the past to enact representation of the past and visions of the present (Bauman 2004; Bauman and Briggs 1990; Lakoff and Johnson 1980; Johnson 1987).[11] History and geography may acquire "a center of value" through performance and enactment, but this acquisition of value is nevertheless temporary. The center of value is constantly challenged, shifted, and contested. Examining a work of art—in particular, examining the moving and sonic forces that constitute a staged performance—involves studying the sounds and movements of power as it emerges.

## Contemporary Performance and Theory

Performance theory identifies structural devices within performances to understand the structures of power and its networks of distribution (Stone 2007: 136–140). The structures and networks of power that have shaped the creation of *Dunhuang bihua yuewu* and staged Dunhuang arts have developed for a long period and have affected expressive arts. In the 1960s and 1970s in China, the state was the dominant agency of power, responsible for reconstructing and maintaining ideas of a Chinese musical identity. By strategically reconstructing the performances of middle-level music workers, the state reconstructed the performances of what it considered to be popular, folk, and ethnic minority musics and created a national discourse through the performing arts.

The recreation of the staged Dunhuang arts in the late 1970s was driven by the state's desire to reconstruct the Dunhuang arts as Chinese national arts. The concept of "ethnic minority" was important throughout much of the twentieth century (and remains so today), in relation not only to the labeling of music but, more importantly, to the classifications of peoples within the borders of China. The national government recognizes fifty-five officially classified minority groups in China today. In much contemporary Chinese discourse, relations between the Han population and the non-Han minorities are commonly explained to be a result of China's history of interactions between the Chinese heartland and the settlement of China's borders (*siyi* 四夷). Some anthropologists in the West have questioned the validity of China's classification system regarding ethnicity, which is "based on Stalin's definition of 'nation' and on a notion of fixed racial categories rather than recognizing ethnicity as a fluid, situational and changeable" (M. Yang 1996: 121; see also D. Wu 1990, 2004; Gladney 1991). More recent studies have been conducted by Uradyn Bulag (2012), Jing Li (2013), and others. Bulag's (2012) article on tourism sheds light on the country's political processes for managing ethnic minority relations by curating touristic spectacles for the ethnic minority elites from the peripherals, thereby enforcing the traditional Chinese tributary system or the center-peripheral hierarchy.[12] Li's (2013) study of the Yunnan provincial government's presentations of minority folk song and dance performances at the 2007 Smithsonian Folklife Festival in Washington, DC, shows how local governments program ethnic performing arts to achieve political and economic goals.

The categorization of the people living within the political borders of China into two primary categories (Han Chinese and ethnic minorities) and the further classification of ethnic minorities into fifty-five minority nationalities remains part of the dominant discourse in China and beyond, and these categories frame the construction of discourse about the staged Dunhuang arts: "We still have a great deal of work to do to decouple ethnicity, as it functions in the dominant discourse, from its equivalence with nationalism, imperialism, racism and the state. . . . What is involved is the splitting of the notion of ethnicity between, on the one hand the dominant notion which connects it to nation and 'race' and on the other hand what I think is the beginning of a positive conception of the ethnicity of the margins, of the periphery" (Hall 1996: 442).

The staged Dunhuang arts thus help perpetuate the dominant discourse of the state as nation, but they complicate these discourses: rather than being "a unified corpus of symbols and meanings that can be definitively interpreted" (Clifford and Marcus 1986: 18), the multifaceted culture they perform is temporal and emergent, created and transmitted through historical processes. The distinctive aesthetic ideal embodied in the staged Dunhuang arts enacts the meta-elements suggestive of the Mogao Grottoes and beyond. The genre incorporates a unique politics of aestheticization within and through the manifestation of *tianxia*.

## *Nationalism, Modernity, and* Tianxia

Prasenjit Duara (1996), Ulrich Beck (2006), Craig Calhoun (2007), and others have approached nationalism—a concept that emerged in late eighteenth- and early nineteenth-century Europe—as a historical phenomenon. They analyze the continuous writing of national history as part of the creation of nations, and they consider cosmopolitanism and nationalism as mutually constitutive.[13] Scholars who write in the presence of nationalism are frequently drawn to the history of the nation and choose to adopt or incorporate a historical approach in their research. Nonetheless, "the nation," argues Duara, as "the subject of History" is "never able to completely bridge the aporias between the past and the present" (1996: 29).

Other key concepts, however, can be brought to bear to understand the relation between past and present, such as the concept of *tianxia* (天下), which is interesting because it was key to the governance and self-understanding of three millennia of the Chinese empire and discussion of it is becoming popular again in the twenty-first century (Callahan 2007: 2). Along with the concept of the Mandate of Heaven, a ritualized process that legitimatized the ruler as the "Son of Heaven" (*tian zi* 天子) to rule a centralized kingdom and its outstretched, reutilized agrarian borderland states, the *tianxia* system emerged during the Zhou dynasty (1045–256 BCE), embodying a Chinese vision of world order that subsequently grew.[14]

The idea of *tian* itself may be traced back to the Zhou dynasty. The prevalence of ritual systems and practices in the Zhou dynasty marked China as a land of ceremony and propriety (Yong and Peng 2008: 41). Nevertheless, ancient Chinese scholars' examination of earlier textual references led them to believe that the idea of a celestial realm may be traced back even further than the Zhou dynasty. For example, the first chapter of the *Classic of History* (*Shangshu* 尚書, 772–476 BCE), titled "The Canon of Yao" (*Yao dianpian* 堯典篇), includes the statement "By order of Yihe, the royals like heaven, and the sun and moon and constellations record historic fact, to bestow time to the people" (乃命羲和, 钦若昊天, 历象日月星辰, 敬授人时). This statement is a record of the celestial realm before what we now call China had become a social state (Wang 2001). In texts found on Shang dynasty (1600–1046 BCE) oracle bones, although the character *tian* (天) was primarily used to express a meaning of "grandness," it also could mean "the supreme one." At times, it was even inscribed with the character *di* 帝, an imperial ruler. At the same time, *di* also functions as a name for a sacrifice and a signal to burn a sacrificed item at a high place.[15] This interpretation is supported by historical references dating to the early Qin dynasty (221–210 BCE). By the Han dynasty, Chinese thinkers had already articulated the profound interdependence between humans and the subcelestial realm. Scholars like Yang Xiong 揚雄 (53—18 BCE) argued that without a profound interconnection between humans and the subcelestial realm, the very purpose of human creations would be rendered meaningless. The celestial realm's fabrications would lack purpose without human understanding. This delicate relationship underscores how notions of the subcelestial emerged only after the establishment of philosophical frameworks focused on the celestial sphere. It was only when theories centered on the celestial realm matured that concepts regarding the subcelestial could come to fruition. Consequently, only when a philosophy of the celestial realm was established could the idea of the subcelestial come into being. (Yong and Peng 2008)

Staged Dunhuang arts are thus intended to contemporize a historical past and crystallize a vision of a multicultural China and Chineseness in the present, as well as to recontextualize the *tianxia* system within contemporary geopolitical, economic, and cultural-historical discourses. Ethnographic research and the analysis of discursive and performative forms show that staging the Dunhuang arts resembles what Michel Foucault calls a process of creating a countermemory, a transformation of history into a different form of time (Foucault 1977; Aylesworth 2010). For audiences familiar with what Susan Blum and Lionel Jensen (2002) called "an image of China as a homogeneous society and culture," the processes of developing and institutionalizing the *Dunhuang bihua yuewu* as a genre within the category of Chinese classical dance (*Zhongguo gudian wu* 中國古典舞) demonstrate the attempt to recreate a multicultural national identity. In staged Dunhuang arts performances, the countermemory reasserts the authenticity of a history shaped by a monolithic value system. To stage a vision of a historically cosmopolitan Chineseness, creators require an other to legitimize the notion of a self—of being Chinese.

In the foreword to *China Off Center: Mapping the Margins of the Middle Kingdom*, Prasenjit Duara (2002) begins a discussion of conceptions of Chineseness by asking why "the enduring image of China as a homogeneous society and culture—Chin as a distinctly 'centered' society—persists? What are the conditions and causes of its production in China?" He points out the importance of examining the "complexity and contradiction of any view of [China]" (xiii–xvi). Chineseness has been approached by modern scholars as a concept that allows people of the English-speaking world to participate rhetorically in the processes of understanding who (which people) and what (which territory and polity) are being referenced by the term *Chinese* in different historical and discursive contexts (Chow 1998, 2001).

It is difficult for scholars to map the conceptual territorial space within which research can be situated, and the expression of Chinese civilization and its usage in academic discourse are still being contested, but the term *Chineseness* has nevertheless been intertextually incorporated into the processes of assimilating and appropriating diverse elements into the modern, contemporary, and living signifiers of *tianxia* (天下).

## Key Concepts in Historical Context

As noted in the first chapter, the sources of the *Dunhuang bihua yuewu* genre are primarily images, narratives, and musical tunes depicted in the wall paintings and documents discovered in the Mogao Grottoes at Dunhuang. The genre tends to draw primarily from the artistic creations from the Sui (581–618) and Tang (618–907) dynasties, although artistic patterns established earlier, beginning in the Han dynasty (206 BCE–220 CE), are evident in it, as are folkloric motifs from contemporary popular narratives and vernacular literature with nonreligious themes. The Sui dynasty reunified Southern and Northern China after almost three hundred years of fragmentation, and the Tang dynasty is the period most often cited in relation to the idea of cosmopolitanism historically in China (Lewis 2009; Schafer 1985). The Han dynasty, however, inherited a centralized organization from the Qin dynasty (221–207 BCE) and initiated some of the earliest encounters with political powers beyond China proper (Drompp 2005). These historical processes and artistic patterns have long histories and have influenced many artistic forms. For instance, Gao Jinrong (2002) discusses the predominant influences of Sui and Tang on the staged Dunhuang arts. Victor Mair (1989) and Hung Wu (1992) discuss the Tang dynasty's artistic culture and, especially, Dunhuang transformation texts (*bianwen* 變文). Joseph Levenson (1971) and Colin Mackerras (1989), in contrast, focus on the impact of foreign cultures on the rise of modern Chinese theatrical forms. My research on these historical sources has identified "aesthetic suggestiveness," "self-referentiality," and other key concepts associated with the staged Dunhuang arts, as explained below.

*Aesthetic Suggestiveness and Self-referentiality*

Aesthetic suggestiveness (美學暗示) and self-referentiality (自指性) are key concepts associated with my research on the staged Dunhuang arts. "Aesthetic suggestiveness" has been explored extensively in discussions of the arts. It literally means "to show something by indirectly hinting at it" and is often coupled with the word *aesthetic* in artistic discourse, and so it becomes an aesthetic principle (Gu Mingdong 2003).

The prologue to *Chinese Aesthetics: The Ordering of Literature, the Arts, and the Universe in the Six Dynasties*, discusses the appropriateness of applying to the Chinese tradition the term *aesthetics*, a word of Western origin, and lays out some doubts about such practices:[16]

> The philosophical sophistication of such reflection in Ancient Greece is attested by Plato's *Hippias Major* and Aristotle's *Poetics*, which were formative texts for the Western tradition, but until very recently there was nothing in this tradition comparable to the level of Chinese reflection on painting reached in a text such as Chang Yen-yuan's *Li-Tai Ming-hua Chi* (*Records of Famous Paintings*). Yet it would be extremely imprudent to collect these and other examples of reflection on art and beauty under the title of "aesthetics." The latter is not only of modern origin, but its preoccupations, direction of analysis, and consequently its internal system of division and classification are specifically European and should not be applied to either pre-modern or non-European materials. (Elliott 1996, quoted in Zong-qi Cai 2004: 24)

*Aesthetics* is indeed "a term of modern European origin, coined from the Greek *aesthesis* by the eighteenth-century thinker Alexander Gottlieb Baumgarten to designate contemporary studies of art and beauty as a distinct discipline of systematic, scientific inquiry," and if "'aesthetics' refers exclusively to this modern European discipline, of course, one would have to allow Elliott's disqualification of Chinese aesthetics'" (Zong-qi Cai 2004: 24). Nevertheless, the broader meaning of *aesthetics* can fairly refer to all Western philosophies of art and beauty, not excluding those surviving from earlier times, given that "there are serious practices and theories of art in any given tradition" (Zong-qi Cai 2004: 24). This broader concept is important here, if only because the notion of aesthetics is central to the discourse of contemporary China and to the creators of the *Dunhuang bihua yuewu*.

Aesthetic suggestiveness is considered to be "the ideal of all Chinese art" by Feng Youlan (馮友蘭), a renowned historian of Chinese philosophy, who notes that the writings of the *Analects* and the *Laozi Text* (also known as the *Daodejing* 道德經) are "aphorisms full of suggestiveness. It is the suggestiveness that is attractive" (1983: 12–13). Gu Mingdong quotes Feng Youlan's interpretation of aesthetic suggestiveness as a poetic technique: "In poetry, what the poet intends to communicate is often not what is directly said in the poetry, but what is not said in it." He [Feng] also considers it an artistic effect: "'According to Chinese literary tradition, in good poetry the number of words is limited, but the ideas it suggests are limitless.' So an intelligent reader of poetry reads what is outside the poem; and a good reader of books reads 'what is between the lines'" (2003: 490–491).

Feng argues that this inarticulateness is what makes Chinese philosophy uniquely Chinese (Wu Xiaoming 1998). Gu compares the Chinese concept of aesthetic suggestiveness with the postmodern conception of openness: "Within the broader context of Chinese tradition, the Chinese concept of suggestiveness is a product of the interpenetration of and exchanges between philosophical and artistic discourses. It is a symphony performed by metaphysics and aesthetics in harmonious accord[, and it] comes very close to the postmodern conceptions of unlimited semiosis and 'openness'" (2003: 490–491).

These discussions on self-referentiality in performing arts and the Chinese concept of aesthetic suggestiveness show that, while the Chinese concept of aesthetic suggestiveness leads to unlimited semiosis and openness, self-referentiality in the performative Dunhuang meta-elements provides an a priori historical reference for the production and authentication of suggestiveness, transforming them within pertinent frameworks. The *Dunhuang bihua yuewu* dancers and the wall painting of two apsaras in the theatrical drama *Dunhuang, My Dreamland*, for instance, are meta-elements strategically staged for their suggestive self-referentiality.

Self-referentiality has been a central issue in postmodern studies of the arts (Chow 2005; Gu 2003; Spanos 1990; H. Wu 1996, 1997). In the staging of Dunhuang expressive arts, I consider self-referentiality to be both a Foucaultian process, which emerged as a key problematic in language as the outcome of a shifting relationship confined by historical forces, and a process of transferred designations of meta-elements (Baert 1998; Chow 2005; Foucault 1977, 1990, 1991).

The self-referential meta-elements reveal the aesthetic suggestiveness unique to Dunhuang and, most importantly, to Chinese artistic philosophy. These performative, self-referential images, styles, gestures, discourses, narratives, tunes, and musical instruments were employed and embodied by actors involved in the processes of staging Dunhuang arts. These meta-elements thus informed a conceptual landscape of Dunhuang on the contemporary stage and became strategic and communicative devices employed to create metaphors for imagining and enacting a historically cosmopolitan Chinese culture.

Pictorial self-reference and self-referentiality in artistic performances have been studied by W. J. T. Mitchell (1995), Elin Diamond (1996), and others. Diamond points out that "every performance, if it is intelligible as such, embeds features of previous performances: gender conventions, racial histories, aesthetic traditions—political and cultural pressures that are consciously and unconsciously acknowledged" (1996: 1). In staged Dunhuang arts, through historical, performative, and rhetorical processes, actors stage and simultaneously become self-referential meta-elements, disclosing the aesthetic suggestiveness unique to the Dunhuang materials. The meta-elements fundamental to the *Dunhuang bihua yuewu* are defined essentially by their features of pragmatic use and suggestive functionality in forming a cosmopolitan image of China.

### *Vision, Conceptual Landscape, and* Tianxia

In my examination of the processes through which the *Dunhuang bihua yuewu* recreates a vision of China, I employ the concept of Chinascape, understood in relation to notions of vision (*yixiang* 意象), conceptual landscape, or world of ideas (*yijing* 意境), and the subcelestial (*tianxia* 天下). The notion of vision (*yixiang* 意象) is derived from "idea" (*yi* 意) and "image/figure" (*xiang* 象). Pauline Yu, Martin Powers, Stephen Owen, and others have explored the dynamic performativity of image in ancient Chinese poetry and literature in general. Yu has argued that *xiang* "does not correspond to 'representation' in the European sense but is more integrally related to its object than 'representation' implies" (1987: 57). Powers argues that *xiang* is an "expressive figure" and "configuration," a "consequence or result of some other activity," and is a verb meaning "to express" (2000: 219–235). Owen, connecting poetry and painting, argues: "By leaving the mimesis of sensuous surfaces . . . and learning to represent the norm within the visual particular, painting is able to have conceptual content embodied in 'images,' *xiang*, as poetry does" (2000: 219). Yu (1987) argues that mimesis is predicated on a fundamental disjunction between two realms of being, one of which is replicated in the verbal product, regarded by Plato, for example, as but a pale shadow of some timeless truth. In contrast, implicit through-out the classic Chinese text "The Great Commentary" within the "Great Preface" to the *Book of Odes* (*Shijing* 詩經) is the assumption of a seamless connection, if not virtual identity, between an object, its perception, and its representation. This perception is aided by the semantic multivalence of the term *xiang* (象).

In a discussion of the "interplay between image and concept," Hellmut Wilhelm (2011) argues that the impulse in "The Great Commentary" seems to assert correlations between image and concept. This idea was developed in an essay titled "Elucidating the Image" (*Ming xiang* 明象) by Wang Bi 王弼 (226–249), who annotated *The Book of Changes* (*Yi jing* 易經), which was said to have been completed during the Zhou dynasty (1066–256 BCE). Wang Bi opens by declaring:

夫象者，出意者也；言者，明象者也。盡意莫若象，盡象莫若言。言生于象，故可寻言以觀象，象生于意，故可寻象以觀意。意以象盡，象以言著。故言者所明象，得象以忘言；象者所以存意，得意而忘象。

Images are the means to express ideas. Words (i.e., the texts) are the means to explain the images. To yield up ideas completely, there is nothing better than the images, and to yield up the meaning of the images, there is nothing better than words. The words are generated by the images, thus one can ponder the words and so observe what the images are. The images are generated by idea, thus one can ponder the images and so observe what the ideas are. The ideas are yielded up completely by the images, and the images are made explicit by the words. Thus, once the words are the means to explain the images, once one gets the images, he forgets the words, and since the images are the means to allow us to concentrate on the idea, once one gets the ideas, he forgets the images. (Wang Bi 1976, translated in Lynn 1994: 25–46)

## *"Return to Antiquity"* (Fu-gu 復古)

The key concept of "return to antiquity" motivated, at least in part, the creation of the *Dunhuang bihua yuewu* in the twentieth century, but this concept itself is embedded within a much longer history. Niall Ferguson's (2010) review of Thomas Cole's *The Course of Empire* (*1833–36*), a series of five American landscape paintings conserved by the New-York Historical Society,[17] states that Cole's paintings display foresight of the complexity and collapse emerging from the life cycle of a great power. Ferguson conceptu-ally reframes these paintings through a discussion of the current affairs of the United States and recreates for his contemporaries another vision of the country, based on what he sees captured in these images: "a perception not only of the pastness of the past, but of its presence" (2010). T. S. Eliot (1888–1965) called this sort of perception "the historical sense" (1920: 43). Whereas Eliot considered this sense indispensable for defining tradition, I consider it fundamental in some of the contemporarily created expressive arts staged to legitimatize a particular pastness that could enact the history of China's present. "Archaism" (*guyi* 古意) was this perception in its Chinese context.

Zhao Mengfu 赵孟頫 (1254–1322), a Han literatus-painter during a century of Mongol occupation (1279–1368),[18] drawing on the aesthetic values of the ancient masters, invoked *guyi* to recreate an artistic tradition resembling the image of the thousand-armed and thousand-eyed Avalokiteśvara in the now-famous Dunhuang Mogao Cave No. 3. This image is one of the most studied wall paintings in the Mogao Grottoes and a prominent inspiration for the *Dunhuang bihua yuewu*.[19] Zhao and a group of Yuan dynasty literati-painters set a course for future scholar-painting (*wenren hua* 文人画) by highlighting the essentiality of archaism (H. Wu 2008: 106; Ortiz 1999: 166).

Zhao was not the first to advocate a concept of archaism in Chinese history. The earliest known reference to this concept can be traced to the Western Zhou dynasty (1046–771 BCE) in *The Book of Odes* (*Shijing* 詩經). Nevertheless, the reinvigoration of the tradition occurred in southern China, where the people who had resisted the Mongol invasion the longest faced official discrimination. This concept eventually had unforeseen effects on the recreation of one of the most studied wall paintings at Dunhuang.

From very early on in the Confucian tradition, the Zhou rituals were the foundation of the polity, as the state rituals were categorized according to the ancient classic *Rituals of Zhou* (*Zhouli* 周禮).[20] The rituals were measurements for circumstantial calculations in state matters and power struggles. The regulatory functions of music, as an emblem of political authority, are emphasized in Chinese classics such as the *Chronicle of Zuo* (*Zuozhuan* 左傳) and the *Discourses of the States* (*Guoyu* 國語). Music is a key to understanding past, present, and future developments in the history of Chinese aesthetic thought. In the *Book of Rites* (禮記 *Liji*, p. 1013), for instance, Prince Wen of Wei asks Confucius's disciple Zixia: "When I put on the ritual cap and listen to ancient music, my only fear is that I will doze off; but when I listen to the notes of Zheng and Wei, I do not know fatigue. May I ask why ancient music is like that? Why is new music like this?" In response, Zixia describes ancient music as solemn and stately, as "expansive in harmonious rectitude" (*hezhengyiguang* 和正以廣), and as instilling respect for tradition, vigilant self-cultivation, and just government.

By contrast, new music "overflows with deviant sounds, and its overwhelming extravagance has no limits" (*jianshengyilan, ruoerbuzhi* 姦声以滥,溺而不止; W. Li 2007: 118–146), "indulging in sensual excesses and harming virtue" (*yingyuseerhaiyude* 淫於色而害於德). Fast and stirring music is linked to sexual license, not only analogically, as in parallel modes of excess, but also literally, as in descriptions in early texts of men and women consorting freely to the accompaniment of musical entertainment in aristocratic chambers or in some vaguely folk or rustic settings. The "Great Preface" to the *Book of Odes* states, "Emotions are stirred within and take form in words. When words are not enough [to express emotions], one sighs about it; when sighing is not enough, one sings them in songs" (情動於中而形於言。言之不足故嗟嘆之, 嗟嘆之不足故永歌之) (Cai 2001: 44–45). According to classical Confucian theories, music resonates with internal emotions and the external world; therefore, it has the power to influence the body and the mind.

## The Genealogy of Philosophies of the Body and Ritual

The human body became a central issue in Chinese thought in the fourth century BCE, when the school of Yang Zhu and the practice of self-cultivation described in the *nei ye* 內業 theorized it as the natural and necessary center for organizing space. The *Mencius* (*Mengzi*) 孟子 [21] and the *Chronicle of Zuo* (*Zuozhuan* 左傳) presented the body as the source of virtue and ritual order. Several of these ideas, however, were anticipated in the Confucian *Analects* (*Lunyu* 论语), compiled during the Spring and Autumn period through the Warring States period (475–221 BCE). Correcting the body is the basis of social order, according to two notable passages that discuss explicitly ritual and the concept of the "true gentleman." These texts emphasize the importance of physical refinement and self-improvement and evaluate the body and its components as indicators of worth or value. Cultivating the body serves as the foundation for maintaining social harmony (Lewis 2005: 14–15).

Performing rituals in ancient China demanded precise bodily control. Texts emphasized specific postures—kneeling, bowing, turning, and more. Consequently, Confucius and his followers elevated ritual to a fundamental category, assigning the human body a central role in their social framework. Within the *Analects*, for instance, some passages cleverly linked the term for ritual (*li* 禮) to words related to the body or its manipulation. These texts established a close phonetic and visual connection between ritual and the body (*ti* 體). An essay in the *Book of Rites* (*Liji* 禮記) juxtaposed "bodiless ritual" (*wutizhili* 無體之禮) with "soundless music" and "mourning without mourning garments," emphasizing the body as the essence of ritual. Although this gloss is not explicitly suggested in the Analects, certain passages hinted at a link between *li* (meaning "ritual") and the verb *li* 立 (meaning "to stand"), signifying both physical and social positioning. One such text described the process of cultivating full humanity: "Inspired/initiated (*xing* 興) by the odes; established (*li* 立, 'made to stand') through ritual; completed in music." The correct alignment of the body, even without the character *li* 立, played a crucial role in the legendary ruler Shun's method of governance—simply by "making himself reverent and facing south."

The link between ritual and body also figures in the passage on the Confucian doctrine of the "rectification of names" (*zhengming* 正名): "If affairs are not completed, then ritual and music will not arise [*xing* 興]. If music and ritual do not arise, then punishments will not be correct. If punishments are not correct, then the people will have no place to set their hands and feet." Again, the definition of true humanity as "taming the self and restoring the rituals" defines this injunction through an itemized list of the control of the body by ritual: "If it is not ritual, do not look at it; if it is not ritual, do not listen to it; if it is not ritual, do not say it; if it is not ritual, do not move." This pattern of itemizing the body as a set of discrete units that must be separately controlled became fundamental to Warring States accounts of both corporal and social order (Lewis 2005: 73–74).

My research on the *Dunhuang bihua yuewu* shows that the body has been an important subject in discussions of the genre because it is an embodiment of multifaceted cultural ideas and meta-elements. Throughout my interviews with dance scholars and Dunhuangologists, the theme of expressing through the body consistently emerged. Dance scholars, notably Gao Jinrong, emphasized the significance of self-cultivation for dancers aiming to portray Buddhist deities. Meanwhile, Dunhuangologists have intently studied the physical attributes and attire of performers and divine figures depicted in the Dunhuang wall paintings to learn more about their historical context and ethnic origins.

*Selection of Images from the Mogao Wall Paintings*

Not only do the creators of the *Dunhuang bihua yuewu* make connections between their aesthetics and those of the Chinese past but the material from which they draw—the wall paintings within the Dunhuang caves—provides them with examples from antiquity, including the depiction of a variety of people and deities engaged in ritual and music performance. The musicians thus depicted are of various types, such as gandharvas (*xiangyinshen* 香音神), kinaras (*jinluona* 緊那羅), and kalavinkas (*jialinpinjia* 伽陵頻伽). The gandharvas are one of the eight categories of deities who serve the Dharma; kalavinkas are celestial beings with a bird's body and an angelic head. Gandharvas in the earlier caves, built during the Northern Wei (439–534) and Western Wei (535–556) dynasties, are "deity-musicians," playing instruments while staying behind the windowsill in the heavenly realm of the Buddhist cosmos; however, gandharvas from the Sui (581–681) and Tang (618–907) dynasties fly freely in the heavenly realm while playing instruments. The last set of musicians depicted in the paintings accompany dancers serving the Dharma: they sit in groups, and their positions on the stage in the paintings resemble those of court entertainers during the Sui and Tang dynasties. Additionally, secular themes include musicians playing instruments, usually to accompany a dancer performing next to them.

Dancing figures in the Mogao wall paintings consist of gandharvas, apsaras (*abushaluosi* 阿布沙羅斯), yakṣas (*yaocha* 藥叉), and kalavinkas (*jialinpinjia* 迦陵頻伽), as well as secular dancers with physical appearances and outfits of ethnic groups found along the Silk Road. Like the gandharvas, the apsaras fly in the heavenly realm, usually empty-handed but sometimes strewing flowers. These celestial beings (*yuren* 羽人), popularly known in China as apsaras (*feitian* 飛天), a term originating from Buddhism, are among the most representative and studied images from the Mogao Grottoes; once a hybrid of folklore, myth, Daoism, and Buddhist beliefs, they have served as an icon of modern China and as an important element of *Dunhuang bihua yuewu* performances. The yakṣas are twelve divine generals who serve Bhaiṣajyaguru (*yaoshi liuliguang rulai* 藥師琉璃光如來), the Medicine Master of Vaidūryanirbhāsa (Lapis Lazuli Radiance); the yakṣas in the wall paintings are portrayed as males. The kalavinkas are usually positioned in the center of a courtly dance performance.

Secular dancers usually appear in the Dunhuang murals in performative events, as in the celebration of a wedding or a drinking party. For instance, a marriage ceremony between a Tibetan man and a Han woman appears in the Amitāyurdhyāna Sūtra mural, found on the southern wall of Dunhuang Yulin Cave 25. In addition to depicting performative events that would allow viewers of the paintings to share knowledge of sociocultural

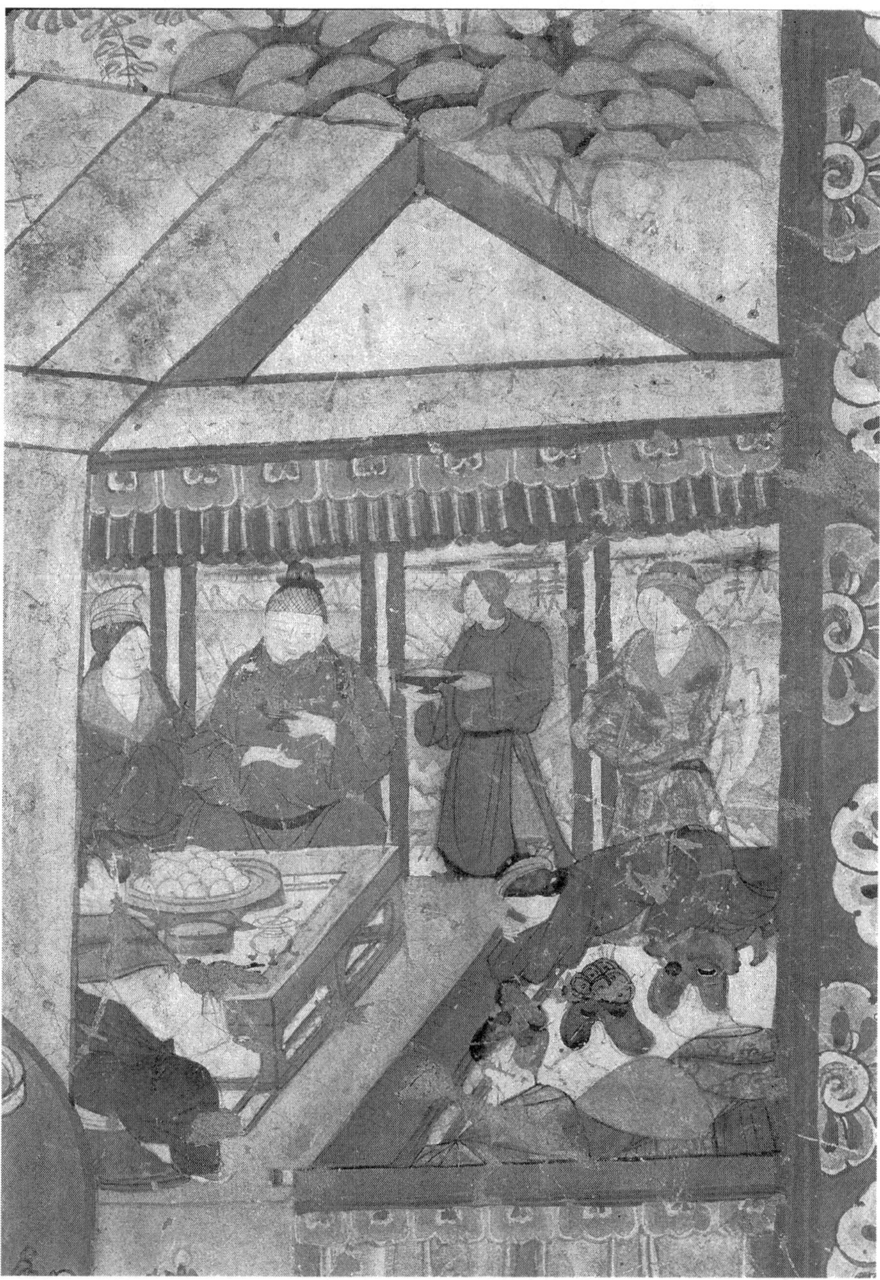

Figure 2.3. Yulin Cave 25, southern wall, mural of the marriage of a Tibetan man and a Han woman in the Amitāyurdhyāna Sūtra. Permission to use image granted by Dunhuang Academy.

conditions during the time when the caves were created and decorated, some of the paintings contain important data on political events, reflecting the multiethnicity and multiculturality of the environment from which the Dunhuang arts drew their elements and inspirations. For instance, dancers dressed in Tufan (*Tubo* 吐蕃) outfits in the wall paintings in Cave 156 are presented as part of a group celebrating and welcoming the return of Zhang Yichao 張義潮 (799–872), a Han general and a resident of Dunhuang. According to the *Comprehensive Mirror to Aid in Government* (*Zizhi tongjian* 資治通鑑), a historical reference text, Zhang led a rebellion against the Tufan and returned the region to allegiance to the Chinese empire. He subsequently conquered the region of the Hexi Corridor (*Hexi zoulang* 河西走廊) and ruled it as the military governor (*jiedushi* 節度使) of the Guiyi Circuit (*Guiyi Jun* 歸義軍; also translated as "Return-to-Allegiance Army") under the nominal authority of the Tang emperors.

The central themes of the wall paintings created in the Northern Liang dynasty (421–439 CE) during the Sixteen Kingdoms period were jātaka tales recounting the previous births of Śākyamuni Gautama Buddha, in both human and animal forms, as well as illustrations of Buddha preaching Dharma teachings. Each image of Buddha, whether the Lord of the Eastern Realm of Pure Lapis Lazuli or various Bodhisattva figures, was created to fit the spatial design of the cave, which changed according to the period of construction. The interiors of the caverns, where these visual narratives resided, served as theatrical stages for worship and reimagination. Here, the Buddhist deities and their attendants invite the gaze of visitors who are effectively worshipping them as they arrive.

## Music Archaeology and the Reconstruction of Historical Music

Those involved in reconstructing historical music today can refer to a wealth of examples from antiquity that comment on music and its connections to political states and to history itself. One of the most famous examples of the judgment of causes and consequences through musical performance was made by Wu Gongzi Jizha 吳公子季扎 during the Spring and Autumn period (771–476 BCE). His observation (*guan* 觀) of dance and music from various states and periods while visiting the state of Lu led him to comment on the power of music as a reflection of the state and its ruler. He hailed from Wu, a state sometimes characterized as semibarbarian in the *Chronicle of Zuo*

(*Zuozhuan*, or *ZZ*), yet he possessed superior knowledge of the rituals, traditions, and history of the central states. Lu received from the Zhou court the musical traditions of the Yu, Xia, Shang, and Zhou eras (*ZZ*, p. 1161) and is adduced elsewhere in the *Chronicle* as the guardian of Zhou rites (*ZZ* Min 1.5, p. 257), Zhou music (*ZZ* Xiang 10.2, p. 977), and Zhou texts (*ZZ* Zhao 2.1, p. 1227). In the concert for Jizha, the sequences of performance correspond in part to the Mao tradition of the *Odes* and may have reflected the order of presentation in the Lu exegetical tradition of the *Odes*, now no longer extant.[22]

Many of Jizha's comments begin with an immediate appreciation of the affective power of the music: "Beautiful indeed!" (美哉!); "How profound!" (遠乎!); "How expensive!" (洋洋乎!); "How pervasive!" (蕩乎!); "Great indeed!" (廣乎!); "How joyous!" (熙熙乎!); "Supreme indeed!" (至矣乎!) His aesthetic judgments soon fuse with moral and political evaluations. As Du Yu 杜預 (222–285) observes, he relies on musical notes to ruminate on political situations (*yishenglaicanzheng*, 依聲來參政) in a manner reminiscent of the delineation, in exegetical traditions of the *Odes*, of the sociopolitical context of the poems. By watching musical performances, he divines particularities of the geographical and historical forces of these performances and summarizes the past, present, and future of the various states of origin.

The destiny of the Zhou state receives more of Jizha's attention than any other political entity. Jizha recapitulates significant moments in Zhou history when relevant sections of the *Odes* are performed. He intersperses judgments of other states, in which memory and predictions, as well as perspectives on the past, present, and future, are more freely and variously mixed. The following passage from *Chronicle of Zuo* (*Zuozhuan*) records an event during which he identified and interpreted the performances from different historical time periods and regions:

> Jizha asked to observe Zhou music. The musicians sang for him "Zhounan" and "Shaonan," and he said, "Beautiful indeed! The beginning foundation is being laid down, but the task is not yet accomplished. There is industry but no rancor!" The "Airs of [the states of] Bei, Yong, and Wei" were sung for him, and he said, "Beautiful indeed! How profound! There is anxiety but no despair. I have heard that such is the virtue of Wei Kang Shu and Lord Wu. This is likely the 'Airs of Wei!'" The "Airs of the Royal Domain" were sung for him, and he said, "Beautiful indeed! There is longing but no fear. This is probably after Zhou moved east!" The "Airs of Zheng" were sung for him, and he said, "Beautiful indeed! The fine points are extreme; the people would not be able

to bear it. It would likely perish first!" The "Airs of Qi" were sung for him, and he said, "Beautiful indeed! How expansive! Great airs indeed! Exemplar of the states by the eastern sea—surely this is the state of Taigong! Its greatness cannot yet be fathomed!" The "Airs of Bin" were sung for him, and he said, "Beautiful indeed! How pervasive! There is joy but no licentiousness. This must be when the Zhou Duke moved east!" The "Airs of Qin" were sung for him, and he said, "This is called the Sounds of Xia [the west]. For to be capable of *xia* [meaning 'grand' or 'imposing' in the Qin dialect] is to be great. The epitome of greatness—this could well be where Zhou was formerly!" The "Airs of Way" were sung for him, and he said, "Beautiful indeed! How fluid and flowing! Forceful yet gentle. [The rules are] demanding yet easy to carry out. Aided by virtue, these would be enlightened rulers." The "Airs of Tang" were sung for him, and he said, "Profound longing indeed! These are probably descendants of the people ruled by the house of Tao and Tang! Otherwise why would their concerns reach so far back? If they are not descended from [the line of] prime virtue, how can they be capable of this?" The "Airs of Chen" were sung for him, and he said, "The state has no master, how can it last long!" From the "Airs of Hui" on, Jizha did not give any comments.

The "Lesser Odes" were sung for him, and he said, "Beautiful indeed! There is sadness but no disaffection, rancor but no expression thereof. Is this perhaps the decline of Zhou virtue? There are yet descendant of people ruled by the ancient kings!" The "Greater Odes" were sung for him, and he said, "Great indeed! How joyous! Involute but straight in nature, surely this is the virtue of King Wen!" The "Hymns" were sung for him, and he said, "Supreme indeed! This is upright but not arrogant, involute but not bent, close but not invasive, afar but not alienating, moving yet not licentious, recurrent yet not tiresome, grieving yet not disconsolate, joyous yet not wild, put to use yet not exhausted, expansive yet not revealing, giving yet not extravagant, taking yet not avaricious, staying yet not stagnant, proceeding yet not wantonly flowing. The five sounds harmonize; the eight winds are even. The notes have proper measure, the gradations are in right order: this is the common ground of great virtue." (Translated by Kuang based on Zhongde Cai 1995 and Zong-qi Cai 2001)

Jizha's divination of the geographical origins of the music meant that his judgments of historical and political contexts were authoritative, despite his use of the syntax of conjecture about the polities of the regions noted in the passage. In his judgments, he frequently invoked beginnings.

The founding of a state or a decisive event in its history—such as the Zhou Duke's eastward expedition or the Zhou court's eastward move—becomes an enabling movement of meaning against which later developments are considered. The virtue of founders lingers on, and moral-political judgments on remote pasts often are applied to more recent events or to the present (ZD Cai 1995; ZQ Cai 2001). For example, the greatness of Qin, manifested in its grand (*xia* 夏) sounds, is a function of its possession of lands that formerly belonged to Zhou.

In the fourth edited volume of *Music from the Tang Court*, Laurence Picken (1988: 1–87) presented writings on music from the Sui and Tang courts, listing them under subject titles such as "Sogdians Drinking Wine" and "Bodhisattvas." Picken's collections of writings feature the Japanese court music that borrowed from the Sui and Tang courts, but they provide insights into the construction of dances and music influenced by the central Asian states and Buddhist elements. In his collections, manuscripts from Dunhuang have been primary sources, as the Japanese court musicians long recognized the cultural elements preserved in the Dunhuang materials. The *Dunhuang bihua yuewu* may be approached in a similar fashion in terms of the selection of images and notations, especially as the choreographers who were responsible for recreating the genre studied in Japan. Information on the Chinese Tang court dance was preserved in manuscripts written between the eighth and thirteenth centuries and can be seen today in the library of the Imperial Palace in Tokyo and in other Japanese libraries.

## Heritage, Tradition, and Authentication with a Historical Sense

In 1943, the Dunhuang Academy was founded to protect and study the Dunhuang relics, and the Mogao Grottoes were included in the first list of National Cultural Relics established by the Chinese government, in 1961. In 1987, when *reform* was one of the most common words in China's socio-political vocabulary, China's post-Mao leaders began to reformulate their foreign policies and their involvement in United Nations cultural programs (Shichor 1991). China has since sought to foster international relations and enhance its social and economic development. As in many other multiethnic states, the Chinese government continually works to strengthen internal cohesion (Gill and Huang 2006; Kurlantzick 2007a, 2007b; McGiffert 2009; Nye 2004a, 2004b, 2004d; Shirk 2007).

Beginning in the late 1980s, China began participating in international cultural and educational organizations, undertaking a "metacultural operation" by using world heritage as "a vehicle created for envisioning and constituting a global polity within the conceptual space of a global cultural commons" (Kirshenblatt-Gimblett 2006: 1). It eventually persuaded UNESCO to declare the Mogao Grottoes a World Heritage Site.

## Heritage, Tradition, and Performance-Based Legitimacy

Today, heritage and tradition are among the most popular subjects of contemporary cultural display and representation, whether through UNESCO heritage projects or through tourism, museums, and so on. Among the issues to be considered when analyzing the processes of representing heritage and tradition in contemporary society are the (re)invention of history and authenticity, the (re)identification of geographic or conceptual territory, the (re)creation of symbolical systems, and the (re)construction of identity or the human body.

Scholars have increasingly defined culture as an economic and political resource in the modern era (M. Brown 2004; Graham 2002; Ingram, Robinson, and Busch 2005; Kirshenblatt-Gimblett 2006), analyzing heritage and tradition as layered representations of the past. In popular usage, the terms *heritage* and *tradition* imply the idea of continuity with a real or imagined past that occupies a conceptual space. Time (history) and space (the body/site where a meaningful existence is produced) are therefore considered essential to an understanding of the nature of heritage, tradition, and their representations: "The interest in displaying performance or in using performance as a way of displaying culture is, like the series of objects are arranged to show a continuous historical process, linked to particular theoretical orientations" (Kirshenblatt-Gimblett 1998: 74–75), yet neither history nor the boundaries of space are fixed. Scholarly criticisms of ahistorical constructions of a hegemonic past must be faced as a challenge by those who wish to claim the authenticity of a heritage. The contestability of time and space create challenges in the contemporary display and representation of heritage and tradition:

> Much of the recent literature on the management of the past, especially of its physical remnants, has concentrated on the various attempts that political elites have made to "fix" history in a partial, highly selective presentation. These formulations, while useful as a critique of statist ideology, entail two closely interwoven dangers. It is being invented and reinvented as a continuous, creative process and in this case, to authenticate a heritage. First, such terms as "the invention of tradition" (Hobsbawm and Ranger 1993) suggest the possibility of an ultimately knowable historical past. Although traditions are invented, the implicit argument suggests, there ought to be something else that represents the "real" past. But if any history is invented, all history is invented. (Herzfeld 1991: 12)

Heritage and tradition are in themselves layered representations—the products of layered representational processes—of perceptions intended, contested, and recreated by social actors who have the power and authority to perform a symbolic action. Heritage is a value-added industry, "a mode of cultural production in the present that has recourse to the past" (Kirshenblatt-Gimblett 1998: 7), that has been supported and generated by a global institutional apparatus: "Heritage is created through a process of exhibition (as knowledge, as performance, as museum display)" (149). In this sense, staged Dunhuang arts as a form of exhibition exemplify a performative process implemented by social actors to contribute to the creation of a national heritage. In short, this genre is intended to add value to the national heritage while being framed as an authentic representation of a national tradition.

Employed within discourses of heritage, tradition is a contested concept. Multiple concepts of tradition have been proposed by scholars approaching the term from an anthropological view, including those who define tradition as a set of situated practices inherent in a cultural form—a definition that tends to "foster a conception of intergenerational transmission as the replication of uniformity" (Bauman 2001a: 15819). This concept of intergenerational transmission often involves a historical sense, of something set in the past but carried on into the present. Heritage and tradition are almost always discussed in association with the concept of authenticity: "A hallmark of heritage productions—perhaps their defining feature—is precisely the foreignness of the 'tradition' to its context of presentation" (Kirshenblatt-Gimblett 1995: 374). Since tradition has been viewed as "invented" and heritage as a value-added industry, it is unsurprising that the issue of the real and the fake always exists within the discourse of cultural production, including that of the *Dunhuang bihua yuewu.*

### *Authenticity*

The idea that authenticity is a construct that emerges in the process of interpretative performance—that meanings and authenticity are created in social interactions—is not new. Scholars have argued that authenticity emerges through dynamic interactions across places as a hybrid, creative process situated in local contexts while retaining distinct identities. Non-Western expressions participate in broader exchanges yet chart their own trajectories, forging multiple histories from grounded, lived experiences. In effect, it "is located not in the artifacts *per se* or in the models on which they are based but in the *methods* by which they were made—in a way of doing, which is a way of knowing, in a performance" (Kirshenblatt-Gimblett 1998: 196).

An intriguing example of the use of history in the rhetorical construction of authenticity is described in Ben Hillman's "Paradise under Construction: Minorities, Myths and Modernity in Northwest Yunnan" (2003). Hillman sheds light on how the local people and the government of Deqin County in the Diqing Tibetan Autonomous Prefecture of Yunnan, China, underwent reconstruction by adopting the name Shangri-la—an evocative and mythical imaginary landscape. This strategic renaming aimed to attract tourism and investments to the region. Diqing thus became "authenticated" as Shangri-la, a name that comes from the novel *Lost Horizon*, published by British author James Hilton in 1933. Building on a boom in Yunnan tourism in the 1990s, the Deqin County and the Diqing prefecture governments thus have capitalized on an exotic, fictional name and on its Tibetan population and cultural heritage to bring in tourists. In turn, this Shangri-la not only provides a space for economic and cultural development but also allows the new touristic force to strengthen ethnic identities.

Hillman (2003) quotes from the discourse of corresponding agents who facilitated the authentication of an imagined past within a fictional (literarily) time frame. He explains the naming process in detail. In a proposal that the county and prefecture government sent to Yunnan provincial government, the local officials of Deqin County (now Shangri-la) suggested that the name Shangri-la would "embody the unique characteristics of the land and people . . . and [the name change would] also demonstrate the Party's and the government's concern and commitment to the area and speed the development (*fazhan*) and civilizing process (*wenming*) of the Tibetan nationality" (178). In the provincial government's application to the China State Council, "the name represents what people of all races are searching for—a desire that among people and between people and nature there be no conflict, no chaos (*qingluan*), only economic prosperity, national unity (*minzu tuanjie*), and social stability," and the name makes Diqing "a 'leading' Tibetan area in China" (179). Hillman's analysis of such discourse shows how agents involved in representing ethnic cultural identity acted according to power relations: they constructed a tangible site on the basis of an imagined site, creating an imagined time-space—a crystallized past of Shangri-la.

The selective representation of China's cultural heritage in Ann Anagnost's *Splendid China* (1997) conveys how the desire for and ambivalence about a national past are displaced onto commodified forms along with the expansion of a market economy. Both Anagnost and Hillman illustrate ways that themes such as modern national history and ethnic diversity have been adopted from a reconstructed past to display China as a developing and unified state. Anagnost and Hillman question the motives and effectiveness of these themes by examining them within their specific sociopolitical and economical contexts. They point out that these themes are constantly under contestation among those who have the power to represent, those who are being represented, and those who mediate the contests over meaning. These themes are equally presented in the display and representation of intangible cultural heritage in China.

## Coda

In this chapter, important notions for understanding the recreation and staging of the *Dunhuang bihua yuewu*, such as the concept of aesthetic suggestiveness, have been explored in association with self-referentiality in the meta-elements that constitute the Chinascape. I have provided an explanation of some of the key concepts and terms that provide the fundamentals for understanding the formation of the *Dunhuang bihua yuewu* through performances and discourse. This chapter is critical for interpreting the analysis of *Dunhuang bihua yuewu* techniques and case studies.

In the next chapters, combining methodologies of performance studies and ethnographic research, I examine the ways that ideas about the classical, multicultural, and cosmopolitan Chinese past are enlisted in the staging and representation of the modern nation through the *Dunhuang bihua yuewu*, and I identify moments in which the creation and representation of Chinese expressive arts are continuously transformed within it.

Since "joining the politics of history and of performance rests upon a specialized application of dance analysis" (Martin 1995: 111), ethnographic research is here the most appropriate procedure for exploring the relating of agency and history that is simulated in performance. Further, unlike language, where a discernible relationship between signifier and signified is at least identifiable and not immutable, dance resists representation. In this sense, ethnographic research highlights what is lost in representation, akin to the intricate performer-audience relationship in dance (109–111). My research combines historical and ethnographic methods to show how the politics of history and representation are implicated in the contemporary creation, performance, and discourses of the staged Dunhuang arts.

# Notes

1.  In addition to NBC's broadcast, live broadcasts occurred in Europe and on the internet.

2.  According to Zhang Yuanlin, deputy director of Dunhuang Academy, "Flying apsaras embody freedom and beauty. All that can touch hearts and bring joy will be welcomed. . . . People of different nationalities and cultures nowadays should achieve understanding and show tolerance by participating in the Games." See Zhang's interview in the *China Daily* article "Similarity of Frescoes to Winter Sports Raises Intrigue" (Ma and Cang 2022). Ye (2020: 3–26) calls the BRI a "state-mobilized globalization campaign."

3.  For firework photos, see Bi Nan (2022).

4.  Chinese president Xi Jinping's speeches and public diplomacy narratives frequently mention the Silk Road and the *tianxia* concept (Jiang 2022).

5.  Michelle Wang has examined the history of esoteric Buddhism in Dunhuang murals in her book *Maṇḍalas in the Making* Maṇḍalas in the Making study on (2018).

6.  *Xinhua*, "Xi Focus-Profile: Xi Jinping and His Fondness for Culture," *China Daily*, last modified May 19, 2022, https://www.chinadaily.com.cn/a/202205/19/WS62851d33a310fd 2b29e5d916.html.

7.  "20th CPC National Congress: Delegate from Dunhuang Academy on Building Cultural Confidence, Developing Socialist Culture," *CGTN*, last modified October 18, 2022, https://news.cgtn.com/news/2022-10-18/VHJhbnNjcmlwdDY4ODQy/index.html.

8.  Rendanheyi 人單合一 is a management model employed by Chinese companies such as Haier; it is considered a leading model in the Internet of Things (IoT) era by Zohar (2022).

9.  Zhao Tingyang published *Lishi shanshui quqiao* 歷史山水漁樵 (History, mountain, water, fisherman, woodcutter) in 2019 and presented his latter approaches to *tianxia* through the Chinese literati tradition. This work is discussed further in the concluding chapter.

10.  China's open-door policy in 1978 invited foreign investors to operate in the country through joint venture, licensing, and other collaborative efforts.

11.  Lakoff and Johnson (1980: 117) argued that experiential gestalts, based on interactions, serve as the grounding of conceptual metaphors. Johnson (1987) developed the idea as "image schemata" or "embodied schemata," which structure our perceptions, as evident in the metaphoric patterns in language (1987: 23–29).

12.  Bulag (2012, 135) describes this as an "aspect of the Chinese state 'centripetalism'—a political desire for a gravitational orientation from the margin to the center."

13.  Duara (1996) suggests giving greater attention to alternative principles for grouping "marginalized others" as a way of resisting totalizing ideologies in China. Beck (2006) argues that methodological cosmopolitanism—a cosmopolitan frame of reference—enables empirical investigation of the renationalization or reethnification of minds, cultures, and institutions. Calhoun (2007) situates nationalism and ethnicity in relation to the idea of a cosmopolitan global order and argues that the opposition of ethnic and civic nationalism is part of a framing of cosmopolitanism within the nationalist imaginary.

14.  The concept of realm not only highlights an association with the level of human consciousness at which aesthetics is developed but characterizes the Chineseness of Buddhism—the religious art source that inspired the *Dunhuang bihua yuewu*.

15.  For translation and reference, see Jao Tsung-I's "Moral Speculation and the Conception of a Sky God" in *Space, Time, Myth, and Morals: A Selection of Jao Tsung-i's Studies on Cosmological Thought in Early China and Beyond* (2022).

16.  Zong-qi Cai (2004: 23) also put forth the question regarding the usage of the phrases "Chinese aesthetics," "Six Dynasties aesthetics," and "Wei-Jin aesthetics."

17.  Niall Ferguson, "Complexity and Collapse: Empires on the Edge of Chaos," *Foreign Affairs,* March/April 2010, http://www.foreignaffairs.com/articles/65987/niall-ferguson/complexity-and-collapse.

18.  The two principles established by Zhao Mengfu are renewal through the study of ancient models and the application of calligraphic principles to painting.

19.  Zhao Mengfu was primarily inspired by the masters of traditional Chinese paintings from the Northern Wei (439–534), Western Wei (535–556), Western Jin (265–317), Eastern Jin (317–420), Southern and Northern (420–589), Sui (581–681), and Tang (618–907) dynasties.

20.  On the history of classification of state rituals into five categories, see Wechsler 1985: 49–50.

21.  *The Mencius* is a Confucian classic, a collection of texts written by the philosopher Mencius in the second half of the fourth century BCE.

22.  Different versions of the *Odes* (Shi 詩) survived. They were compiled under the patronage of the Lu 魯, Qi 齊, and Han 韓 exegetical lineages. In the year 1 BCE, the Mao tradition of the *Odes* received a dominant place at the imperial academy of the Western Han dynasty. For details on the Mao tradition of the *Odes*, see Kern 2005 and 2007.

# 3

# IMAGINING DUNHUANG

## *Literary Topography*

THE CONCEPT OF "RETURN TO ANTIQUITY" (*FU-GU* 復古) is a critical factor in some of the contemporarily created expressive arts staged to legitimatize a particular pastness that could enact the history of China's present. This chapter, examining the practices of textual production and transmission, the cultivation of literary tastes, and the role of Han (206 BCE–220 CE), Sui (581–617 CE), and Tang (618–906 CE) poetry in the cultural construction of China's borderland frontier culture, reads deeply and intertextually through an ethnopoetic lens the performative processes of a contemporarily created staged Dunhuang arts program labeled a theatrical dance drama of the Chinese nation and an artistic form with distinctive ethnic features. Investigation of the historically and discursively formed frontier culture—literary topography created and consisting of time, space, cultural agents, signs, and metaphors—addresses my research questions on the aesthetic ideals and materials from the past selected during the staging processes of the contemporarily created Dunhuang arts.

History and geography—aspects commonly considered constituents of a nation—are "invariably aestheticized to a certain degree" (Bakhtin 1995: 208). Historically, Dunhuang was a multiethnic, cosmopolitan frontier metropolis (*bianjing dushi* 邊境都市) strongly imbued with the customs and institutions of central China (Duan 1997; Mair 1989; Shi 2002; Q. Sima 1959).

In a study of anthropological time in ancient Greece, Claude Calame points out that "the simultaneously spatial and referential aspect of discursive temporality has thus led us back to places of memory. . . . The work of the *historiopoietes* is largely based on material indices which are conventionally understood as traces; by their concrete and tangible nature, the traces correspond to meaningful spaces, spaces on which interpretation of the indices confers a temporal dimension" (2009: 30). Influenced by Heideggerian phenomenology, Calame cites Bloch (1964), Foucault (1969), and Ricoeur (1985) on the importance of the trace "for return to the past" and offers his own interpretation:[1] "As a vestige, the trace would be an element of mediation between the *hic et nunc* and the reality of things past; as an index, it would constitute the material place of the semiotic reference to the past, and at the same time the operand of the historiographic research and deciphering that it prompts" (30).

In his chapter titled "Eavesdropping on Zhang Xiaoxiang's Musical World in Early Southern Song China," for instance, Joseph Lam (2017) uses the sounds, sights, and smells in historical texts to introduce the categories of sound culture, musical world, and soundscape and to guide our thinking about the experience of sound in the Southern Song.

In the following sections, I analyze the received rhetorical strategies for representing the frontier cultures during the Han, Sui, and Tang dynasties and the ways these strategies were deployed, transformed, and complicated in intertextual historical references.

## Poetic Narratives of Sui-Tang Dynasty Musical-Theatrical Cosmopolitanism

The Tang dynasty was arguably the pinnacle of imperial Chinese culture. Its empire expanded far beyond the Central Plain, while its scholar-officials, the Tang literati, produced some of the finest literature in Chinese history. Written Chinese, partly because of its geographical spread, served as a prestigious, cosmopolitan script across medieval Asia, and music and other expressive arts from central Asia entered China, where they were heavily favored at the Tang court and popular in broader urban settings.

Chinese emperors and states used music to represent power and social status long before the Tang dynasty. A theory about the relation between dynastic policy and music during the early Sui dynasty was proposed by Yan Zhitui 颜之推 (531–591), a Han scholar-official, musician, and supporter of Buddhism who served four different Chinese states during the late Southern and Northern dynasties (the Liang dynasty in southern China, the Northern Qi and Northern Zhou dynasties of northern China, and their successor state that reunified China, the Sui dynasty) (Wang 2001; Wang 2003; Wang 2004). Yan was fully aware that the Northern Zhou dynasty emperor, who was of Xianbei 鲜卑 descent, had allowed many expressive art styles from non-Han groups in court performances.[2] This fact was later mentioned in the *Comprehensive Institutions* (*Tongdian* 通典), a Chinese institutional history that recorded historical events from high antiquity down to the reign of Tang dynasty emperor Xuanzong (r. 685–756):

> Later, Emperor Wu of Northern Zhou [r. 543–578] married his queen from the Turks, and obtained music from Samarkand (Kangguo 康國), Kösän (Qiuci 龜茲), and other places; [he] combined [the newly obtained ones] with the ones already processed from Qočo (Gaochang 高昌), [and the music and dances] were studied under the music ministry, which used their tones, applied them [the tones] to instruments, and presented them within the structure set by the Zhou officials. (*Comprehensive Institutions*, 142.2 on Music, translated by Kuang)

> 其後，帝聘皇后于突厥，得其所獲康國、龜茲等樂，更雜以高昌之舊，并于大司樂習焉。采用其声，被于鐘石，取周官制以陳之。

The Tang dynasty was one of the most cosmopolitan ages in Chinese history. Elements of various foreign cultures had been transmitted into the Central Plains along the northwestern borderlands for thousands of years, but the Tang dynasty was particularly powerful and prosperous, and the infusions of various cultures and arts at that time were distilled into a rich and diverse cultural content.

The Tang dynasty was an era of rapid transformation in Chinese poetry. This period not only established the model of regulated verse but also saw innovations in poetry that would greatly influence later times. The Tang dynasty was a golden age of music and dance, which were present at court and in the homes of officials, in drinking establishments, and in temples and religious festivals. Several Tang emperors' enjoyment of music led them to promote and engage in music—which in turn elevated the musicality of Tang poetic content. The *New Book of Tang* notably describes Emperor Xuanzong as a music enthusiast who took part in performing:

> Xuanzong knew music well and especially enjoyed *faqu*. He even selected three hundred musicians from the "string division" to be trained in Liyuan. Whenever a musician made a mistake in a performance, the emperor would always correct the error.[3] (Translated by Kuang)

> 玄宗既知律，又酷爱法曲，选坐部伎子弟三百教於梨园，声有误者，帝必觉而正之。

Music and dance thus occupied an indispensable position in the life of Tang court royalty (Shigeo 1940; E. Schafer 1985). Cui Lingqi's (fl. 713–765) *Record of the Imperial Academy of Fine Arts* (*Jiaofangji* 教坊記) is one of many historical records of Tang musical cosmopolitanism in an urban setting. This collection of documentation on musicians and their careers contains some of the music and tunes found in the Dunhuang region.[4]

## The Expressive Arts in Sui-Tang Frontier Poetry (*Biansai Shi* 邊塞詩)

Frontier poetry (*biansai shi* 邊塞詩) came into being as a genre in Chinese literary history in the Southern dynasties. It contributed to the poetic imagination and cultural constructs associated with fixed characteristics or gender stereotypes: the tough, austere, and masculine (the North) versus the soft, sensuous, and feminine (the South). Frontier poetry reached its heyday in the Sui and Tang dynasties, owing to constant warfare at the northwestern borders. The characteristics and stereotypes of the genre became firmly established, and they continue to influence the literary construction of Chinese frontier imagery.

The northwestern frontier was a popular theme in poetry of the High Tang period (ca. 713–766). "Life on the frontier," which includes vivid narratives describing departure for the frontier, the difficulties of life in the deserts, and scenes of battle, became a particularly important theme during the Tang. Dynasties in northwestern China since the Han established a military defensive zone, the so-called border fortified zones (*sai* 塞 and *bianting* 邊庭), between the hinterlands of the Central Plains and the northern nomadic nations. Poems with titles such as "At the Frontier" (*Saishang qu* 塞上曲) would use the immense territories of lands bordering the Great Wall as their setting. The present-day Gansu, Ningxia, and Qinghai regions in the Northwest, Xiao Pass in the northern Central Plains, and Dazhen Pass in the West form the inner borderlands of this zone. The external north–south and south–northwest boundaries were composed of concentric circles of defensive zones forming a tiered regional structure, with Hexi 河西 and Longyou 隴右 in a surrounding defensive formation for the Central Plains region.

Under the administration of Emperor Wu of the Han (Han Wudi, r. 140–87 BCE), at the end of the Western Han, Dunhuang Prefecture had a mostly Han population of more than thirty-eight thousand. Immigrants and resident troops from the Central Plains brought Han culture, which flourished and established a solid foundation in Dunhuang, becoming dominant from then on. By the time of the Wei, Jin, and Northern and Southern dynasties, the Dunhuang region had seen, for a time, intermarriages between Xiongnu and Han and a rise in the popularity of Buddhism, Confucianism, and Daoism.

The arts became integrated according to imperial state policies aimed at governing the ethnic populations of the Han, Sui, and Tang dynasties. Emperor Wu was the first ruler to bring the Music Bureau (*yuefu* 樂府) to full development. The bureau collected poems and folk ballads and provided music for court ceremonies and state sacrifices. During the Sui and Tang dynasties, urban civilizations centering on the metropoles of Chang'an 長安 and Luoyang 洛陽 produced profound effects throughout the empire.

In 633, the Tang court annihilated the Eastern Turkic Khaganate in the north and challenged Tuyuhun in the west. In 711, it established the Tang dynasty's first military commissioner of Hexi. The Western Regions became a border city hub that melded different cultural systems, including Han of the Central Plains, Greek, Indian, central Asian, and West Asian, before transmitting them to other border cities.

Interactions between the Central Plains and the Western Regions during the Tang dynasty have received the most attention from scholars, largely because of the Chinese-Western exchanges taking place there. Tang dynasty frontier poems made up a significant part—one to two thousand texts—of *Complete Tang Poems* (*Quan tangshi* 全唐詩), an early eighteenth-century compilation. Moreover, according to Zhang Tongsheng (2014), frontier poems existed in both a narrow sense and a broad sense. Narrowly defined, they refer primarily to areas along the Great Wall and in fortified borderlands in the Hexi 河西 and Longyou 隴右 region in modern Qinghai and Gansu Provinces; their authors had personally experienced frontier living. Broadly defined, Tang frontier poetry arose at the end of the Sui and the beginning of the Tang. It reached its zenith during the Kaiyuan 開元 (713–741) and Tianbao 天寶 (742–756) era and persisted in dissemination throughout the middle and late Tang Dynasty. Therefore, it is critical to acknowledge that as a literary genre, frontier poetry embodies historical prescriptiveness. The topical content of frontier poetry as a genre was prescribed—it must relate to frontier living—but many poems expressed emotions, described objects and natural scenery, embodied correspondence between friends, and depicted spousal love without directly invoking the war or the preparations for war that influenced the shape of the Chinese empire and the lives of its people during the Tang dynasty.

As identified by Zhang, frontier poetry expresses emotions or describes events relating to the frontiers of the dynasties:

> The nation-state is a new concept of the contemporary era, so if our viewpoint is based on a unified dynasty, the border fortifications and poems of the fragmented feudal states should perhaps not be referred to as frontier poems; frontier poems refer to poems and chants of border defenses of unified dynasties. Thus, border defenses are a necessary condition for frontier poems, because how can there be frontier poems without border fortifications? However, borderland fortifications are not borderlands. Since the borderlands of various dynasties were different, and even the borderlands of the same dynasty may be changing, migrating, or in flux, the mental history of frontier poems for a certain dynasty is also always evolving. (Zhang 2014, translated by Kuang)

In other words, given territorial fluctuations across and within Chinese dynasties, the psychological terrain—and related literary representations—of any dynasty's frontiers constantly evolved. As a result, the portrayal of non-Han performing arts in frontier poems exhibited remarkable variability, imbued with an atmosphere of potentiality and artistic freedom. . Even more broadly speaking, frontier poetry emphasized expressions of various subjects relating to the frontier, with the premise and background of frontier defense (Yan 2014).

Numerous ancient Han essays and poems relate to dance. The northwestern region of China, where Dunhuang is situated, served as a geographical, cultural, and imaginative wellspring for Tang dynasty frontier poems. Renowned Tang poets such as Wang Wei 王維 (701–761), Zhang Yue 張說 (666-730), Li Bai 李白 (701-762), Du Fu 杜甫 (712-770), Bai Juyi 白居易 (772-846), Yuan Zhen 元積 (779-831), and Liu Yuxi 劉禹錫 (772-842) all composed verses that vividly depicted the Western Regions. These frontier poems, which portrayed life and landscapes in the remote borderlands, offer a fascinating contrast to the music and dance flourishing in the bustling metropolis of Chang'an. These literary works allow us not only to comprehend the beauty of dance from hundreds or a thousand years ago but also to choreograph dramas of the Dunhuang performing arts: they contain descriptions of ancient music and dance, particularly the content and form of music and dance during the Han and Tang dynasties. These ancient poems, especially those depicting the multinational music and dance performances of the Western Regions, provide the best materials for our present-day deconstruction, imagining, and reconstruction of cosmopolitan musical arts. As the overall research standards for dance arts have increased, the most profound effects of poetry on dance and the intrinsic relationship between dance and poetry have received greater levels of attention.

## Poetic Narratives of Tang Dynasty *Hu* Dances (胡舞)

*Hu xuan* dance was extremely well received at court during the Tang dynasty. According to the *Old Book of Tang*, in the "Biographies of Imperial Relatives" chapter,

> Empress Wu Zetian's grandnephew Wu Yanxiu went to visit the Turks to establish a close relationship with them.[5] When he returned, he was fluent in the Turkic language and good at singing Turkic songs and performing the *hu xuan* dance. Emperor Zhongzong [656–710] enjoyed his performances and assigned court musicians to [accompany] his dance. This was a few decades before the Tianbao reign [742–756]. (Abridged translation by Kuang)

> 延秀, 承嗣第二子也。則天时, 突厥默啜上言有女請和親, 制延秀与阎知微俱往突厥, 将亲迎默啜女为妻。既而默啜执知微, 入冠赵、定等州, 故延秀久不得還。神龙初, 默啜更請通和, 先令延秀送款, 始得歸, 封桓國公, 又授左卫中郎将。时武崇訓为安樂公主婿, 即延秀从父兄, 数引至主第。延秀久在蕃中, 解突厥語, 常於主第, 延秀唱突厥歌, 作胡旋舞, 有姿媚, 主甚喜之。及崇训死, 延秀得幸, 遂尚公主。

Bäkçor Qapaǧan of the clan Ašina (r. 692–716), the khan of the Second Turkic Empire, detained Wu Yanxiu until 703. Having returned to the Tang court, Wu Yanxiu sang Turkic songs and performed the *hu xuan* dance, enchanting his audience.

The Tang dynasty poet Bai Juyi identified in his narrative poem "Hu Xuan Lady" the origins of the female artists proficient in the *hu xuan* performance style, indicating they came from the region of Kangju 康居, also known as Kangguo 康國, corresponding to modern-day Samarkand in Uzbekistan. The Qing dynasty scholar Wei Yuanda 魏遠達 (1794–1857) investigated the evidence in *Records of Military Accomplishments of the Empire* 《聖武記》: "The Middle zhuz of the Kazakh *jüz* or hordes is nomadic in pursuit of water and grass and lived in Kangju since the ancient times" (1984).[6] This suggests the *hu xuan* dance in Tang poetry may have depicted dances by ancient Kazakhs that were introduced to Tang territories by relocated artists. Thus, the Hu Xuan ladies likely referred specifically to those dancers. Because this kind of dance, introduced by the so-called Hu people, had strong and forceful tempos, with galloping and joyous movements involving spins and steps, it was known as *hu xuan*. The Tang dynasty *Comprehensive Statutes* (*Tongdian* 《通典》) by Du You 杜佑 (735–812) states: "The dance involves spinning quickly like the wind; thus it was commonly known as *hu xuan*."

Bai Juyi, in his famous poem "The Nomad Whirling Dancer: Against Adopting Foreign Customs at the End of the Tianbao Reign, the Northwestern Kingdom of Kangju Sent the Dancer as a Tribute" (胡旋女-戒近习也 [天宝末, 康居国献之]), wrote of the *hu xuan* dancer:

> Whirling dancing girl, whirling dancing girl. Heart as strings, hands as drums.
> Sleeves raised as strings and drum sound, her skirt flutters like snow blowing in the wind.
> Spinning left and turning right, thousand times round, then ten thousand more.
> Nothing like it in this world, a spinning wheel: slow were the winds around her.
> She thanked the Son of Heaven twice at the end; the Son of Heaven smiled only mildly. This whirling dancing girl traveled thousands of miles east from the Kangju tribe, but in vain.
> The Central Plains already had whirling dancing girls; in comparison, she is not as talented.
> Since the Tianbao reign, officials and consorts learned this spinning dance for a change.
> Taizhen [Consort Yang] and An Lushan: the two were known for their engagement over the whirling dance.
> Amid the Pear Blossom Gardens, she acted as his queen, and Lushan as her son.
> Lushan's whirling dance blinded our emperor, who did not even question when soldiers had crossed the Yellow River.
> Consort Yang's whirling dance deluded our lord's heart; dead and abandoned at Mawei, his yearning only grew deeper.
> Since then, the earth kept on spinning and the heavens revolved; for fifty years, no imperial edict was ever issued to ban it.
> Oh, whirling dancing girl, please do not dance in vain: just sing this song a few times to awaken our wise lord. (Translated by Kuang)

胡旋女, 胡旋女。心應弦, 手應鼓。弦鼓一聲雙袖舉, 回雪飄颻轉蓬舞。
左旋右轉不知疲, 千匝萬周無已時。人間物類無可比, 奔車輪緩旋風遲。
曲終再拜謝天子, 天子為之微啟齒。胡旋女, 出康居, 徒勞東來萬裡餘。
中原自有胡旋者, 鬥妙爭能爾不如。天寶季年時欲變, 臣妾人人學圜轉。
中有太真外祿山, 二人最道能胡旋。梨花園中冊作妃, 金雞障下養為兒。
祿山胡旋迷君眼, 兵過黃河疑未反。貴妃胡旋惑君心, 死棄馬嵬念更深。
從茲地軸天維轉, 五十年來製不禁。胡旋女, 莫空舞, 數唱此歌悟明主。

From Bai Juyi's poetry, we learn that the dancers performed *hu xuan* 胡旋, the nomadic style of whirling dance from Kangju 康居, as indicated by a short note on the dancers' origin, which states that at the end of the Tianbao reign, the northwestern kingdom of Kangju sent the dancers as a tribute.

From depictions of musicians and dancers in Mogao Cave 200 at Dunhuang, we know that the *hu xuan* dance was popular in the Hexi Corridor during the reign of the Tang emperor Taizong. "Hu Xuan Lady" was included in the collection of *Complete Tang Poems, Tang Dynasty Grand Councilor.*[7]

We learn from Bai Juyi's poem that those performing the *hu xuan* dance had been sent to the Central Plains as tribute. The poet mentions the appearance and postures of the "Hu Xuan Lady" in textual form: "I can convey the appearance of Hu Xuan." (胡旋之容我能傳) The dancer's appearance was eye catching and beautifully described: "A dancer's accessories and jewels traced lines of light, dazzling as she spun; the light fabric draping her danced with the wind, shining like lightings caught in her hands" (骊珠 进珥逐飞星，虹晕轻巾掣流电).

Most performers of *hu xuan* dance were women; the dance could be performed individually or collectively. *Hu xuan* dance was characterized by light motions, rapid spinning, and a clear tempo. It was generally accompanied by drums to accentuate its robustness and force. Today, the northwestern folk dances of Uighurs, Kazakhs, and Uzbeks have retained the feature of rapid spinning and are generally accompanied by drums. Bai starts with a vivid, elegant description of the performance: "In the music of resonant strings and drums, Hu Xuan Lady lifts her sleeves in the air, dances with quick movement, lightly spins" (弦鼓一聲雙袖舉); "she is like falling snowflakes, tumbling grasses" (回雪飄颻轉蓬舞), full of dynamic beauty. In the poem, she spins back and forth without weariness; here, Bai writes with exaggeration, "She spins left and right without knowing fatigue" (左旋右轉不知疲，千匝萬周無已時); "nothing can compare with her in the world; she makes spinning wheels, and tornados seem slow" (人間物類無可比，奔車輪緩旋風遲). Spectators were so dazzled that they could not distinguish between her front and her back: "After ten thousand turns, who can tell the beginning or end; no one sitting on the four sides can tell where her back is" (萬過其誰辨終始，四座安能分背面).

The Dunhuang murals, which show the combination of dancers and musicians presented to the Buddha, also depict this dance. Two dancers in the middle face each other; the painters chose to express the spinning dance by depicting the front of one dancer and the back of the other. This can be compared with the textual descriptions of the *hu xuan* dancer cited above.

The *hu xuan*, because Emperor Xuanzong of the Tang greatly favored it, became especially popular at court. People of Chang'an learned it, and it remained popular for half a century. To please Xuanzong, his favorite consort, Consort Yang ("Taizhen" in the poem), and favored minister, An Lushan (d. 757), frequently performed the dance at court. Once when Consort Yang danced, Emperor Xuanzong played the drums, hitting them so hard that he smashed through the membrane.

After Bai describes the *hu xuan* dance performance, the focus of "Hu Xuan Lady" changes. Bai points out that although her beautiful dance enjoyed the emperor's favor, ironically, she could not "compete with the talent of" certain *hu xuan* dancers in the Central Plains—meaning Yang Guifei. Yang Guifei not only was exceedingly beautiful but could play the flute, percussion, and pipa and perform various kinds of dance. She was especially exquisite when dancing the *hu xuan*. Chinese dance scholars such as professors Dong Xijiu and Gao Jinrong believe that the beautifully plump bodhisattva form we see in Tang dynasty Dunhuang murals was inspired by her countenance; this was the reason for the phrase "Bodhisattva seemed like a court lady," which came up during my interviews with the choreographers of the *Dunhuang bihua yuewu*. At the time, Buddhist art in Dunhuang murals had become secularized on a great scale, to the point that the artists would introduce images of court ladies in their (non-Buddhist) paintings.

The introduction of the *hu xuan* dance into the Tang imperial court is notably associated with one of the most turbulent and violent periods of Chinese dynastic history, an era defined by the An-Shi Rebellion 安史之亂 (755–763). Erupted in the year 755 CE, the An Shi Rebellion is named after the two former Tang militants of Turco-Sogdian descent, An Lushan 安祿山 (703–757) and Shi Siming 史思明 (703–761). Emperor Xuanzong consequently fled from the capital city Chang'an during the calamitous war, seeking refuge in Sichuan in southwest China. Although the Tang defeated the Rebellion and ended the war in 763, the foreign heritage of An and Shi and the catastrophic Rebellion became a turning point in the Tang Dynasty's acceptance of foreigners. The once cosmopolitan and open Tang dynasty unfortunately became conservative and xenophobic.

Toward the end of this poem, representing the Tang intellects who were dissatisfied with the imperial court's showing of corruptive favoritism toward foreign general An Lushan and Consort Yang Guifei since the early eighth century, Bai writes, "Lushan's whirling dance blinded our emperor, who did not even question when soldiers had crossed the Yellow River. Consort Yang's whirling dance deluded our lord's heart; . . . Oh, whirling dancing girl, please do not dance in vain: just sing this song a few times to awaken our wise lord." In this context, the *hu xuan* dance serves as a metaphor warning that changes were afoot and that such actions of court favorites were causing the fall of the Tang dynasty. China has a long history of using such kind of metaphors to drew parallels between contemporary political issues and events from the previous dynasties.

Aside from the *hu xuan* dance, which is often associated with female dancers, the *hu teng* dance was transmitted from Uzbekistan by foreign merchants on the Silk Road at the time of the late Northern dynasty. In it, men exhibited strength and passion by leaping rapidly in a fast tempo. As the Silk Road reaches through Ciscaucasia, some of the musical and choreographic characteristics of the ancient *hu teng* dances found in the Western Regions were recorded in literary references: the shuffling, pacing, tapping, stepping, stomping, and acrobatic leaping show similarities to the hopak, which was known to be performed originally by male participants.[8]

*Miscellaneous Notes on Songs from the Music Bureau* (*Yuefu zalu* 樂府雜錄) by Duan Anjie 段安節 (fl. 894–898) lists the *hu teng* dance among the Tang dances as one of the "robust dances." Tang dances could be stylistically classified as robust or soft: the former was free and unrestrained, robust and bold, with a heavily marked meter; the latter was elegant and graceful, delicate and soft, with a lightly marked meter. The actions of the *hu teng* dance involved twisting one's hands inside one's sleeves, bobbing one's head while twisting one's legs, and lifting one's knees and hopping; it was characterized by rapid lifts and stomps of the legs and feet. It featured, according to the description by Liu Yanshi 劉言史 (742–813) in *To See Hu Teng Dance in Official Wang's House One Night* (《王中丞宅夜观舞胡腾》), "quick feet in soft and beautifully decorated boots 弄腳繽紛錦靴軟." In Liu's poem, *hu teng* dancers wear roll-brimmed hats with pointed ends adorned with bells, along with light, woolen, narrow-sleeved "foreign shirts," belts, and embroidered boots: "The woven hat was pointy, and the sleeves of the barbarians were tight" (织成蕃帽虚顶尖，细氎胡衫双袖小). They danced on floral carpets.

"Hu Teng Er" 《胡腾兒》, by Li Duan 李端 (738–786), another well-known Tang dynasty poet, gives an even more nuanced depiction of *hu teng* dance, providing us with precious textual evidence. Like the poetry excerpted above, the text featured metaphors, allowing the audiences of poetic music and dance scenes to develop their imagination of the cosmopolitan multicultural landscape. Li Duan's poem opens by saying, "The *hu teng* dancer is a young man from Liang Prefecture 胡腾身是凉州兒, with jadelike skin and a sharp nose 肌膚如玉鼻如錐. A light cotton shirt tied in the front and back 桐布輕衫前後卷, a grapevine-pattered belt hung on one side 葡萄長帶一邊垂."9 The image of a non-Han Liangzhou dancer from the Western Regions with white skin and a long nose leaps from the page. Rather than woolen foreign clothing, the dancer wears a long light cotton shirt that is soft and tied in the front and back, with a grapevine-patterned belt. Although a word for *grape* is a detail in the poem, it enhances the reader's impression of Hu Teng Er as being from the borderlands, with "delicious grape wine in a luminous chalice," and of the material cultural interactions on the Silk Road. Thus, as depicted in the poem, the decoration on the dancer's long belt was full of symbols: the image would have induced in the reader an image of the multiethnicity of Tang China.

In the poetry of Duan Li, we not only see the dance forms of a central Asian people but learn about the performance etiquette of the time: the dancer "knelt before the tent and spoke his native language; he danced for you after making sure his collars and sleeves were well ordered." The description is of the dancer before he began a performance; he spoke in his native language, made sure his clothing was in order, and then began the dance performance with "lifted brows, moving eyes, and steps on the floral carpet." Hu Teng Er, an outstanding dancer with great skill, "circling and rapidly stomping on the beat, turning hands akimbo like the half-moon," became personally caught up in the performance. From time to time, he tipped right and left as if intoxicated, as his boots flickered under the lights; then he jumped up in the air, with a lively countenance, raising his eyebrows and moving his eyes while stomping and leaping on the carpet, "pouring sweat from his pearled hat askew."

Hu Teng Er in the poems of Li Duan demonstrates the national character and vitality of the nomadic peoples in the Western Regions under the Tang; however, Li did not forget to locate the diasporic life story of Hu Teng Er in the greater context of history. He ended the poem with the question "Did he know that the road home was in ruins?" (胡鄉路斷知不知) to note the suffering of the wandering peoples of the Western Regions at the time.

Cen Shen was another outstanding producer of High Tang frontier poems. He visited the northwestern borderland fortifications twice and experienced the folkways of the minority nationalities in the Northwest. His frontier poems not only reflected his personal experiences, senses, emotions, and thoughts but concentrated the representation of details of the landscape and of life during the Kaiyuan and Tianbao eras. These poems include extensive descriptions of music and dance performances by various nationalities. For example, "Song about Governor Tian's Consorts Who Danced like Lotus Flowers Whirling to the North"《田使君美人如蓮花舞北旋歌》 depicts the *hu xuan* dance.[10] These works provide us with valuable materials for researching Chinese-foreign exchange in the Tang dynasty.

## Poetic Narratives of Musical Performance

The poems of Yuan Zhen (779–831), another leading poet of the New *Yuefu* 新樂府 movement and Bai Juyi's close friend, demonstrate similar ways of using poetry to express emotions and of using music and dance scenery to construct historical landscapes, as in Yuan's "In Response to the Twelve Poems Composed by Li, the Collator of Texts."[11] Yuan grew up in the Northwest and had submitted memorials to discuss military service in the northwestern borderlands during the reigns of Tang emperors Xianzong and Muzong. He was therefore familiar with borderland fortification landscapes.

Yuan's "In Response to the Twelve Poems Composed by Li, the Collator of Texts" describes other contemporary music and dance performances than "Hu Xuan Lady" and "Hu Xuan Dance," which were popular for a time. The depiction in the following passage of "The Huayuan Chime Stone" (*Huayuan qing*《华原磬》), for instance, was not simply an image of "new music" transmitted to the Central Plains with the culture of the Western Regions but also a record of ancient musical instruments and their effect on social change:

> Chime of Huayuan, Chime of Huayuan, ancients never listened [to your sound], but people do now.
> Stone of Si and Bin, Stone of Si and Bin, people never drummed of them now, but ancients did.
> The difference between people then and now? It all depends on the musicians' preferences.
> A musician may be considered deaf if he lacks the ability to distinguish pure and impure sounds.
> The disciples of Pear Garden tuned their instruments and knew that the new sounds are not as good as the old.
> In ancient times, it was said that the floating chimes emerged out of Si and Bin, its distinct sound so moving. (Translated by Kuang)

華原磬，華原磬，古人不聽今人聽。
泗濱石，泗濱石，今人不擊古人擊。
今人古人何不同，用之舍之由樂工。

樂工雖在耳如壁，不分清濁即為聾。
梨園弟子調律呂，知有新聲不如古。
古稱浮磬出泗濱，立辨致死聲感人。
宮懸一聽華原石，君心遂忘封疆臣。
果然胡寇從燕起，武臣少肯封疆死。
始知樂與時政通，豈聽鏗鏘而已矣。
磬襄入海去不歸，長安市兒為樂師。
T華原磬與泗濱石，清濁兩聲誰得知。

Here, we can witness the poets, heirs of ancient styles, using "ancient music" and "new music" as metaphors for changes in the times and in politics. The Si and Bin stones have a history that carries back to the Xia dynasty (2070–1600 BCE), but the chime stone was replaced by those of Huayuan during the Tang emperor Xuanzong's reign.[12]

The poet Bai Juyi suggested metaphorically in this poem that the An Lushan Rebellion was caused by replacing the Si and Bin chime stones with the chime stone of Huayuan in the imperial court music. Such literary narrative shows how closely Tang intellectuals were observing shifts in state affairs by changes such as those in the musical arts. In addition, the lines "Emperor Xuanzong loved music and loved new music" (玄宗爱樂爱新樂) and "the barbarian riders were led away by the barbarian dancers" (霓裳才彻胡骑来) introduce the poet's own experiences. Forms of music and dance, as well as the social audience in the changes of the Tang dynasty, were thus intricately turned into art forms that carried the national history.

If "The Chime Stone of Hua Yuan" presents a poet's mournful thoughts about the Confucian music and dance culture of the Central Plains being replaced by non-Han forms, then "Model Music" (*Faqu*, Beautiful and holy, a truly flourishing voice《法曲 - 美列聖, 正華聲也》) was a reaction to the rise of "barbarian-influenced" banquet music in China:

*Faqu, Faqu,* the song of great peace, amassing virtue, asserting with prosperity, and more than enough joy to celebrate.
The people of Yonghui [650–655] danced and sang: *Faqu, Faqu,* they danced the Rainbow Skirt [title of a famous *Faqu* song and dance].
Harmonious government-ordered world, the people of Kaiyuan era are healthy and happy.
*Faqu, Faqu* the song dignified, so grand the celebration without end.
Emperor Zhongzong and Suzong restored the empire; on the throne of the Tang, this prosperity was to go on for thousands of years.
*Faqu, Faqu,* mixed with barbarians' songs, and those foreign tunes disrupted the harmonious sound.

At the end of our Tianbao reign, it was only a year later that the Imperial Palace
  was sullied with foreign dirt; we then knew *Faqu* to be a song of prosperous
  airs.
If you understand the music, you will find its principles are the same as those
  for government.
Yet since those barbarian tunes were wrongfully mixed in, no longer could we
  distinguish between prosperity and decline, sadness and joy.
We yearn for the true and flourishing voice of Bo Ya and Shi Kuang,
  undisturbed by barbarian tongues. (Translated by Kuang)

法曲法曲歌大定，積德重熙有餘慶。永徽之人舞而詠，法曲法曲舞霓裳。

政和世理音洋洋，開元之人樂且康。法曲法曲歌堂堂，堂堂之慶垂無疆。

中宗肅宗復鴻業，唐祚中興萬萬葉。法曲法曲合夷歌，夷聲邪亂華聲和。

以亂干和天寶末，明年胡塵犯宮闕。乃知法曲本華風，苟能審音與政通。

一從胡曲相參錯，不辨興衰與哀樂。願求牙曠正華音，不令夷夏相交侵。

In this poem, Yuan mixes foreign Buddhist, indigenous Daoist, and traditional Confucian elements of the Central Plains. He uses music and dance
performances and ritualistic tones to express his political views. His poetry
considers the old and discusses the present in an accommodating spirit.

Instead of viewing Yuan's yearning for the "true and flourishing voice
of Bo Ya and Shi Kuang" as a desire to repel the cultural elements from
outside the Central Plains, we could perhaps understand it as a reaction
to the less apparent instabilities in the court. For decades after the An Shi
Rebellion, the Tang court found itself constantly under attack by hostile
foreign powers: the Khitans of the northeast, the Uighurs of the north,
and the Tibetans of the west. Many intellectuals at the time shared the
sentiment and hope that could be seen in "Song of My Cottage Unroofed
by Autumn Gales" 《茅屋為秋風所破歌》 by Du Fu 杜甫 (712–770): "If I could get
a mansion with a thousand, ten thousand rooms, / A great shelter for all
the scholars in *tianxia*, together in joy, / Solid as a mountain, the elements
could not move it" (安得廣廈千萬間, 大庇天下寒士俱歡顏, 風雨不動安如山). As one of
the most celebrated Chinese Tang dynasty poets, Du lived through the An
Lushan Rebellion and, as a scholar-official who had been affected by the
turbulence of constant warfare between a weakening Tang court and the
so-called barbarians, often expressed his wish for a peaceful and prosperous country.

Building on the historical references presented in this chapter, the next
chapter examines the institutionalization of ethnic populations and their
artistic productions by analyzing music suites that show similarities and

differences in the administration of multiethnic groups and their cultural heritage, in the past and in the present.

## Notes

1. See Calame 2009 for discussion on Bloch, Foucault, and Ricoeur's interpretation of the trace.

2. Xianbei 鮮卑, one of the neighboring states on the Central Plain, was inhabited by a Mongolic nomadic people, believed to be descendants of the Donghu federation in Manchuria. The Xianbei Empire became fragmented in 235 CE.

3. *Faqu* is a type of long, multisectional musical piece performed in a grand style uniting the singing of poetic verses, instrumental playing, and dancing. It belongs to the *daqu* genre, popular in China since the Han dynasty.

4. See Ren 1962.

5. Wu Yanxiu was selected to be married the daughter of Bäkçor Qapağan of the clan Ašina by Wu Zetian.

6. "哈薩克左部遊牧逐水草，為古康居。"

7. Poems cited in this chapter are from Zhongguo wudao yishu yanjiu hui and Wudao shi yanjiu zu 1958 and Cao et al. 1960.

8. The *hopak*, still one of the most visually recognizable dance genres found in the central Eurasian regions, is associated with the Cossacks (Pivtorak 2016).

9. "胡騰身是涼州兒，肌膚如玉鼻如錐。桐布輕衫前後卷，葡萄長帶一邊垂。帳前跪作本音語，拾襟攪袖為君舞。安西舊牧收淚看，洛下詞人抄曲興。揚眉動目踏花氈，紅汗交流珠帽偏。醉卻東傾又西倒，雙靴柔弱滿燈前。環行急蹴皆因節，反手叉腰如卻月。絲桐忽奏一曲終，嗚嗚畫角城頭髮。胡騰兒，胡騰兒，胡鄉路斷知不知?"

10. "美人舞如蓮花旋，世人有眼應未見。高堂滿地紅氍毹，試舞一曲天下無。此曲胡人傳入漢，諸客見之驚且歎。曼臉嬌娥纖複穠，輕羅金縷花蔥蘢。回裾轉袖若飛雪，左旋右旋生旋風。琵琶橫笛和未匝，花門山頭黃雲合。忽作出塞入塞聲，白草胡沙寒颯颯。翻身入破如有神，前見後見回回新。始知諸曲不可比，《採蓮》、《落梅》徒聒耳。世人學舞只是舞，姿態豈能得如此。"

11. *Xin yuefu* (*New Music Bureau* 新樂府) poetry, recording the poets' experience of war, is often dedicated to social criticism.

12. *Chime stone* refers to a lithophone.

# 4

# INSTITUTIONALIZING THE *DUNHUANG BIHUA YUEWU*

## *Past and Present*

The *Dao* is always nameless, plain and simple. Even so,
nothing overranks it all-under-heaven (*tianxia*).
If the nobles could safeguard it, all that in the myriad world
will defer of their own accord.
Heaven and Earth collided, bringing forth sweet shower,
[which is] already balanced without demand from the people.
To rule, names are given,
once named, one would know the existence of boundaries
and limitations, only then destruction can be avoided.
The *Dao* is to/for *tianxia* as the River and the Sea
are to/for rivulets and streams.

道常無名，樸。雖小，天下莫能臣也。
侯王若能守之，万物将自宾。
天地相合，以降甘露，民莫之令而自均。
始制，有名，
名亦既有，夫亦将知止，知止可/所以不殆。
譬道之在天下，猶川谷之於/與江海。

THE EXPRESSIVE ARTS MAY EMBODY A FULL ENSEMBLE of intellectual, aesthetic, and moral values, but these in turn are shaped by and represent power. As seen in the *Dunhuang bihua yuewu*,[1] music, dance, theatrical drama, and other forms of expressive art are a means through which archaeological materials reveal the shapes and movements of emergent power. Rhetorical gestures, such as naming, discussing, and negotiating, help define a genre. In the *Dunhuang bihua yuewu*, they associate power with a nation and the representations of its history.

This chapter focuses on the interplay of institutions and agents that embody the historical processes through which the *Dunhuang bihua yuewu* serves as a state-building cultural device. Ethnographic writing has typically given special attention to analyzing the discursive aspects of cultural representation, the narrative characters of cultural representation, and the stories built into the representational process itself (Clifford 1986a and 1986b). To represent national traditions or heritages, ethnographic playwriting necessarily presents selectively imagined and created memories. A pertinent example of this from the Pacific Islands, the play *Think of a Garden* by John Kneubuhl (1997), poignantly interweaves the playwright's childhood memories with historical events, sometimes colored with the sounds of singing, to explore the psychology of cultural change and identity.

Ethnomusicologists, espousing a discipline whose conceptual focus tends to emphasize both society and the individual and both synchronicity and diachronicity, have attempted to outline models that take account of the historical and individual dimensions of music (Merriam 1964; Rees 2000; Stone 2007). As early as 1940, Charles Seeger was addressing the idea of music as historical evidence, and in 1980, Kay Shelemay was pointing out that "an ethnomusicological study of a living music culture provides a multi-faceted and unique database, which in its totality may well illuminate important aspects of a culture's history" (1980: 235). The study of any artistic tradition inevitably implicates historical processes. These are not always the focus of research, but they often come into play in studies of specific genres. In the Pacific Islands, for example, in the late 1960s, Adrienne L. Kaeppler (1967) was tracing the history of Tongan dances, and in the early 1970s, Jacob Wainwright Love (1991: 218–280) was tracing the evolution of Samoan children's songs.

During my work in China, I traveled extensively between Beijing, the national political center, and the borderland frontier region of Gansu Province. The repeated shifting of geographic, cultural-economic, and sociopolitical backgrounds brought to my attention the roles that the *Dunhuang bihua yuewu* plays, depending on location. It also brought to my attention the shifting roles that my interviewees play, depending on their social and economic situation. Ultimately, I realized that these shifts would have been caused by the process of institutionalization in a general sense.

Institutionalization generally involves complex dynamic processes through which an emerging field, a movement, or, in the case of the *Dunhuang bihua yuewu*, a genre that has established and developed its own paradigm will be legitimized by formal rules and laws. The processes of institutionalization related to the recreation of the *Dunhuang bihua yuewu* as well as the genre's categorization were influenced by various factors. There are several key questions regarding these factors. Do the cultural agents of modern China discursively or in practice model themselves on the successful artists from the Han, Sui, and Tang dynasties, when the arts were incorporated into imperial policies for governing its multiethnic populations? What are some of the similarities? What are some of the differences? To answer these questions, in this chapter, I analyze the politicization of aesthetics, or rather, the political economy of power, in terms of its manifestation in the performances of the *Dunhuang bihua yuewu*. It is through the embodiment of artistic time and space within layers of performances that history and geography acquire "a unique center of value" (Bakhtin 1995: 208)

To show how, through performance and enactment, we can see the intersection of the past and the future and the politicization of aesthetics, I here compare the musical suites recorded in historical references, including the *New Book of Tang*, and performed on the contemporary stage in *Dunhuang bihua yuewu* drama.

In *The Political Essence of Zhenguan* (*Zhenguan Zhengyao* 貞觀政要), Tang emperor Taizong Li Shimin 李世民 expressed his beliefs about the relations between music and state politics while giving instruction to the government officials who were supposed to make new music (*xinyue* 新樂) for him. The institutionalization of new music into the old system revealed the nature of the Tang court's foreign policies relating to trade, diplomacy, and war with the frontier minorities, the so-called barbarians from the borders surrounding China (*siyi* 四夷). Here, music, dance, and the expressive arts were written as embodiments and demonstrations of power hierarchies formed through encounters between cultures and civilizations.

As seen in the case of Empress Wu Zetian's grandnephew Wu Yanxiu, arranged marriages were especially common for sons and daughters of the social elite in a political marriage market during the Han dynasty, paralleling the situation of imperial princesses, who were often married off to the rulers of non-Han ethnic groups. Musicians and other professional artists were often sent as a part of the princesses' dowry. The historical materials I translated and quoted in chapter 3 indicate that, as early as the Zhou dynasty, the imperial court had already obtained new musical forms from Samarkand (*Kangguo* 康國) and Kösän (*Qiuci* 龟兹) because of the marriage between the emperor and a Turkish queen.

In 582, about the same time that the Kaihuang Code (*Kaihuang lü* 开皇律), a series of civil laws, was formulated at the request of the Sui dynasty emperor Wen of Sui 隋文帝 (r. 581–684 CE),[2] Yan suggested that a reconstruction of court music be done by reviewing the traditional music of the Han groups from the Southern Liang dynasty (502–557). Emperor Wen of Sui supported the idea because he did not enjoy permitting "the division in charge of ritual and music to praise the merits of a former ruler" (translated by Kuang based on the classical text found in Cai Zhongde 1995 and Wang 2003).[3] A primary outcome of this discussion about proper court music was the establishment of the Yellow Bell, or *huangzhong* 黄钟, a tone in the Chinese musical scale used as the only official and dominant tonal temperament. This decision was intended to strengthen tonal unison and avoid any transition and modulation (*xuangong zhuandiao* 旋宫转調).[4]

On the surface, this discussion focused on the matter of resetting the temperament to be used for music, on the basis of laws from the North Qi and North Zhou dynasties, yet it was primarily a political debate and power struggle. The Sui dynasty emperor Wen of Sui Yang Jian 杨坚 revealed his interest in favoring the officials who had served the court of the North Zhou dynasty (*beizhoujiuchen* 北周舊臣) by employing their opinions in setting the temperament. Later historians and musicologists have interpreted this action as a political gesture that illustrates Emperor Wen of Sui Yang Jian's monolithic style of making policies (L. Wang 2003; S. Zheng 2001; Z. Zheng 2001).

Music and dance were essential to performing rituals, formal feasts, sacrifices, warfare, and education. As such, they resided at the core of the moral, sociopolitical, and cosmic order. The Han court incorporated dance suites representing various non-Han ethnicities into its musical system by institutionalizing them. Throughout Chinese history, the establishment of a new imperial reign often spurred the emergence of novel expressive art forms. The intriguing aspect of these phenomena is not the genesis of new court performance genres timed with political shifts. Rather, analysis on such historical phenomena could focus on the specific mechanisms by which the governing power integrated each innovative style into the existing expressive arts framework of their society. Examining how distinct ethnic and regional music and dance forms underwent selection and adaptation to align with dominant musical institutions provides insight into the country's cultural politics.

## Institutionalization of New Music and Dance Performances during the Tang Dynasty

The institutionalization of new music during the Tang dynasty reflected the cultural complexity of the Chinese empire at the time. When Tang emperor Taizong Li Shimin was still a general for his father, Tang emperor Gaozu Li Yuan 李淵, he was rewarded with the "Nine Musical Suites" (*Jiubu yue* 九部樂) for his achievements in warfare.[5] A passage from *The Old Book of Tang* recorded the event:

> In June, [Li Shimin] returned in triumph. . . . Emperor Gaozu . . . granted [him] a golden carriage, costume, a set of jade ornaments, six thousand *jin* of gold, [a ceremonial band consisting of] front and back percussion and reed players, and "Nine Musical Suites," along with forty sword carriers. (Abridged translation by Kuang)

> 六月, 凱旋。太宗亲披黄金甲, 阵鐵馬一萬騎, 甲士三万人, 前後部鼓吹, 俘二伪主及隋氏器物輂辂献于太庙。高祖大悦, 行饮至礼以享焉。高祖以自古旧官不称殊功, 乃别表徽号, 用旌勋德。十月, 加号天策上将、陝东道大行台, 位在王公上。增邑二万户, 通前三万户。賜金辂一乘, 袞冕之服, 玉璧一双, 黄金六千斤, 前後部鼓吹及九部之樂, 班剑四十人。

According to historical references, such as *The Old Book of Tang*, the "Ten Musical Suites" affiliated with the Tang court are *Suite Qingshang* 清商, *Suite from Western Liang* (*Xiliang* 西凉), *Suite from India* (*Tianlan* 天竺), *Suite from Goryeo* (*Gaoli* 高麗), *The Whirling Dance Suite of Foreign Barbarians [from Uzbekistan]* (*Hu Xuan* 胡旋), *Suite from Kösän* (*Qiuci* 龟兹), *Suite from Bukhara* (*Anguo* 安国), *Suite from Kashgar* (*Shule* 疏勒), *Suite from Samarkand* (*Kangguo* 康国), and *Suite Wenchang* 文康.[6] Together, they represent the imperial culture of the Tang dynasty and its expansion since its founding. Seven of the ten suites listed as the "Ten Musical Suites" were named according to the geographic region where the expressive art form originated. *The Whirling Dance Suite of Foreign Barbarians* was clearly named according to a sociocultural perception.

The Old Book of Tang elucidates how Tang emperor Taizong Li Shimin recognized from his ancestors the intricate link between authoritative rule and the performing arts presented at state ceremonies. Building on the "Ten Musical Suites" (*Shibuyue* 十部樂) established by his forebears, he incorporated music and dances from regions that had come under Tang imperial sovereignty. This artistic adaptation and cultural synthesis embodied Tang ideals of inclusivity while signaling to former regimes that a new era had begun. Curating and categorizing these dance suites exemplified Taizong's governing approach of strategic cultural integration. The structural changes made in the "Ten Musical Suites" after the Tang settlement in Qočo (Gaochang 高昌) in East Turkestan in 640, during Taizong Li Shimin's reign, exemplify an institutionalization process. The process is recorded in the chapter on music in *The Old Book of Tang* (*Jiu Tang shu* 旧唐書).[7]

> Communications with Qočo (Gaochang 高昌) had been established since the West Wei dynasty, and since then there were musical and dance performances from Qočo. Our emperor Taizong conquered Gaochang, collected its music completely, composed *yanyue* [banquet music] in addition, and dismissed the musical piece "Libi" [the final ritual]. Presently, the ones that have been composed and recorded textually (*zhuoling* 著令) were only these ten suites. (Translated by Kuang)

西魏与高昌通, 始有高昌伎。我太宗平高昌, 盡收其樂, 又造《宴樂》, 而去《礼毕曲》。今著令者, 惟此十部。

In 640, Emperor Li Shimin conquered the Eastern Turkic Khanate and forged the Tang state into an imperial power, which the Turks could neither manipulate nor ultimately withstand. It was then that he ordered the reconstruction of the "Ten Musical Suites."

Official imperial histories include detailed descriptions of the suites from Qočo (Gaochang 高昌). This was a way to introduce and incorporate through written texts the geographical and cultural Qočo as a part of Tang imperial history. For instance, *The Old Book of Tang* (*Jiu Tang shu* 旧唐書) includes the following discussion:

> Suites from Qočo, two dancers, [each dressed in] a white jacket with embroidered sleeves, red leather boots, a red leather belt, a red headband. For music [they] use one *dala* drum, one set of waisted drums, one *jilou* drum, one *jie* drum, two vertical notched flutes, two horizontal flutes, two *bili*, two four-stringed pipas [from China], two five-stringed pipas [from central Eurasia], one bronze bell, and one angular harp. Angular harps are not extinct. (Translated by Kuang)

《高昌樂》, 舞二人, 白襖錦袖, 赤皮靴, 赤皮帶, 紅抹額。樂用答臘鼓一, 腰鼓一, 雞婁鼓一, 羯鼓一, 簫二, 橫笛二, 篳篥二, 琵琶二, 五弦琵琶二, 銅角一, 箜篌一。箜篌今亡。+

The instruments used to perform *Suite from Qočo* are characteristic of the Eastern Turkic people. During the Tang dynasty, one of the most important changes in musical culture was the incorporation of foreign instruments into imperial court music. Musicians from Persia, central Asia, India, and Southeast Asia traveled along the Silk Road and eventually lived and performed at Chang'an (now Xi'an), the Tang capital, and influenced the musical tastes of the ruling classes (Schafer 1963: 50–57). These musicians introduced new instruments into China, most notably the Persian *barbat*, which developed into the pipa of China, the *biwa* of Japan, and the *ty-ba* of Vietnam (Shigeo 1940). Musicians began to incorporate foreign instruments, mainly central Eurasian ones, into pieces that had been composed for traditional Chinese instruments. Percussion instruments are among the most adaptable, and dances are believed to have become a main part of performances because of the selection of instruments. Instruments originating from regions along the Silk Road have been integrated into the performative genre now known as Chinese classical dance (中國古典舞). This occurrence is evident in the staging processes of the Dunhuang expressive arts, and a more detailed examination of this phenomenon will be presented in the subsequent section of this chapter. Music and dance performances during Li Shimin's reign were constructed to serve the needs of the ruler and state politics (Zhongde Cai 1995: 589–93). In the chapter on rites and music in *The Political Essence of Zhenguan* (*Zhenguan Zhengyao* 貞觀政要), Li Shimin expressed his beliefs about the relations between music and state politics in his instructions to the government officials ordered to construct new music (*xinyue*新樂) for him. He stated that music reveals the harmony or disharmony of a state:

> How can music move people? One who is happy shall be happy when he/she hears [music], one who is sad shall be depressed when he/she hears [music], and happiness and sadness are in one's heart, which should not be altered by music. With the effeminate rule of a polity, its people have a sorrowful heart; with sorrowful hearts accompanying each other, therefore [whatever music is] heard sounds sorrowful. What kind of music so depressing could make a happy man sad? (Abridged translation by Kuang)

> 不然，夫音声岂能感人？欢者聞之則悦，哀者听之則悲，悲悦在於人心，非由樂也。将亡之政，其人心苦，然苦心相感，故闻而则悲耳。何樂声哀怨，能使悦者悲乎？今《玉树》、《伴侣》之曲，其声具存，朕能为公奏之，知公必不悲耳。

The structural transformation of the "Ten Musical Suites" thus demanded was therefore particularly important in demonstrating the emperor's favored musical aesthetic. In particular, he emphasized the feelings of imperial subjects and the social function of music. This incorporation of new music into the old system reveals the nature of the foreign policies the China Tang court used in trade, diplomacy, and war with the minorities inhabiting the frontiers (*siyi* 四夷). The changes to the titles, the structures, and the order of the "Ten Musical Suites" since the beginning of the Tang dynasty reflect the complex process of institutionalizing artistic forms and expressions originated from a foreign culture. Here, staged performance of the musical suites is viewed as an embodiment and display of power hierarchies formed through encounters between cultures and civilizations, both peaceful and violent.

Tang literati long incorporated elements from musical events into their poetry and essays, as the expressive arts in general were treated and administrated as state affairs. The narratives of musical performances seen in *The Old Book of Tang* (*Jiu Tang shu* 舊唐書), the *Complete Collection of Tang Dynasty Poetry* (*Quan tang shi* 全唐詩), and *The Political Essence of Zhenguan* (*Zhenguan Zhengyao* 貞觀政要) thus have a performative function in representing and constructing the imperial rulers' aesthetic and governing styles. These genres were institutionalized historically and rhetorically when relevant events were categorized and recorded in state historical references as a part of the state's chronological discourse.

My research on the contemporarily staged *Dunhuang bihua yuewu* shows these performative narratives of a musical cosmopolitanism as a continuous, active process. The institutionalization of the *Dunhuang bihua yuewu* as a new dance genre within the Chinese classical dance tradition in contemporary China reveals the nature of the nation's current sociopolitical and cultural situations (Zhongde Cai 1995; Kuang 2016a; Picken 1997; E. Schafer 1985).

## Performative Narratives of *Dunhuang bihua yuewu* as a Classical Dance Genre

Performance theory helps identify structural devices within performances to show the structures of power and its networks of distribution (Stone 2007: 136–140). The structures and networks of power that have shaped the creation of *Dunhuang bihua yuewu* have been developing in China for a long period and have affected the expressive arts. Images of nationalist ideologies as cultural devices can be designed to make explicit some aspects of collective self-redefinition and to cast essentialist pride or epochalist hope into symbolic forms (Geertz 1973: 252).

In the 1960s and 1970s, the Chinese state was the dominant agency of power, responsible for reconstructing and maintaining the ideas of a Chinese musical identity. By strategically reconstructing the performances of middle-level music workers, the state reconstructed the performances of what it considered popular, folk, and ethnic minority musics and created a national discourse through the performing arts. The recreation of the *Dunhuang bihua yuewu* in the late 1970s was driven by the state's desire to reconstruct the Dunhuang arts as national arts.

The concept of an ethnic minority was important throughout much of the twentieth century (and remains so), in relation not only to the labeling of music but, more importantly, to the classification of peoples within the borders of China. Fifty-five officially classified national minority groups exist in the People's Republic of China (PRC) today. In much contemporary Chinese discourse, the relations between the Han population and the non-Han minorities are explained as a result of China's history of interactions between the Chinese heartland and the settlement of China's borders. Present-day researchers from the PRC believe (or at least are trained to appear to believe) that each of these minority groups has maintained its own ethnicity and cultural identity, including what ethnomusicologist Yang Mu (1996) called musical identity, but anthropologists in the West have questioned the validity of this classification system, which is "based on Stalin's definition of 'nation' and on a notion of fixed racial categories rather than recognizing ethnicity as a fluid, situational and changeable" (H. Wu 1996: 12; see also Gladney 1991; Yang Mu 1996). Nonetheless, the division of the people living within the political borders of China into two primary categories—Han Chinese and ethnic minorities—and the further division of ethnic minorities into fifty-five minority nationalities remain part of the dominant discourse in China and beyond. These categories frame the construction of discourse about the *Dunhuang bihua yuewu*.

According to Stuart Hall, "We still have a great deal of work to do to *decouple* ethnicity, as it functions in the dominant discourse, from its equivalence with nationalism, imperialism, racism and the state. . . . What is involved is the splitting of the notion of ethnicity between, on the one hand the dominant notion which connects it to nation and 'race' and on the other hand what I think is the beginning of a positive conception of the ethnicity of the margins, of the periphery" (1996: 442).

The *Dunhuang bihua yuewu* participates in perpetuating the dominant discourse of the state as a nation, but it complicates these discourses: the culture performed through it, rather than being "a unified corpus of symbols and meanings that can be definitively interpreted" (Clifford and Marcus 1986: 18), is temporal and emergent, created and transmitted through historical processes over time.

My research on the *Dunhuang bihua yuewu* and the institutionalization of new music during the Tang dynasty sheds light on a similar pattern in the administrative policies and styles of the cultural values and ethnic elements in present-day China. Although the *Dunhuang bihua yuewu* uses folk and ethnic elements, it is not listed as a genre in the folk dance and ethnic minority dance categories. How did it become a genre in the Chinese classical dance category?

Dong Xijiu 董錫玖, the late professor emeritus at the China Arts Academy and one of my primary interviewees, said the term *Chinese classical dance* 中國古典舞was coined in the 1950s by Ouyang Yuqian 歐陽予倩 (1889–1962). She explained that Chinese classical dance was developed "as part of the founding of the People's Republic of China after 1949" (Dong Xijiu et al. 2001: 78): "The term *classical* in a foreign country would mean 'classical ballet.' In Japan, classical dance is referred to as Noh, or Kabuki. [The Japanese] think this is classical, Noh [and] Kabuki. This is its classical dance. Then what is our classical dance? We have no such expression; the word [*classical dance*] was actually coined by Professor Ouyang Yuqian. I was his secretary for ten years" (video recording clip 1, March 17, 2009).

Scholars of modern Chinese history consider Ouyang Yuqian, a native of Liuyang, Hunan Province, a founder of modern Chinese drama (Cody and Sprinchorn 2007). During his time as president of the Central Drama Academy, he served in several political positions, including National Congress representative, vice president of the Chinese Drama Union, and chair of the Chinese Dance Union. At the age of fifteen, he traveled to Japan to study. In 1907, after graduating from the Meiji University and Waseda University there, he joined the amateur drama troupe Spring Willow Society (*Chunliushe*春柳社), the earliest Chinese drama community in Japan. He returned from Japan in 1911 and started acting in plays. In 1932, he joined the Union of Left-Wing Drama Writers.[8] He then went to Britain, France, Germany, and Russia to study their drama. In the autumn of 1934, he went to Shanghai and began to direct films. He was appointed president of the Central Drama Academy after the founding of the PRC in 1949. Before then, he organized new drama communities, directed plays, and trained young actors and actresses in various drama schools, becoming a pioneer of modern Chinese drama.

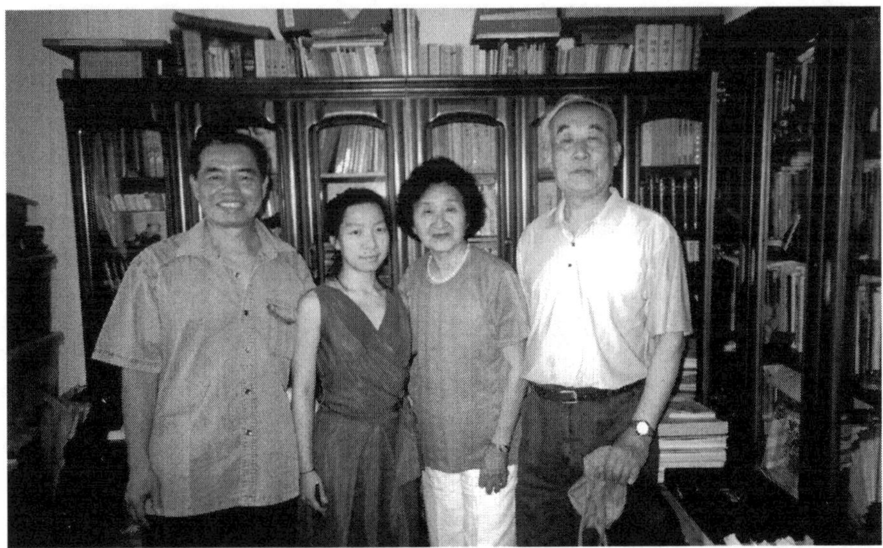

Figure 4.1. Image of the author with her late father, Kuang Jianren, who introduced her to the late professors Dong Xijiu and Liu Enbo. China Arts Academy, Beijing. © Lanlan Kuang, 2020.

Professor Dong recalled the details involved in the process of naming Chinese classical dance in relation to the newly established Central Drama Academy and the interactions between performers of different dramatic genres:

> At the time of the founding of the new People's Republic of China, he [Professor Ouyang] asked the dancers, because he was our president [at the academy], and we were the first dance troupe established since the founding of the new PRC—he invited many dramatic actors [as instructors] for us, such as Liu Yufang, who was as famous as Mei Lanfang at the time, famous *kunqu* opera performers,[9] such as Han Shichang, Bei Yusheng, Hu Yongkun, and Ma Xianglin. At this time, he said: "Dancers should never forget their traditions; they should learn [about/from] their own tradition. [There is much to learn from] the dramatic opera [and] *kunqu* opera." (Video recording clip 1, March 17, 2009)

What difference, then, is there among Peking opera, *kunqu* opera, and Chinese classical dance? I expressed my confusion to Professor Dong, and she explained:

> At this time, what names were there to use? Call it theatrical drama? Call it *kunqu* opera? One could certainly do that, [use the names of existing genres, such as] Peking opera, *kunqu* opera. However, it was necessary to draw from

them the dance of China, the Chinese [dance]. Therefore, he [Professor Ouyang] proposed one name, Chinese classical dance. That was how [the term Chinese] *classical dance* came about. Therefore [I must say that] this classical dance, ours is unique and different from those of other countries. [For instance], in France or Britain, ballet was [their] classical dance. For the Japanese, Noh and Kabuki were their classical dance. What about us in China? It would be the classical dance that was put forward after the liberation of the republic [from the Chinese Nationalist Party, also known as the Kuomintang], in the 1950s—around 1950, 1949, 1950, when Professor Ouyang suggested it. (Video recording clip 1, March 17, 2009, 07:10:00)

Professor Dong went on to describe the current development of Chinese classical dance in China: "Currently, the [Beijing] Dance Academy has become the base for [developing] the Chinese Classical Dance, our classical dance. Professors Ye Ning (葉寧), Li Zhengyi (李正一), and Tang Mancheng (唐满城) drew from Peking opera and traditional Chinese opera, including martial arts, and even from ballet" (video recording clip 1, March 17, 2009, 07:11:00).

According to Professor Dong and other Chinese dance scholars I interviewed, such as Gao Jinrong, the idea and name *Chinese classical dance* were not traditional but were introduced into Chinese contexts in the 1950s. Although the Chinese translation of *classical* (*gudian* 古典) may also be glossed "ancient institutions," "ancient books," "classical allusions," or "laws," the idea of classical used by Ouyang appeared to be setting a new standard of canons to serve the PRC. The historical authenticity of the *Dunhuang bihua yuewu* is therefore an invented authority.

While the construction of Chinese classical dance drew many of its elements from Peking opera and traditional Chinese opera, it was heavily influenced by Western art forms, such as ballet and modern dance. Aaron Avshalomov (Russian: Аарон Авшаломов) (1894–1965), for instance, was a Russian-born composer who contributed extensively to the formulation of Chinese classical dance. Born in the Amur basin or Heilongjiang regions, he grew up listening to Peking opera and Chinese folk songs.[10] Attracted by Peking opera actors' postures, movements, and facial expressions, as well as the genre's unique integration of singing and dancing, he decided to develop Peking opera further by conducting research on Chinese folk songs. His goal was to make Peking opera more colorful and less restrained by a simple repeated melody, which he thought dull at times (Messmer 2012).

In 1916, Avshalomov went to China to live and work in Beijing, Tianjin, and Qingdao, and he used this opportunity to study folk songs and

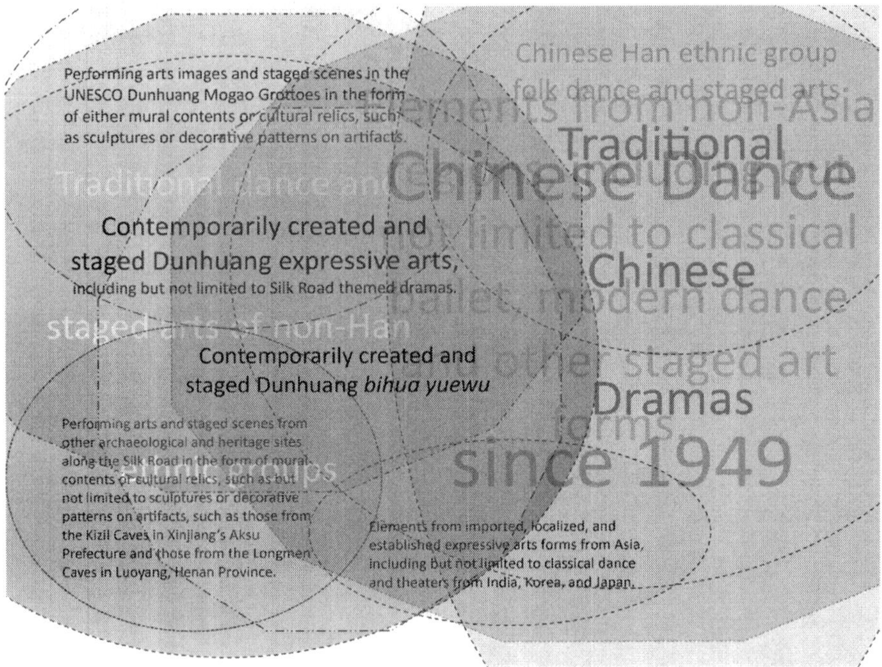


Figure 4.2. A working metagraph loosely demonstrates the intertextual relations between the staged Dunhuang expressive arts, with the *Dunhuang bihua yuewu* genre at its core, and the various fields of dances from China that became key components in Chinese dance formed during the founding years of the People's Republic of China. © Lanlan Kuang, 2024.

folk music and to create music with Chinese characteristics. Among his first works of this type was an opera, *Guanyin* 觀音, which premiered in Peking in 1925; it was named after *Guanshiyin* 觀世音, a female depiction of Avalokiteśvara common in East Asia, referring to the Mahāyāna bodhisattva of the same name. He cooperated with Peking opera actors to stage several dances with stylizing characteristics of Peking opera, as well as the three-act dance drama *A Dream in the Buddhist Temple* (香篆夢, also known as 古刹驚夢 or 香煙繚繞) and the opera *Lady Mengjiang* (*Mengjiang nü* 孟姜女). Each of the three acts of the former, staged in March 1935, displayed what Chinese scholars consider to be signature traditional Chinese dance programs that are still being performed today, such as the dance depicting the revelation of the Thousand-Handed and Thousand-Eyed Avalokiteśvara in act 1, the long-sleeved dance and fan dance in act 2, and the martial arts with acrobatic actions in act 3. Avshalomov also produced and staged

*Buddha and Stars of the Five Elements*, a short dance drama based on a diagram of the five elements discovered in the Mogao Grottoes. Inspired by Chinese Daoist astrology and representing the five planets, the five elements were distinguished by different colors and enacted by actors in costumes designed according to images found in the diagram, with Mercury holding a pipa, Pluto holding a peach, Venus holding stationery, and Saturn holding a flag; Mars, who started a war among the stars, was holding a weapon (Chen and Huang 2022: 11).

Another important figure who had a long-lasting impact on the formation of Chinese classical dance was Choe Sung-Hee (Korean 최승희; Chinese 崔承喜, 1911–1969), a Korean dancer who taught briefly at the Central Academy of Drama in 1951. Ouyang Yuqian, who directed the academy at the time, invited her to conduct workshops. An outstanding dancer of modern and Korean dance, Choe was a student of Ishii Baku (Japanese いしいばく; Chinese 石井漠, 1886–1962) who pioneered modern dance in Japan. Her visit to China was driven by the Korean War (1950–1953). The Chinese dancers and scholars who established the field of modern Chinese dance learned from her, Dai Ailian, and other dancers who traveled to China, and learned from them techniques and methodologies that are still influencing dancers and choreographers (Wilcox 2019).

During my earlier ethnographic research in China, none of the interviewees I met questioned the origin of the term *Chinese classical dance*, and none proposed an alternative source. The term has gained legitimacy regardless of its complexity in correlation to modern China's national history, as it was coined by an authoritative figure at a time when the history and traditions of a country now called China were being vigorously reconstructed. Folkloric research and Dunhuangology received the attention and support of the state government at that time, as the government understood that the discursive formation mobilized by scholars in academic fields would greatly affect the formation and historic legitimacy of China as a modern nation. Professor Dong stated in *Dance and Communication in Chinese Culture*: "The development of Chinese classical dance has mostly been supported by the activities of the new Beijing Dance Academy, which has concentrated on reinterpreting Chinese dance to reflect the spirit of a China renewed by revolution and proud of its monumental history. . . . The principal inspiration is the entire span of China's performance traditions, and so many of the dances return to ancient, and even prehistoric, themes and forms" (Dong Xijiu et al. 2001: 78).

If Chinese classical dance included new dance forms that constituted a departure from earlier forms of drama and opera, with movements borrowed from characters in Peking opera and *kunqu* opera, was the *Dunhuang bihua yuewu* then also characteristic of traditional Chinese opera? Why was *Dunhuang bihua yuewu* considered a genre of Chinese classical dance? According to Professor Dong, who first encouraged Gao Jinrong in her work to develop the genre, the pertinent repertoire was "a notable example of the synthesis of history and innovation in contemporary classical dance in China" (Dong Xijiu et al. 2001: 78). In an interview, Professor Dong explained at length what she thought would help me understand the nature of the *Dunhuang bihua yuewu* as a Chinese classical dance genre. She first made a clear distinction between music and dance portrayed in the murals of the Mogao Grottoes and music and dance presented in staged *Dunhuang bihua yuewu* programs.

> We should approach the *Dunhuang bihua yuewu* this way: first there was the music and dance itself [the contents from Mogao wall paintings]. The construction of it [the Mogao Grottoes] began in 366, starting with three caves built during the Sixteen Kingdoms period and followed by Northern Wei, Sui, Tang, Five Dynasties, Song, Yuan, and Qing dynasties. There were no caves built during the Ming dynasty, because during the Ming dynasty, the power [of the Ming court] did not reach beyond Gate Jiayu 嘉峪關.[11]
>
> Therefore, you must remember, there was no [influence from the] Ming dynasty, but they [the contents in the Mogao Grottoes' wall paintings] [have elements spanning] one thousand years, starting from 366 [and going] all the way to the Qing dynasty. This was the music and dance from Dunhuang itself [depicted in the wall paintings].
>
> Why does [the *Dunhuang bihua yuewu*] belong within the field of Chinese classical dance, or to be considered a classical dance genre? We just discussed the original body, the source, the corpus of artistic works of the Dunhuang wall painting. We [dance scholars] absorbed the dance movements portrayed in the Dunhuang wall painting, and created, you could say, by imitating the ancient corpus and reviving [the contents of the Dunhuang wall paintings] on stages or in classrooms. This kind of dance we now refer to as the Dunhuang dance, right? Yet that was after [the staging of the first Dunhuang-themed dance drama]; I thought the starting time should begin with [the dance drama] *Along the Silk Road* [*siluhuayu* 絲路花雨]. (Video recording, November 22, 2008)

The *Dunhuang bihua yuewu* had a stunning start as a newly created dance form and was considered a genre of the Chinese classical dance, but its creator encountered numerous challenges trying to institutionalize it within the academic system. One reason was that, at the time when *Along the Silk Road*, then considered one of the earliest programs associated with the *Dunhuang bihua yuewu*, was being staged domestically and internationally, many people working in literature and the arts (*wenyi jie* 文藝界) were uncertain whether state officials and policies would agree with and permit the institutionalization of such a new art form. It is not unusual to witness the impact of sociopolitical changes on the creation of expressive art forms, as the examples from the Wei and Tang dynasties illustrate above. After the Great Cultural Revolution (1966–1976), during which many historical and religious art forms were destroyed, *Dunhuang bihua yuewu*, historically influenced and inspired by religious art, did not appear to be the likeliest form to be institutionalized and taught formally in dance academies. The influence brought by the Great Cultural Revolution was so great that people were still uncertain about what might be considered forbidden. The cultural damage caused by "ten years of chaos" (*shinian dongluan* 十年動亂) was reflected not only in the material destruction and stagnation of existing traditional art forms but also in the choices made by the generations of scholars and artists who experienced the revolution.

In 1977, the year after the downfall of the Gang of Four (*Sirenbang* 四人幫), who stood accused of implementing strategies that had led to the Great Cultural Revolution, Professor Dong and a group of scholars from Beijing went to Dunhuang to investigate the performing arts depicted in the murals of the Mogao Grottoes. Excited by their discovery, they suggested to the local and central government officials that they should create a dance drama based on the performative images in the murals, yet they were nevertheless concerned about the potential repercussions of their activities: "I had doubts and fears when I went to investigate [Dunhuang in 1977], because [I still thought that] religion was considered taboo. While the Gang of Four [was in power], it was taboo. How dare I?" (video recording, March 22, 2009).

In fact, some authorities did question the investigation conducted at Dunhuang in 1977. In our interview, Professor Dong laughed at this incident and said she had "equipped herself with the words of Marshal Ye" (interview note, 2008). Ye Jianying 葉劍英 (1897–1986) was one of the ten veteran generals from the People's Liberation Army who had received the title of marshal in 1955 and was hence known as Ye Shuai 叶帅. Named minister of defense of the PRC in 1975, he was one of the few remaining marshals in China to stay in power after the fall of the Gang of Four in 1976.[12] It was not a coincidence that Professor Dong quoted him in defense of the investigation into the Dunhuang arts in 1977. He became the second most powerful figure after Hua Guofeng 華國鋒 (1921–2008), Mao Zedong's designated successor as the paramount leader of the Communist Party of the PRC.

Professor Dong explained the words that she was prepared to borrow: "Once I got there, I saw an inscription written by Marshal Ye Jianyin, which says: 'Dunhuang was the wisdom of the working-class people.' I then had in my mind 'a sword of state' [*shangfang baojian* 尚方宝剑]. I said [to other scholars] that if anyone wished to criticize our investigation at Dunhuang, I should use the words of Marshal Ye Jianying, 'wisdom of the working-class people,' and of course it [Dunhuang] was the creation of the working-class people. So I have 'a sword of state.'"

*Sword of state* was a term used frequently to suggest having obtained executive power from an imperial ruler; the sword was a symbol of authority and power. Like other monarchs, imperial rulers in China proper used a sword as part of their regalia to show the privileges of a sovereign. Professor Dong used Marshal Ye's reference to working-class people to refer to those who had constructed the Mogao Grottoes. In her study on Chinese dance from the 1930s to the 2010s, Emily Wilcox (2019) also explores the birth of Chinese dance as a modern creation in the backdrop of socialism.

## The Earliest Performances of the Genre

Despite the sociopolitical difficulties, Professor Dong and other early Dunhuang expressive arts scholars continued with their work and went on to stage one of the first *Dunhuang bihua yuewu* performances. *Along the Silk Road* was a benchmark for Dunhuang-themed dance dramas staged by the Gansu Provincial Dance and Song Troupe in 1983. Its creation was overseen by Wu Jian 吴坚 and Chen Shuiyao 陈水谣, then chairs of the Gansu Provincial Chinese Communist Party Committee for Publicity. The staged performance was so well received that it was later made into a film with the same title.

*Along the Silk Road* is set in the northwestern Hexi Corridor during the Tang dynasty. A Persian merchant named Enus travels to China for trade, and he is saved from a sandstorm by Zhang, a painter nicknamed Magic Brush for his skill. Five years later, after learning that Yingniang, Zhang's daughter, was kidnapped as a child by an acrobatic troupe, Enus pays a large ransom to rescue her. *Along the Silk Road* consists of six acts, and "Playing Pipa in Reverse Position" (*Fantan pipa* 反弹琵琶), one of the most elegant images from the Mogao Grottoes, was made famous by a solo dance in it with the same title.

He Yanyun, the woman who danced the role of Yingniang in *Along the Silk Road*, once taught the *Dunhuang bihua yuewu* at the Beijing Dance Academy. She was among the dancers I interviewed. She has become so well known that she has been addressed as First General Yingniang—which suggests that *Along the Silk Road* was so successful that it has indeed become what Yang Chengwei, director of the Gansu Provincial Peking Opera Troupe, described as "a trademark product" and "a tradition" (video recording, November 22. 2008).

The impact of *Along the Silk Road* was huge. It became one of the first artistic works created since the Great Cultural Revolution that presented China's intent to forge relationships with foreign nations. According to Professor Dong, its staging may be considered a diplomatic strategy, or what many called soft power in contemporary international relations: "This way, it made an impact, an impact in Beijing. In addition, all foreign ambassadors were excited after they saw it, because China has often been staged with an unpleasant image [*fanmian xingxiang* 反面形象], but now the foreign relations, in this case [the story line of *Along the Silk Road*] the relation [of] Enus with Iran, or Persia, the friendship among China, Persia, and Iran, has greatly improved. [The Gansu Provincial Dance and Song Troupe] were immediately invited by more than twenty countries to perform overseas" (video recording, November 22, 2008).

Gao Jinrong 高金榮, the former president of the Gansu Provincial School of the Arts, was known as the creator of the *Dunhuang bihua yuewu*. In the early 1970s, while she was president of the school, she recreated, primarily using the three-volume collection of *Ancient Dance-Movement Pictographic Images*, the first systematic training course for the dance, which laid the foundation for the development of the *Dunhuang bihua yuewu* as a unique and independent genre on the contemporary stage.

Before Gao's development of the training course, the *Dunhuang bihua yuewu* could hardly be described as a dance genre; instead, it consisted of a few dance programs inspired by the Dunhuang materials and the history of the region. Gao's contribution to the development is remarkable, yet it took years for her to gain recognition from scholars and audiences beyond the Northwest on account of the comparatively poor financial and instructional resources and the city of Lanzhou's geographic location in an underdeveloped region.

It is not unusual to find intangible cultural heritage transmitted in a family. In fact, well-known Chinese expressive art genres—such as Peking opera, *kunqu* opera, and even the Chinese martial art *taiji*—often pass from one generation to the next as a family treasure, a way of living, and a way to make a living. Those who wished to study with a master but were not a member of the master's family might be adopted into the family with a change of last name, depending on the student's willingness and talent. In Gao Jinrong's case, her own daughter, as well as her daughter in-law, were trained dancers of the *Dunhuang bihua yuewu*. Such kin-oriented heritage transmission is less common today because of the availability of public education and job opportunities. Only Gao's daughter-in-law is still practicing the genre as a dance teacher, formerly at the Gansu Vocational School of the Arts and now at the new Lanzhou University of Arts and Sciences.

## Institutionalizing *Dunhuang bihua yuewu* in Present-Day China

The advantages and disadvantages of long-term research in a single location have been compared by Anthony Seeger (1998, 2008), J. Lawrence Witzleben (1997, 2010), Deborah Wong (2001, 2006), and others. As the *Dunhuang bihua yuewu* continues to grow into a more developed and recognized subfield of Chinese classical dance in the academic world in present-day China, I start to become more self-conscious of how my positionality as an ethnomusicologist-in-the-field affects ethnographic and epistemological practice. My long-term interactions with leading scholars and administrations inevitably affect the research phenomena. Reflexivity, emblematic of anthropologists' disciplinary identity, was emboldened by postcolonial scholarship in the 1980s and 1990s, when awareness and discussion of the field researcher's positionality became increasingly salient as a prerequisite to the analysis of and theorizing about social experience. The relationship between music and identity became a commonplace theme in ethnomusicology beginning in the early 1980s (Rice 1987). Revealing the conditions of possibility through which researchers objectify social reality is inevitable in producing objective knowledge, as ethnographers' intellectual biases take form in their educational background (Bourdieu 1991). In my research on the institutionalization of *Dunhuang bihua yuewu* in contemporary China, scholarly communications occurred frequently, almost daily, as a critical part of my work in northwest China. In 2022, my research on staged Dunhuang arts—especially the staged Chinascapes concept featured in my 2016 monograph—was cited in the description of Northwestern Minzu University's new Dunhuang dance studies graduate degree program. This was the first Dunhuang dance studies graduate degree program since the genre began to be taught as a subfield of Chinese classical dance.

Being cited by the graduate program curriculum is arguably one of the strongest validations of my long-term research on staged Dunhuang arts and the Chinascape concept.[13] I have argued in the past, from an existential point of view, that an ethnomusicologist's *being*-in-the-field also means *be-coming* the field as an embodied way of *being*, but I am starting to see even more precisely the criticality of organized reflexivity in future ethnographic work. For instance, in a Heideggerian and a Merleau-Pontian sense, my physical presence in the staging process of the Dunhuang arts means that I have been engaging with and living in the time-space through bodily experience and constituting spatiality. In other words, the ethnographer's spatial presence becomes a particular and concrete moment in the processes of staging: "[One] can convey the idea of space only if already involved in it, and if it is already known. Since perception is initiation into the world, and since, as has been said with insight, 'there is nothing anterior to it which is mind,' we cannot put into it objective relationships which are not yet constituted at its level" (Merleau-Ponty 1962: 257).

My research and ideas have left in the staging process traces that continue to emerge; the ethnographer's presence though media such as text and film thereby continue *be-coming* elements of the Chinascape. The emergence of *Chinascape* as a key term in the process of institutionalization signifies the continuous staging of new visions of multicultural China in domestic and international media and performance spheres through discursive formation. The next chapter continues to investigate key concepts and terms related to staging the Dunhuang arts on the basis of long-term multisite research in China.

## Notes

1. The *Dunhuang bihua yuewu* is defined in the earlier chapters as a multifaceted genre of music, dance, and dramatic performances that was created in the twentieth century primarily on the basis of artifacts excavated from the northwestern frontier metropolis of Dunhuang, China.

2. The *Kaihuang Code*, considered an example of the Chinese legal system and the origin of Han dynasty Chinese law, served as a blueprint for the legal institutions of the Tang and later the Song, Ming, and Qing dynasties.

3. 隋文帝開皇二年，尚因周樂，命工人齊树提檢校樂府，改換聲律，益不能通。俄沛公郑譯奏上，请更修正。于是诏太常卿牛弘、國子祭酒辛彦之、國子博士何妥议正樂。然沦謬既久，積議不定。帝怒曰：“我受天命七年，樂府犹歌前代德。”命治書侍御史李谔引弘等下，将罪之。谔奏曰：“武王克殷，至周公相成王制礼樂。斯事体大，不可速成。”帝意稍解。九年，平陈，获宋、齊旧樂，詔于常置清商署以管之。求得陳太乐令蔡子元、于普明等，复居其职。

4. 隋代雅樂，唯奏黄钟一，郊廟朝飨用一調，迎氣用五調。旧工更盡，其餘聲律皆不複通声律皆不复通。或有能为蕤宾之宫者，享祀之际肆之，竟無覺者。

5. The number of suites rewarded indicates the importance of the official; for example, if the emperor himself may be entertained with ten musical suites, then the reward of nine musical suites confirms Li Shimin's high status in the political hierarchy.

6. The term *Yiliang* refers to Yizhou and Xiliang; the former is now called Hami in Xijiang, and the latter is in Gansu. See *Jiu Tang shu* and *Xin Tang shu* for details.

7. Qočo (Gaochang 高昌) refers to present-day Turfan. See *The Old Book of Tang* (*Jiu Tang Shu* 旧唐書), chapter on music, vol. 4, p. 1069.

8. Also known as the League of Left-Wing Writers, the union, founded in 1930, adopted the Soviet doctrine of socialist realism.

9. Proclaimed by UNESCO in 2001 as a Masterpiece of the Oral and Intangible Heritage, *kunqu* 崑曲 is an operatic singing style that developed in the town of Kunshan 崑山, near Suzhou 蘇州, China, in the sixteenth century.

10. The land mentioned here refers to the Amur basin or Heilongjiang regions, which belonged to China under the Treaty of Nerchinsk (1689) until the Qing government ceded the lands north of the Amur (1858) and east of the Ussuri (1860) to Russia.

11. Jiayu Pass (*Jiayuguan* 嘉峪關) is a fortress located at the narrowest point of the western section of the Gansu Corridor. It was built as the westernmost fortification of the Ming dynasty Great Wall.

12. Wang Hung-wen, Zhang Chun-qiao, Chiang Ch'ing, and Yao Wen-yuan were to become known collectively as the Gang of Four, a sobriquet coined by Mao Zedong himself. After Mao's death, the Gang of Four was accused of a multitude of crimes, which included keeping a nation of eight hundred million living in constant fear, ruthlessly attacking Communist Party members, nearly destroying an economy, threatening civil war, committing national betrayal, hampering foreign trade, ruining the educational system, and preventing a single poem or play from being printed, much less published, without their approval.

13. An even earlier adaptation of the term *Chinascape* can be traced to an exhibition staged by China's Central Academy of Fine Arts (CAFA) at Italy's Istituto Garuzzo per le Arti Visive (IGAV). According to IGAV curator Alessandro Demma, "Chinascape: From Rural to Urban" (2017) showcased "the new visions that the artists have of a contemporary national and international system subject to constant evolution and metamorphosis." See "Chinascape: From Rural to Urban—Exhibition of Chinese Contemporary Photography," *Five Columns*, December 1, 2016, https://www.cinquecolonne.it/chinascape-from-rural-to-urban.html.

# 5

# CREATING *DUNHUANG BIHUA YUEWU*

## *Key Concepts and Terms*

ONCE AESTHETICIZED ONSTAGE, THE HISTORICAL AND topological land-scape of Dunhuang becomes a conceptual landscape, developing and expounding its own key concepts and terms. These inform this chapter, which interweaves discourses and narratives from Dunhuang with schol-ars' comments, using a performance-based, ethnopoetic approach.[1] By de-scribing and analyzing the rhetoric occurring in the process of teaching, transmitting, and authenticating, this chapter shows how the *Dunhuang bihua yuewu* has been staged as a representation of a historically multifac-eted and cosmopolitan Chinese nation.

### Archaeological Sources and the Creation of the Genre

*Yue* (樂) and *wu* (舞) are the Chinese characters for music and dance, re-spectively. Music and dance have essentially been bounded in China since ancient times, as they were essential parts of shamanistic rituals long before the rise of the Zhou dynasty (ca. 1045–256 BCE), when civil officials, en-gaged in the central administration to organize religious affairs, established the Zhouli 周禮, the Rites of the Zhou. Before then, Chinese religion had been a religion of shamans, known as *wu* (巫).

According to etymologist and lexicographer Xu Shen (ca. 58–148 CE), who compiled *Shuowen jiezi* 說文解字 (The origin of Chinese characters, also known as Discussions of writings and explanations of characters), a *wu* is a woman who serves invisible spirits and can invite them by dancing. The term *wu* (巫) is related to its homophone *wu* (舞), the word for "dance," and it has been explained as referring etymologically to the raising of one's sleeves in a dancelike gesture. *Wu* itself can refer to both a person skilled in dancing and someone holding in two hands the instruments of magic or divination (Ching 1997).

A straightforward, word-for-word translation of *Dunhuang bihua yuewu* (敦煌壁画乐舞) is "Dunhuang murals music [and] dance." The Sinitic name of Dunhuang 敦煌/燉煌 first appeared in the *Collective Biographies of Dayuan* by Sima Qian (ca. 145–86? BCE) in the *Shiji* (Records of the grand scribe), which documented the diplomatic mission of Zhang Qian (d. 114 BCE), a Chinese envoy twice dispatched by the Han emperor Wudi (141–89 BCE) to the Western Regions between 139 and 125 BCE. This mission played an important role in the opening of the Silk Roads, which linked the Mediterranean coast with central China and beyond via oasis towns such as Samarkand. Dunhuang, a cosmopolitan enclave closely associated with the history of transcontinental relations and the propagation of Buddhism in China, was plagued by frequent conflicts among many groups living in, passing through, and attempting to control the region. It was one of the four prefectures established by Wudi about 121 BCE and was a vital political, social, economic, and religious center in the northwestern periphery of the Chinese empire (Sima Qian et al. 1959).

An original quality of the *Dunhuang bihua yuewu* is the capability of staging, through bodily enactment, the multifaceted as synthetic and the fragmented as linear. The genre's appeal arises from the complexity and sophistication said to be born of centuries of conflict and negotiation among different civilizations along the Silk Road. While it tends to draw primarily on images from the Sui (581–617 CE) and Tang (618–906 CE) dynasties, patterns established in the Han dynasty (206 BCE–220 CE) are also evident. This selection of historical references for recreating dance differs from that of Han-Tang dance 漢唐舞 (*Han-Tang wu*), another genre of Chinese classical dance created in the modern era. Unlike *Han-Tang wu*, inspired by images from the Han dynasty tombs and murals and various Tang dynasty artifacts, the *Dunhuang bihua yuewu* is not constrained by close association with a specific time, even though archaeologists and art historians have labeled its sources from the Mogao Grottoes by dynasties and eras.[2]

Professor Gao Jinrong, one of my primary sources in the field and a dance scholar widely acknowledged for creating a paradigm of Dunhuang dance education, advised me more than once to concentrate on the search for what she called a parallel style after she had examined the developments and changes of the performative images from the wall paintings. By *parallel style*, she meant a similar, shared pattern evident in all the performative images from Dunhuang.

Another important matter to be considered when approaching the staging of the genre is the function of rhetoric, by which I mean the borrowing or sharing of aesthetic terminologies rooted in ancient ideas and laws about the cosmos, rituals, and philosophy. It was through the textual and verbal usage of these shared terminologies in discourses and processes of staging that the dance has been institutionalized and authenticated as a Chinese dance, to take its place among traditional painting and other art forms.

A third original contribution of the *Dunhuang bihua yuewu* caught my attention. The rhetorical use of shared aesthetic terminologies characterized the dance genre as Chinese, but Professor Gao's application of some of the principal ideas embodied by these terms, such as breathing (*qi* 氣), spirit (*shen* 神), and rhythm (*yun* 韻), became instruments to authenticate the genre as being unique. Professor Gao described the process of staging the *Dunhuang bihua yuewu* as "image to image, static to dynamic" (*xingxiang—xingxiang* 形象—形,象 image to image; *jingzhi—huodong* 靜止—活動, static to dynamic).

### *Poetic Imagery and the Concept of Shi* 勢

Poetic imagery has been a center of Chinese critical attention from the earliest times, though scholars disagree on the empirical origin of all images in a poem. Certainly, however, poetic imagery was never regarded as mere description or as simple ornament but was seen as the sine qua non of poetry itself. Curiously, however, just as in the West, the terminology for imagery has proved to be somewhat fluid. Thus, in China, no single word has consistently been used to denote the concept; moreover, some of the most important presumptions about imagery were not even uttered in reference to poetry itself (H. Wu 1996).

Perhaps more than in any other genre of dance, the creators of *Dunhuang bihua yuewu* greatly emphasize the idea of trace—both the physical trace of the brush (*biji* 筆跡) or the ink (*moji* 墨跡) that marked the aesthetic principles and techniques of the paintings done in the Mogao Grottoes and the trace of the historical past, once embodied by the actors who participated in the creation of the Dunhuang arts in general.[3] The current popular term for the *Dunhuang bihua yuewu* often omits the two characters for *wall painting* (*bihua* 壁畫), but Professors Dong Xijiu and Gao Jinrong and other Dunhuang scholars who have studied the figures in the wall paintings have pointed specifically to the role of the images in the process of staging the dance. The painting techniques and aesthetic principles from the Chinese heartland, or China proper, influenced the creation of wall painting in Dunhuang. One of the major influences was the incorporation of calligraphy into painting.

The Dunhuang murals reflect the development of classical Chinese calligraphy, but not many Dunhuang manuscripts feature classical calligraphy specifically. According to Bai Qianshen, Cai Yuandi, and other scholars, the documents can be classified in six types: Suo Jing Yueyitie 索靖月儀帖, Wang Xizhi Shiqitie Copy 王羲之十七帖臨本, Zhi Yong Zhencaoqianziwen Jiang Shanjin's Copy 智永真草千字文蔣善进臨本, Ouyang xun shu Huadusiyongchanshitamin Inscription 歐陽詢書化度寺邕禪師塔銘拓本, Tang Taizong Wenquanmin Inscription 唐太宗溫泉銘拓本, and Liu Gongquan Jingangjin Inscription 柳公權書金剛經拓本. The first three types are manuscripts, and the last three are preserved in the form of rubbings. These manuscripts have long held people's attention and have become models for later penmanship following classical calligraphy. Some of the best-known examples are Xuanshibiao 宣示表, Lantingshu 蘭亭序, and Shangxianghuangqitie 尚想黃綺帖 (Cai Yuandi 2010). Studies of "trace of brush" or "trace of ink" have tried to separate forgeries from authentic sources. An example is Cai Yuandi's (2010) study of excavated fragments of *The Law of Brush-Strokes* (*Bi Shi Lun* 筆勢論).[4]

Some of the manuscripts held at the Dunhuang Academy have been dated to the Wei, Jin, and Southern and Northern dynasties. Among them, the calligraphic scriptures may be described as dignified in regular script, slightly vertical in structure, thick in brushwork, and delicate in stippling. Early sūtra writing, roughly from the period of the Jin dynasty (265–420), blends the characteristics of clerical and regular scripts. The *Nirvana Sūtra* in a calligraphic copy from the Northern Wei dynasty is in a neat and balanced form. The brushstrokes are light and elegant, achieved by moving the tip of the brush quickly at the beginning of the horizontal drawing. Each stroke ends with a decisive and dignified stop. The calligraphic copy therefore appears to be more "official" and worthy of respect. The act of copying Buddhist scriptures requires both stability and speed. Over time, scribes developed the "sūtra writing style" (寫經體), a concise and fluent style of calligraphy different from the style used in daily life.

My research on the *Dunhuang bihua yuewu*, unlike previous scholarship on the brushstrokes, examined the effects of brushstrokes on the

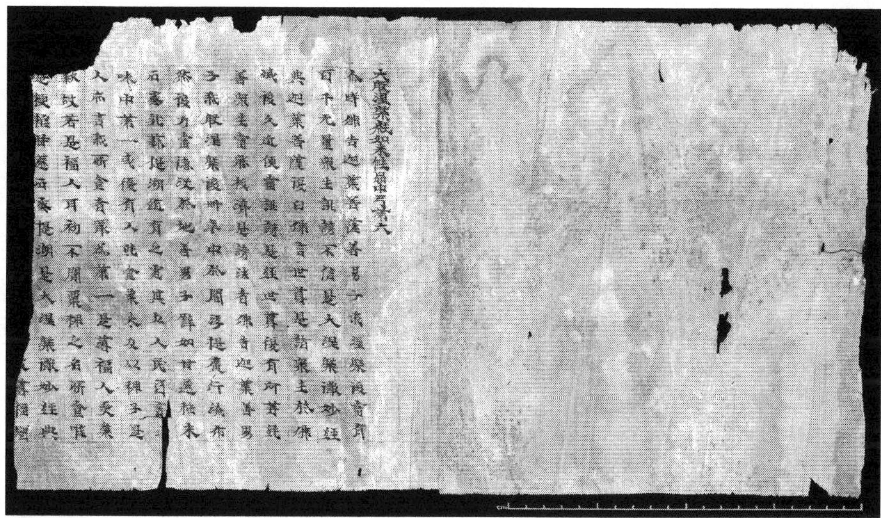

Figure 5.1. *Nirvana Sutra*. Calligraphic copy dated to the Northern Wei dynasty (220–265). Permission to use image granted by Dunhuang Academy.

creation of the *Dunhuang bihua yuewu*. One of the important discoveries I made through on-site work and analysis is that many of the terms used in traditional painting and calligraphy were also used by those involved in the processes of consolidating a theoretical ground for creating and teaching the *Dunhuang bihua yuewu* today.[5] For instance, the term *shi* 勢 (trajectory) was employed in calligraphy treatises and then was widely used in artistic criticism in the Eastern Han dynasty (25–220 CE). Many titles of calligraphy treatises produced between the period of Eastern Han and Western Jin (265–317 CE)—such as *Caoshu shi* 草書勢 (*Shi* of cursive script), *Jiu Shi* 九勢 (Nine types of *shi*), and *Si ti shushi* 四體書勢 (*Shi* of the four scripts of calligraphy)—bear the term *shi*. The concept of *shi* entered into the theory of painting and literary criticism after the Jin dynasty, eventually being absorbed into theories of music and dance.[6] In *Chinese Calligraphy: An Introduction to Its Aesthetic and Technique* (1973), Chiang Yee points out that "it is not unprofitable to compare calligraphy with dancing. The calligraphy of a great master is . . . an adventure in movement very similar to good dancing" when he discusses the writing of Wang Xizhi 王羲之 on *Bi-Shi* 筆勢 (The propensity of brushstrokes). Consequently, Yee introduced the dance-inspired Grass Style 草書 characters of Zhang Xu 張旭, a legendary Tang dynasty calligrapher, and used dance as a metaphor for describing a piece of calligraphy:[7] "A finished piece of it is not a symmetrical arrangement of conventional shapes, but something like the co-ordinated movement of a skillfully composed dance—impulse, momentum, momentary poise, and the interplay of active forces combining to form a balanced whole" (Yee 1973: 44). He compares the movement of the strokes to that of dance: "The movement of the strokes suggests speed, but a dancing rather than a racing speed" (44).

Some of the more recent studies in Chinese language pedagogy and experimental psychology argue that sound coding—both character-level phonological codes and subcharacter-level phonological codes—also plays a role in the identification of Chinese characters as in the identification of words in alphabetic writing systems (Pollatsek, Li, and Rayner 2000). Scholars have made progress in the field of image processing by studying the implied trajectory of the fingertips when writing Chinese characters in the air (Xu, Wang, and Qu 2015). These cross-disciplinary studies suggest the importance of studying the Dunhuang arts through performance-based on-site work.

## The Staging Processes

The *Dunhuang bihua yuewu* synthesizes many different expressive art forms; accordingly, terms used in Peking opera and other traditional Chinese theatrical genres have been used in staging it, and terms even from ballet and modern dance have been translated into Chinese and used for teaching it.

Instead of elaborating on the technical terms found in ballet or modern dance and translated into Chinese, this section focuses on theoretical terms essential in formulating the aesthetic principles of *Dunhuang bihua yuewu*. The monopoly of literacy was one of the most powerful factors in the spread of Chinese, and with it Chinese culture, at the expense of the other languages of the region (Pulleyblank 2002). Terms used in traditional painting and calligraphy were textually based, but when using them to enhance the teaching of the *Dunhuang bihua yuewu*, actors reinvented an oral tradition that was uniquely related to the phenomenon.

Professor Gao's creation of the first systematic training course for the *Dunhuang bihua yuewu* was based primarily on a three-volume collection, *Ancient Dance Movement in Pictographic Images*. As Professor Dong pointed out during one of the interview sessions:

Among the grand achievements of the *Dunhuang bihua yuewu*, we must acknowledge the painters. This is because the Dunhuang wall paintings were the painters' creations. How to combine this Buddhist art form with dances in real life? [The contents of the wall paintings] were representations of the Pure Land of the Mahāyāna Buddhist tradition, right? Or it [the content] would be a representation of the Lotus Sūtra [from the Mahāyāna Buddhist traditions]. Therefore, the wall paintings were religious art. Yet I think they reflect real life as well as the characteristics of music and dance at the time. Why is that? The painters were mostly untrained, local artists; they were painting based on their life experience, rather than making things up. Only if a painter has seen such beautiful, rich dances could he paint it on the wall. (Video recording, March 22, 2009)[8]

Professor Gao, who had worked closely with Professor Dong, acknowledged the importance of the dance images and discussed how the dance scholars used them:

To make full use of all the pictographic dance images found in the treasure house of Dunhuang, which is really a treasure house of Chinese culture, and to make them known to the world, as I was inspired by the dance drama *Along the Silk Road*, I then began to research this with the goal of teaching it. We copied these images overnight. We asked another colleague to trace [the penciled images] with ink. These images are the originals. Therefore, it is not an exaggeration to say that this copy [of *Ancient Dance Movement Pictographic Images*] is the most authentic and most valuable. To avoid damaging this copy, we made an extra carbon-paper copy, which was posted all over in my office [for reference].

[We] must thank Professor Wu Manyin, who took these images from Director Chang Shuhong [of the Dunhuang Research Academy]. We then received these images from him [Professor Wu Manying]. Therefore, we must be thankful to the artists who provided access for us [choreographers]. (Video recording, December 7, 2008)

When making the still images from the wall paintings into dance—not just one dance program but a new genre, which could be taught systematically in classrooms—Professor Gao encountered other challenges, such as the criteria for selecting images.

If aesthetics were discussed in dynastic periods, as in the articles by Cai Zong-qi and other scholars whose writings are reproduced in *Chinese Aesthetics: The Ordering of Literature, the Arts, and the Universe in the Six Dynasties* (2004), as well as in my earlier discussion of the reconstruction of performative suites during the Wei, Sui, and Tang dynasties, I wondered, were the *Dunhuang bihua yuewu* also based on the aesthetic principles that guided each historical period? Was each of the *Dunhuang bihua yuewu* programs created to represent the aesthetic principles and styles of different dynastic periods? This was one of the first questions I asked Professor Gao. To my surprise, I learned that this was not the case.

> GAO: I study the pictographic images and the characteristic of different time periods. I also study the characteristic of the overall image and the general structure. They all look alike, but all are different if examined closely. I always emphasize *the similarity found among the difference*, which is most important. Didn't I tell you that I tried to do it [design the Dunhuang dance] by different historical periods? That was a failure. I think it is not appropriate. Because the Dunhuang wall paintings were done based on a general design, so should the dance be based on [this coherence of] the images.
>
> KUANG: [So] they are not designed by periodic, historical stages?
>
> GAO: Indeed they are not, and I did not [create the *Dunhuang bihua yuewu*] according to dynastic time. I just looked for similarities [among the different images].

What did Professor Gao mean when she said she "looked for similarities?" For instance, she examined and compared the painting in Cave No. 272, created during the Northern Wei dynasty to depict a group of Buddhas attending preaching, with the painting in Cave No. 148, built during the period of High Tang (705–780) to show the group of gandharvas serving the Dharma. During the Northern Wei dynasty, the Buddha's physical attributes, body postures, and overall expression exhibited more foreign characteristics. In contrast, the gandharvas depicted in the murals created during the High Tang period appeared more indigenous. Professor Gao defines "indigenous" as styles and movements traceable to expressive art forms originating in the Central Plateau, far from the borderland regions in the Northwest. For example, bodily movements, hand gestures, and technical terms used in folk dance and classical dramas like Peking opera and *kunqu* opera fall into the category of indigenous elements originating from China's Central Plateau. "Foreign characteristics" refer to a style employed to depict the physical appearance of figures in wall paintings from a time when the aesthetic principles and artistic techniques of central China had not yet significantly influenced Dunhuang. Despite these distinctions, the body lines and movements of these dancing characters remained consistent, as did the positions of their hands.

A second example would be the gandharvas from the murals in Cave No. 288,[9] built during the Northern Wei dynasty, and those serving the

Dharma in Cave No. 205, of the early Tang period. Although the performers' expressions and presentations are different in these groups—the former shows more stylistic influences from India and Xinjiang, and the latter shows more influence from China proper—their bodily movements and their use of long ribbons are quite similar.

Japanese dance scholar Setsuko Ishiguro states in her article on the study of the *Dunhuang bihua yuewu*: "Amongst the postures of flying deities seen in the murals of Dunhuang, those from the early Tang period are said to have developed a style unique to Chinese culture, independent from the influences of India and Uighur. There are also indications that this style has influenced the flying deities in Horyuji in Japan. For this reason, the dance of flying deities we aimed to create was based on the postures from this period" (2004: 80).

In interviews, Professor Gao pointed out five characteristic "outer appearances" that are unique to the *Dunhuang bihua yuewu*:

1. Movements of the hands are slender, elegant, and rich, exemplifying Chinese classical aesthetics.
2. Movements of the arms are flexible and curvy, while the wrist and elbow are arched to an angular position.
3. Feet are bare, with the basic gesture of the feet being "lifting the toes" (*gou* 鈎), "raising" (*ti* 提), or "arching the back of the feet" (*beng* 繃).
4. The body moves downward, with the lower body, especially the hips and legs, twisted into the *tribhanga* position (*sandaowan* 三道彎). There are two ways of moving the legs: one is to push the legs; the other one, to sit on them. Dance movements before the Sui period resemble those of Indian dances and show many traces of foreign influence. After that, movements, fashion, and facial expressions become more individualistic, and as a result, the basic postures of the body are defined, as with the positions of the hands.
5. The use of long ribbons, drums tied to the dancers' wrists, and pipas and other instruments.

### The Three Principal Elements

Outer appearances give only the general form for the *Dunhuang bihua yuewu*. In fact, the characteristics listed above can be found in many other dances around the globe. According to Professor Gao, three principal elements make the *Dunhuang bihua yuewu* unique: "There are three elements; these three elements, if [you] mastered them, [they] will make [my] teaching progress nicely. These elements are drawn from teaching experiences;

Table 5.1 Ancient Chinese Aesthetic Principles and The Three Principal Elements for *Dunhuang bihua yuewu*[1]

| The Three Principle Elements | Translation of the Modern Expressions Used in Teaching | Aesthetic Ideas from Ancient Chinese Philosophy That Are Related to and Used to Formulate the Modern Expressions |
| --- | --- | --- |
| 呼吸 | Breathing | Vital breath (*qi* 氣) |
| 眼神 | Expression of eyes | Spirit (*shen* 神) |
| 三道彎 | *Tribhanga* | Body (*xing* 形) and image (*xiang* 像) |

[1] Recorded discussions and demonstrations of the Three Principle Elements and other multimedia components for *Staging* Tianxia, such as maps, working color metagraphs, audiovisual files, and documentary film clips, can be found at https://lanlankuangofficial .pub/.

[they are] the basic elements. The first one is breathing (*huxi* 呼吸), the second is the expression of eyes (*yanshen* 眼神), and the third is *tribhanga* (*sandaowan* 三道彎), which consists of movements of the upper body, hip, and knees" (video recording from Jinrong Gao interview for the accompanying documentary, 2008).

Because expressive art forms in China are synthetic, as in traditional Chinese theater, the rhetorical expressions embedded within the discourse concerning the staged Dunhuang arts, and especially the staging of the *Dunhuang bihua yuewu* genre, are explicitly tied to aesthetic philosophies from pre-Han and Han dynasties, especially ideas related to traditional painting and political order that have strongly affected the construction of the concept of *tianxia* and, subsequently, the idea of Chineseness over the centuries.

The three elements that many choreographers think define the *Dunhuang bihua yuewu* and differentiate it as a unique genre, unlike any other dance, can be interpreted as in table 5.1.

According to Professor Gao, "breathing" in the *Dunhuang bihua yuewu* emphasizes a deep-breathing technique, which "will [allow the dancer to] create a sentiment that is divine and majestic." To stage the kind, majestic, and tranquil expression of the Buddha and Avalokiteśvara from the Mogao Grottoes, for instance, Professor Gao found it necessary to practice breathing and using the expression of the eyes simultaneously.[10]

The control of breathing is an important technique in other expressive arts in China, including calligraphy, traditional painting, Peking opera, and *kunqu* opera. Breathing practice requires mental and psychological

Table 5.2 Sample Breathing Exercise Instructions for *Dunhuang bihua yuewu* genre[1]

| **Breathing at Normal Speed** | | **Sample Breathing Exercise for the *Dunhuang bihua yuewu*** Students should sit in a crossed-leg position and visualize and module after the facial expressions described below while doing the exercise. | |
|---|---|---|---|
| *Rhythm* | *Two* | *Rhythmic beats* | *Four* |
| Take 1 | Inhale | Expression of the kind and majestic expression of Buddha and Avalokiteśvara | Expression of the lively and graceful gandharvas and apsaras |
| Take 2 | Exhale | 1  Inhale normally | 1  Exhale slightly faster than normal |
| | | 2  Inhale normally | 2  Inhale on the second half of the beat |
| | | 3  Exhale slowly | 3  Exhale slightly faster than normal |
| | | 4  Exhale slowly | 4  Inhale on the second half of the beat |

[1] Recorded demonstrations of the breathing exercises and other multimedia components for *Staging* Tianxia, such as maps, working color metagraphs, audiovisual files, and documentary film clips, can be found at https://lanlankuangofficial.pub/.

power. More importantly, Professor Gao thought that the bodily gesture of the signature *tribhanga* posture, which moves downward, was a natural, physical reaction of the aspirating of air when breathing. Instead of the simple mode of breathing in and out, she designed breathing exercises that would allow *Dunhuang bihua yuewu* dancers to mimic the expression of the imaging of the divine.

The chapter on breathing exercises in Professor Gao's *Dunhuang wudao* opens with the statement, "Deep breathing is the characteristic that created the unique prosodic/resonance (*yun* 韻) rhythm/law (*lü* 律) of the *Dunhuang* [*bihua yue*]*wu*. This is one of the important elements of the *Dunhuang wu* style" (1983: 27).

The breathing exercise should be conducted along with the exercise for eye expressions (*yanshen* 眼神). Professor Gao regarded these two exercises as the most important and the first ones to master in learning the genre. She stated: "Since they are both [exercises for] internal things [understanding and feeling], only after mastering [them] could one accurately revive the dances in the wall paintings, or could one truly express the style and resonance of the *Dunhuang* [*bihua yue*]*wu* and accomplish not only a 'mimic of the body' (*xingsi* 形似) but also 'convey the same spirit' (*shensi* 神似)." She added:

In all kinds of arts, be it painting, sculpture, drama, or dance, as long as the goal is to create a human figure and an image, the spirit (*shen* 神) must be taken into consideration. The wall paintings from Dunhuang were of more than a

> thousand years, each historical period has its own style, there were countless figures and images, yet [they] all focused on conveying the spirit (*chuanshen* 傳神), which means to represent the inner world of the figures, thereby revealing their psychological activities. This is especially obvious in some of the dancing figures in the wall paintings. (1983: 22)

Professor Gao considered the eyes to be one of the most effective instruments to convey the spirit. She identified four primary directions as characteristics of the Dunhuang figures: level, downward, level-sided, and upper-sided sideways (see fig. 5.2).

Conveying the spirit (*chuanshen* 傳神) has been one of the highest aesthetic ideals promoted in the arts of China. Cai Zong-qi (2004: 310–336) has written a comprehensive article on the conceptual origins and aesthetic significance of the spirit in Six Dynasties texts in literature and painting. In it, he explains the notion of *shen* 神 as a conscious supernatural being, anima, élan vital, and daemon. The expression "breathe resonance and lively animation" or "rhythmic vitality" (*qiyun shengdong* 氣韻生動) is frequently used to describe the aesthetic qualities of art. Rhythmic vitality has the highest value in Chinese traditional painting and calligraphy. People therefore often use expressions such as "things change in countless ways" (*qixiang wanqian* 氣象萬千) when they appreciate Chinese traditional arts.

In the *Dunhuang bihua yuewu*, Professor Gao frequently highlighted the phrase "breath resonance" (*qiyun* 氣韻) and especially the concept of resonance (*yun* 韻), which, as stated above, was used with the word *lü* 律, "rhythm/law." Both words are frequently seen in the description of poetical writing because the word *yun* also means "rhyme" and often functions, by extension, as an aural metaphor for describing one's subjective impressions.

The *Dunhuang bihua yuewu* was known for the *tribhanga*, a triply bent pose, consisting of three bends in the body: at the neck, the waist, and the knee. The body is oppositely curved into an S shape (型). Considered one of the most graceful positions in Indian classical dance, *tribhanga* is found in Buddhist arts around the globe. According to Professor Gao, however, the triply bent posture is only one of the main body positions in the *Dunhuang bihua yuewu* dance, which consists of stances of multiple bends, not only at the neck, waist, and knee but also at the ankle and wrist, with the curves extending even to the direction of the eyes.

Since Professor Gao has lived in northwest China for most of her life and has traveled extensively in the region, she could draw elements not only from dances but also from the gestures used daily by members of non-Han

Figure 5.2. Sample Eye Expression Exercise Instruction from Gao (2002: 10–11).[1]

| Direction | Eye Expression | Figure 5.2*A–D* |
| --- | --- | --- |
| Level | Half-opened, straightforward | 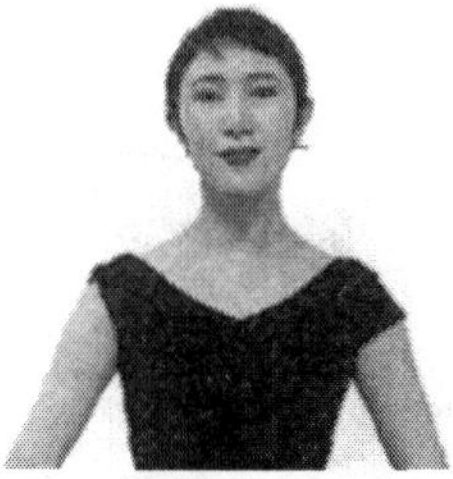 |
| Downward | Half-opened, looking down | 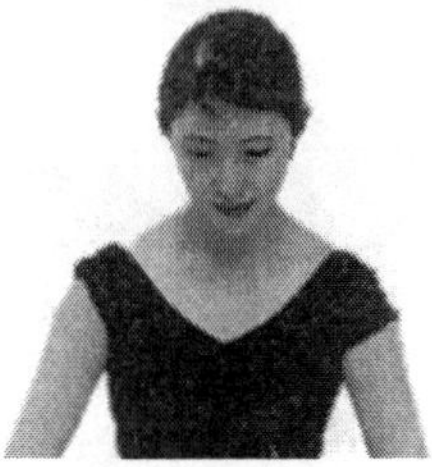 |
| Level-sided | Half-opened, looking aside | 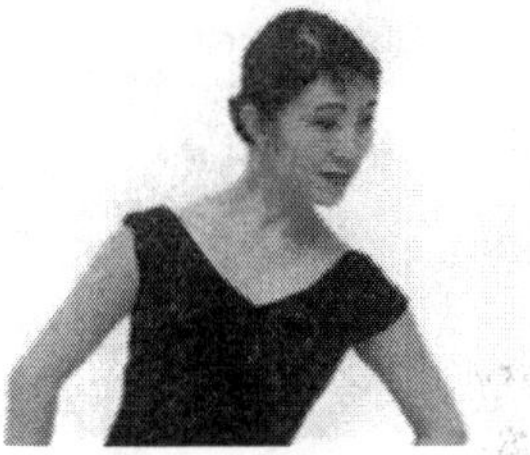 |
| Upper-sided sideways | Half-opened, looking above | 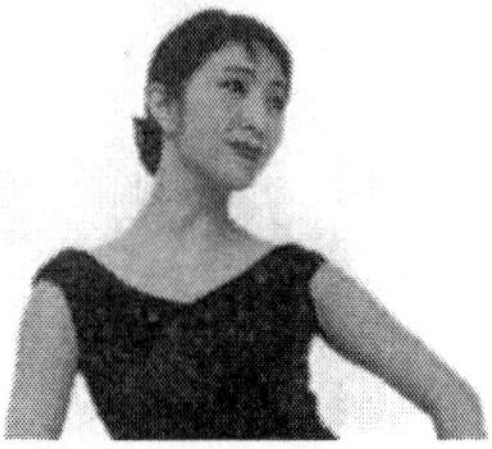 |

Figure 5.2*A*

Figure 5.2*B*

Figure 5.2*C*

Figure 5.2*D*

Courtesy of Gao Jinrong.

[1] Liu Jie 劉潔, the dancer featured in the breathing exercise and eye expression exercise samples, is Gao Jinrong's daughter. Recorded demonstrations of eye expression exercises and other multimedia components for *Staging* Tianxia, such as maps, working color metagraphs, audiovisual files, and documentary film clips, can be found at https://lanlankuangofficial.pub/.

ethnic groups. For instance, during our interview at the Gansu Provincial Radio, Television, Film Service (Gansusheng guangbo dianying dianshitai jituan 甘肅省廣播電影電視總台集團), she demonstrated how the praying stance of the Tibetans—a full bodily bowing gesture, which includes lowering one's arms to the ground and then rising to stand—has inspired one of the movements in the *Dunhuang bihua yuewu*. This adaptation of the Tibetan praying gesture illustrates one of the ways the genre was created.

### *Rhetorical Construction of the* Dunhuang bihua yuewu

Vital mobility is considered one of the essences in the creation of Chinese expressive arts. The movements of lines, spaces, props, actors, and even boundaries are what constitute a work of art. In a review of George Rowley's *Principles of Chinese Painting* (1947), Stephen C. Pepper (1948) translated the concept of vital mobility with the phrase "vividness of quality." Chinese aestheticians have created the principle of "spirit consonance [resonance], life movement" (*qiyun shengdong* 氣韻生動), the first principle of *Six Laws of Painting*, written by the artist and critic Xie He (谢赫 500–535), who explains this principle as that which leads a Chinese artist or connoisseur to connect to the cosmos when the circulation of qi ("breath," "spirit," "vital force of heaven") produces life movement in and through artistic creation (Cai Zong-qi 2004: 310–342; Ding 2010: 63).

Xie He's laws or principles, the fountainhead of traditional Chinese art theory, have been commented on throughout the centuries (Cai Zong-qi 2004). Cai, who quotes a conversation attributed to Xie He, considers "breath resonance and lively animation" to be the first law to explain the metaphorical, descriptive function of *yun*:

> Wang Cheng said, "The ancients spoke about 'breath resonance and animation.' May, for instance, the soaring movement in Mr. Wu's brushwork be considered an example of 'resonance'?" I replied, "'Animation' shows that the daemonic has been attained. If one is talking about the 'daemonic,' that achieves it fully. But it is not necessarily an example of 'resonance.'"
>
> Wang Cheng said, "What about Lu Taiwei's using just a few brush strokes to paint a lion? May that be said to have 'resonance'?" I replied, "Painting a lion with just a few brush strokes is to be abbreviated yet completely capture its underlying pattern. If one is talking about pattern, that achieves it fully. But it too is not necessarily an example of 'resonance.'"
>
> With that, Wang Cheng asked me to explain the matter, and so I told him, "'Resonance' is 'to have more meaning' than what is overtly expressed." Wang Cheng said, "Now I understand. I have noticed that when a bell is struck, after

the initial gong has passed, a residual sound is heard. It wavers and undulates in the air, being a note 'beyond the primary sound.' This must be the meaning of 'resonance.'" I replied, "You've got the gist of it but do not yet grasp its finer points. Where do you suppose this 'resonance' comes from?" Wang Cheng did not answer. I said, "It comes from 'having more' than what is expressed."[11]

Qi, most often translated as "spirit," is more specifically the vital principle or natural energy of all nature—animate and inanimate—not just of living beings, as *spirit* might indicate in English. There are in fact "occasions in which the change/transformation of *qi* is so extraordinary, subtle and mysterious that it transcends our grasp" (Henry 2008: 2). At such moments, qi becomes *shen*, "spirit," in Chinese. This can be the moment when the artist's mind and body become perfectly attuned, resonating with the creative source of the cosmos. The phrase *qi yun*, "spirit consonance," suggests agreement or harmony, and the translation "spirit resonance" suggests an amplification produced by a sympathetic vibration. Qi is the key to understanding *qiyun shengdong* (氣韻生動, "vivid and vibrant spirit") and *qixiang wanqian* (氣象萬千, "nature abounds in changes"). Thus, qi is an important category in Chinese traditional aesthetics. It mandates that true art must express the creative perpetual rhythm of the universe and its omnipresent movement.

Qi is the creative fountain and source of the formed and structured universe. It is not static: it is an eternal creative process. It not only produces the universe but also produces arts within its broad movement, so in Chinese traditional aesthetics, it embraces the fountain of creative energy. Zhong Rong (钟嵘 468–518), a classic theorist of art, said: "*Qi* inspires the universe, then the universe affects human beings, so people's temperaments are agitated by it and they began to sing and dance" (Xie, Zhihe, and Derfer 2006: 53). Qi is the energy that provides productive activities and makes them vivid. Artistic creativity must combine the expression of qi, eternal creation, and vivid process as inherent in the universe and the *yun*, the creative rhythms and vivid beauty of nature and life.

In the preface to *Shi Pin* 詩品, Zhong Rong says, "Artistic creation is also the materialization of vital processes within the Chinese artists themselves" (Xie, Zhihe, and Derfer 2006: 54). This has been especially true since the Ming dynasty, when scholars of the arts discussed "the relationship and interaction and harmony between human, natural and supernatural beings and also the balance between body and mind in humanities" (Ding 2010: 58–59). According to Zhong:

> *Yuanqi* (the primordial *qi* 原氣) of the human body creates a painting by trans-ferring itself to the silk through the harmonious act of the body as an instru-ment. On the other hand, the spirit, thought, sentiment, and emotion of the painter infiltrate the whole process of creating the touch, pattern, temper-ament, sentiment, and verve of an artistic production. With the interaction of the two sides, the artistic life of production is created. Thereby painters make artistic productions with the body and mind, using not only the hands but the hands and brain together. Every expression of pen and ink in the silk is a mark of the painter's burning vitality.
>
> Traditional painters in China used a series of formal procedures for using the brush, wrist, paper, and *qi*. For example, the fingers must hang on to the brush, while the palm should be released, with the wrists functioning hori-zontally. Holding the brush should follow a definite style; sitting and standing should follow a definite attitude; the fingers, wrists, elbow, arm, and the rest of the body should cooperate in mutual coordination. Breath should be even. And *qi* should penetrate the lower part of the abdomen. The artist should gath-er him/herself together in a happy mood, aspiring for the best physiological and mental environment. (Xie, Zhihe, and Derfer 2006: 54–55)

The rich philosophical theories that give the *Dunhuang bihua yuewu* its uniqueness to bind or institutionalize the multifaceted meta-elements from ethnically and culturally diverse Dunhuang within the well-established system of Chinese aesthetics did not merely grant the genre its distinct fea-ture as a representation of Chineseness: these theoretical constructs play a crucial role in discerning the "more authentic" *Dunhuang bihua yuewu* from its "less authentic" counterparts.

## Discursive Formation of Authenticity

While I was conducting research at the Beijing Dance Academy and watching skilled dance students learn the *Dunhuang bihua yuewu* with Professor Gao Jinrong, Professor Dong Xijiu said to me: "[These dance students] are all very good with skills and techniques, but in comparison to the younger and less skillful students from Lanzhou's Vocational School of the Arts, they do not understand the correct 'law of resonance/prosodic rhythms' [*yunlü* 韵律]" (Kuang 2012). Although not as openly as Professor Dong, who was well respected by the faculty members from Beijing Dance Academy and other institutions as a doyenne of Chinese dance theory and history, Professor Gao expressed a similar opinion to me when I was doing research in Lanzhou's Northwestern Minzu University: "The dancers from the Vocational School of the Arts began studying the *Dunhuang bihua yuewu* at a very young age [in comparison to the university students], and

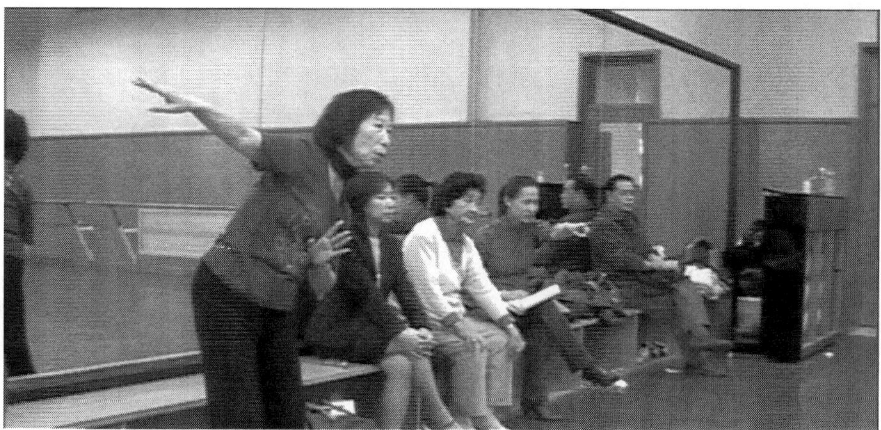

Figure 5.3. Image of the author observing a *Dunhuang bihua yuewu* class conducted by Professor Gao Jinrong, with Professors Dong Xijiu, Jin Qiu, and Kuang Jianren. Beijing Dance Academy. © Lanlan Kuang, 2009.

therefore they have a better understanding of the essences of the genre" (interview, 2008). This is one of the many examples of the ways that individuals discuss their concepts of authenticity within particularly situated contexts.

A pertinent opinion on the authenticity of performers and performances of the *Dunhuang bihua yuewu* was expressed by the director of a dance company in Hong Kong, who had been trained in classical ballet in Great Britain and had studied in the United States. She was a former student of Professor Gao Jinrong. During a meeting of just the two of us before the first Dunhuang Dance Teaching and Academic Conference, held in the Beijing Dance Academy, she asked me: "What do you think of the student dancers who are learning the *Dunhuang bihua yuewu* here?" Before I could answer, she answered: "They do not have the feeling. Unlike the ones from Gansu Province, they [the Beijing dancers] were already molded by the traditional Chinese classical dance. Theirs was not authentic." This was perhaps one of the reasons that dance scholars from Taiwan and Hong Kong would often travel to Lanzhou to study the *Dunhuang bihua yuewu* with Professor Gao, whom they considered the real master of the genre.

Instruction in the *Dunhuang bihua yuewu* in formal university courses at elite institutions outside the Northwest, as at the Beijing Dance Academy, has led to years of academic politics, which have impinged on the teaching of this genre. Professor Gao, to gain recognition as the one who created the "authentic" *Dunhuang bihua yuewu*, with her supporters—mainly from the Northwest, including Shaanxi Province, but also from Taiwan and Hong Kong—thought it essential to focus on the aesthetic principles of Dunhuang and the Northwest in general, which they considered to be unique, local, and regional.

At the end of our visit to Beijing Dance Academy, Professor Dong Xijiu made a brief speech to the student dancers in the classroom:

> You must learn from Professor Gao: What was the *yunlü* 韵律 she dances to? Right? The Dunhuang dance is from the Western Regions, which is Xinjiang. When [the cultural models] from Xinjiang and the heartland Central Plateau clashed, even if there are elements from the Western Regions, [these elements] cannot be seen; [they] have been integrated [so they are invisible]. Therefore, you must study from Professor Gao. What were the things she did that were different from traditional Chinese theatrical drama? What were the things she did that are from Dunhuang? It was for that reason that it [the Dunhuang dance] becomes a genre.[12] You must be able to display its characteristics. Understand its *yunlü* (韻律). This is how you will learn to become excellent students of the *Dunhuang bihua yuewu genre*. (Video-recorded interview for the accompanying documentary; Kuang 2012)

Through my research on ancient Chinese aesthetics, especially the theories that connect the visual arts and elements (in painting and calligraphy) to other expressive art forms (such as dance and music), I have shown that the aesthetic theories and principles that served as the foundation of ancient Chinese philosophy and literary theory were also found in the core of the discourse of contemporarily staged *Dunhuang bihua yuewu* aesthetics and practices. Creators and theorists attach linguistic terms that are fundamental to ancient Chinese philosophy to physical movements, and they use poetic, suggestive metaphors to guide performers. My interviews, participation, and on-site observation with dance scholars allowed me to experience and comprehend the physiopsychological process by which the *Dunhuang bihua yuewu* was translated from static images to dynamic movements. These discoveries helped me develop an understanding of the discursive formation of the *Dunhuang bihua yuewu*. The historical, performative, and rhetorical processes through which the genre was created cannot be approached separately: they must be understood together, as a single coherent process. Thus, I examined aspects such as linear approaches and elements central to the staging of the genre while analyzing the language and metaphors used in the construction of rhetoric about it, including the contexts within which key terms, such as *qiyun shengdong*, were comprehended, interpreted, utilized, and practiced to create the sense and idea of authenticity associated with the genre.

# Notes

1. For an ethnopoetics-centered analysis of performance, see Briggs 1993: 387–434.

2. According to contemporary Chinese dance scholars, twentieth-century Han-Tang classical dance was based solely on dance images from sources from China's Han and Tang dynasties. No techniques were borrowed from ballet or modern dance. Therefore, Han-Tang classical dance is often called a pure Chinese dance form.

3. Fong argues, "The Chinese perceived both calligraphy and painting as having at once a representational and presentational function, i.e., the key to Chinese painting lies in its calligraphic line, which bears the presence, or physical 'trace' (*ji* 跡), of its maker. The spirit [of the artist] is often identified with the Chinese term *qi* (氣)" (2003: 259).

4. *The Law of Brush-Strokes*, also known by Dunhuangologists as P. 4936, is among the Dunhuang manuscripts discovered by Paul Pelliot, a French archaeologist.

5. See Powers 1998 for a "gestural theory of pictorial expression." Powers points out that in the writings of the tenth-century painter-essayist Jing Hao and the eleventh-century essayist on painting Guo Ruoxu, the vocabulary of Chinese painting includes words like *qi* 氣, *feng* 風, *shi* 勢, and *tai* 態, which Powers translates as "character," "manner," "gesture," and "demeanor," respectively.

6. Nancy Rao provides a discussion of *shi* in a poetry-inspired contemporary composition in "The Concept of Shi: Chinese Aesthetics and *Happy Rain on a Spring Night* (2004)" (2020).

7. Zhang Xu 張旭, a legendary Tang dynasty calligrapher from the early eighth century, was known to be inspired by a performance of the "Dance of Two-Edged Sword" by Lady Gongsun 公孫. In Lu Yu's biography of him, Yan Zhenqing (709–785) says: "Aside from observing tumbleweeds and flying sand, Administrator Zhang also watched Lady Gongsun perform her sword dance. This is when he first apprehended the extensions, dips, and swirls of Draft Script." See Cai 1995 for original Chinese text.

8. A study of the paintings on the walls of Buddhist temples in China (Katz 1996) suggests that the painters were not well educated and probably came from the working class.

9. The image of apsaras in Buddhist art at Dunhuang is believed to have originated from gandharvas and kannaras in Indian Buddhist art.

10. See Kuang (2012) for Professor Gao Jinrong's demonstration. Multimedia components for *Staging* Tianxia, such as active maps, working color metagraphs, audiovisual files, and documentary film clips, can be found at https://lanlankuangofficial.pub/.

11. Qian Zhongshu, *Guan zhui pian*, vol. 4, p. 1362. Translation taken with slight modifications from Egan 1998, quoted in Cai Zong-qi 2004: 110–111.

12. This comment is essentially problematic: though the *Dunhuang bihua yuewu* is a genre, it also needs to be categorized within the Chinese classical dance genre.

# 6

## STAGING DUNHUANG ARTS IN CONTEXT(S)
### Case Studies

Through a variety of ethnographic writing styles, this chapter analyzes how programs of the staged Dunhuang arts that have inspired and integrated the genre have contributed to our understanding of the processes through which social actors have staged a historically multiethnic and cosmopolitan Chinese nation. While ethnographies reveal lived experiences embedded within sociocultural contexts, constituting what the anthropologist Clifford Geertz terms an "interpretive science in search of meaning" rather than an experimental science in search of law, ethnographers have also been challenged by the classic dilemma of turning "unruly experience" into "authoritative written account" (1973: 5; 1988: 25). Contemporary anthropological thought has drawn attention to the fact that "ethnography is, from beginning to end, enmeshed in writing" (Clifford 1983: 120), not only because the target culture itself can be seen as an assemblage of texts to interpret rather than a set of facts to command but because any description of that culture is an inescapably rhetorical enterprise. Geertz argues that an ethnographer's capacity to convince readers that he or she has "been there" relies on his or her "being there" on the *page* (131). Anthropological authority is inexorably tied to an act of explicit *authorship*—the authority to "describe" the other. Bernard McGrane (1989) also argues that the composition of an ethnographic account is essentially a *literary* affair. Because the object of ethnographic attention, the exotic "other," is first and foremost a projection of the self anxious to delimit its own identity, the other is less a matter for discovery and description than the product of invention and construction.

Given Geertz's and McGrane's arguments that the legitimacy of ethnographic discourse rests on a creative gesture, I would suggest that by comparing my on-site notes with my ethnographic documentary script and the documentary script for a China Central Television Station program on Dunhuang in the next chapter, we may find a partial yet effective way to theorize intercontextual relations. One of the central issues would be the nature of the ethnographer's presence as a part of the writing. This chapter examines notes on three staged Dunhuang arts programs: *The Thousand-Handed and Thousand-Eyed Avalokiteśvara* (*Qianshou qianyan Guanyin* 千手千眼觀音), *The Flying Apsaras* (*Feitian* 飛天), and, finally, a pedagogical theatrical dance drama, *Lotus Aloft* (*Bubu shenglian* 步步生蓮).

Studies of staged Dunhuang arts narratives can be approached in numerous ways. On-site notes and ethnographic documentary scripts together highlight the intertextuality of ethnographic work. Below, I use a simple, straightforward, less descriptive narration of the performing context, event, date, and time, clearly laid out for the case study on *The Thousand-Handed and Thousand-Eyed Avalokiteśvara*. This writing style provides a comparison to the ethnographic documentary and the postproduction script in chapter 7. My goal is to illustrate how different subjectivities and objectives can be accommodated in ethnographic writing.

In *The Production of Space* (1991), Henry Lefebvre examines the social ontology and history of the body, especially the body's involvement in different social modalities of space and time, and introduces the conceptual triad of social space: spatial practice, representation of space, and spaces of representation. Drawing on the work of Nietzsche and Heidegger, Lefebvre sees space as both a perception and a conception—a producer and a product of the human body—and highlights the spatial notion of "poetic dwelling" (121, 314). To highlight the kinesthetic semiotics—the study of signs through bodily movement in the dance programs—I provide historical references for each selected program, in addition to interviews with the choreographers for the *Flying Apsaras* and *Lotus Aloft* case studies.

## Audiences

Imagined audiences and live audiences are the two types identified in my ethnographic work on the *Dunhuang bihua yuewu* at multiple sites in China, including the Mogao Grottoes, theaters and dance academies in Lanzhou and Beijing, and institutional archives. Imagined audiences include the audiences recorded in the historical references, as well as the potential audiences predicted by choreographers, actors, and producers. When preparing research materials for ethnographic publications such as this book, imagined audiences include potential readers.

In China, dance scholars would discuss with me how each program was designed and staged according to the specific event and audience group. For instance, Professor Gao Jinrong's selection of a program and highlights within the program for a Chinese national dance competition for the schools differed from her selection of a program for a troupe touring in Taiwan. The programs she selected and created for the Chinese national dance competition were usually limited by time, and they often emphasized the demonstration of dancers' techniques. The Taiwan tours were hosted primarily by Buddhist organizations or local art schools. Therefore, she designed programs that would bring forth the religious content, such as a short program portraying dancers offering holy lamps to Buddhist deities.

Imagined audiences include patrons, the composition of the population and audiences of the arts in the caves at the time when they were built, and visiting Buddhist monks and merchants traveling on the Silk Road. Patrons consisted of local residents, including government officials; powerful clans played an important role in the construction of the caves and eventually the Buddhist arts. Unlike the imagined audiences of the past, today's live audiences, especially for the *Dunhuang bihua yuewu*, are no longer limited to Buddhist monks, traveling merchants, and residents of Dunhuang and the Chinese Northwest, nor are they limited to the people who physically visit the caves.

From the depictions on the walls of the Mogao Grottoes, we discern that the painted performances were staged for distinct groups of audiences, such as Buddhist devotees who frequented the site to honor the painted deities. Dunhuang's status as a frontier metropolis also attracted a diverse array of visitors, including individuals from a multiethnic background and adherents of various religious traditions. The meta-elements found in the Dunhuang arts were therefore multifaceted, as they were produced by artists representing diverse ethnicities, intended for varied audiences, and at times, sponsored by wealthy aristocrat patrons.

Similarly, the actors involved in creating *Dunhuang bihua yuewu* programs anticipated different audiences, reflecting the locations of the performances to be staged. The emphasis of each staged performance was unique. Some highlighted the idea of benevolence and the practice of equality that have been associated with the *Thousand-Handed and Thousand-Eyed*

*Avalokiteśvara* in its Chinese Buddhist context, as seen in the staged performance embodied by deaf dancers at the 2004 Paralympic Games in Athens, Greece. The creators of this performance showed their goal of staging the *Dunhuang bihua yuewu* program as a genre capable of delivering ideas beyond the national boundary while reaching international audiences at a transnational event.

In act 3 of *A Grand Dream of Dunhuang*, warlords and princes from nearby regions and from along the Silk Road come to demonstrate their wealth and power to the Great General and his daughter, Yueya, with mesmerizing dances at the competition for the daughter's hand; the stage arrangement of this scene was intended to replicate musical events painted on the walls of the Mogao Grottoes. The Great General, Yueya, and their subordinates sit in the center and upper center stage, displaying an air of authority, and the groups of dancers perform, entering from center-right into the spotlighted down-center area. This event may be interpreted as a diplomatic pilgrimage to the Great General's court, an event that was not uncommon, as such phenomena have been recorded and described in historical references. A similar scene appears in the dance drama *Along the Silk Road*, when groups of diplomats from twenty-seven kingdoms along the Silk Road come to greet the emperor of China in his court.

Music and dance, as seen in chapter 4's discussion of the dance suites from the Sui and Tang dynasties, were an important part of sociopolitical and religious events. Scholar-officials from imperial courts have long incorporated elements from these performative events into their poetry and essays, as these events were part of their daily life. Arts from China shared aesthetic principles and a synthetic nature.

## Case Study 1: *The Thousand-Handed and Thousand-Eyed Avalokiteśvara*[1]

Stage 1, Scenario 1
Media Scope: Local, national, and global
Time: Summer 2008
Location: Beijing National Stadium, People's Republic of China
Event: The Opening Ceremony of the Olympic Games


Dance from Dunhuang came under the spotlight during the opening ceremony of the Olympic Games when a female dancer, dressed in a Tang dynasty costume (its design based on images from the Dunhuang murals) and suspended by a rectangular extension (an imitation of the ancient Silk Road) held by hundreds of performers, tossed a long ribbon into the air, weaving it into flowing movements.

Stage 1, Scenario 1, is a perfect example of *Dunhuang bihua yuewu* programs and Dunhuang meta-elements being used as cultural devices in the staging of a historically cosmopolitan Chinese nation. The setting was the capital, and the performances were part of a global event. Zhang Yimou, director of the 2008 Beijing Olympics Opening Ceremony, was one of the few Chinese directors known by audiences abroad for his cinematographic works. He and a team of experts from around the globe, including the United States and Japan, utilized *Dunhuang bihua yuewu* programs to exhibit the theme of sociocultural and political-economic exchanges in historic China along the ancient Silk Road. The genre was staged for modern international audiences and became an intertextual, self-referential symbol of this concept.

Stage 2, Scenario 2
Media Scope: Local, national, and global
Time: Winter 2008, New Year's Eve according to the lunar calendar
Location: The filming studio of the China Central Television Station in Beijing
Event: The annual Special China Lunar New Year's Celebration Programs

Through the lens of China's state-sponsored China Central Television Station (CCTV), the only channel that could reach people in every big city and small village in China, members of the television audience watched highly skilled dancers from Guangzhou, a southern economically and culturally flourishing harbor city, perform *Apsaras*, a *Dunhuang bihua yuewu* program designed to highlight the launching of a spaceship from Gansu Province, where the Jiuquan Space Center was located.

Stage 2, Scenario 2, showed how a *Dunhuang bihua yuewu* program and elements were utilized as cultural devices in the staging of an event meant to portray national success in aerospace technology. For its audience, it was a form of cultural attraction, a demonstration of soft power (Callahan 2008; Gill 2006; Gill and Huang 2006; Nye 2004a, 2004b, 2004c, 2004d). The space race between the United States and the former Soviet Union was not being overlooked by other countries that had the potential to launch space shuttles. The *Dunhuang bihua yuewu* program demonstrated China's intention of showing its audiences—but primarily the national audience—that the country is advancing technologically.

Stage 3, Scenario 3
Media Scope: Local, national, and global (through my documentary)
Time: Winter 2008
Location: Gansu Provincial Vocational School of the Arts
Event: Practice session of the dancers in a master class by Professor Gao Jinrong

I witnessed this event while working in Lanzhou, Gansu Province. The lens of my video camera followed the movements of a petite older woman as she walked swiftly and carefully (because of an injury to her ankles) through the old campus of Lanzhou Vocational School of the Arts. The woman was Gao Jinrong, a professor and former president of the school. Although she had officially retired and was already in her sixties, she still exhibited the posture and energy of a professional dancer who used to perform genres of dance around the globe, especially the repertories and programs based on the *Dunhuang bihua yuewu.*

It was at the Lanzhou Vocational School of the Arts that Professor Gao became the first person to develop systematically the *Dunhuang bihua yuewu* as a dance genre that could be taught in classrooms and would give birth to many new programs. I made a request to visit the birthplace of the *Dunhuang bihua yuewu,* and she agreed to give me a tour. Her daughter-in-law, once a student of hers, was now teaching *Dunhuang bihua yuewu* in this school.

We were to observe the graduating class that Professor Gao's daughter-in-law Professor Jin Liang was teaching. Professor Gao led me into the school's auditorium, where students were just starting to position themselves on the stage in small groups to practice two of the most representative programs of the genre: *The Thousand-Handed and Thousand-Eyed Avalokiteśvara* and *Percussion Music for Celebrating Happiness* (*Yueguhuanteng* 樂鼓歡騰).[2] They were preparing to compete for the national dance award that they hoped could bring fame to this small, underfunded educational institution.

Through the lens of the video camera, I saw girls in their early teens—from twelve to fifteen—on the stage inside an empty auditorium. They were changing into specially designed metallic gold and jade-blue costumes.

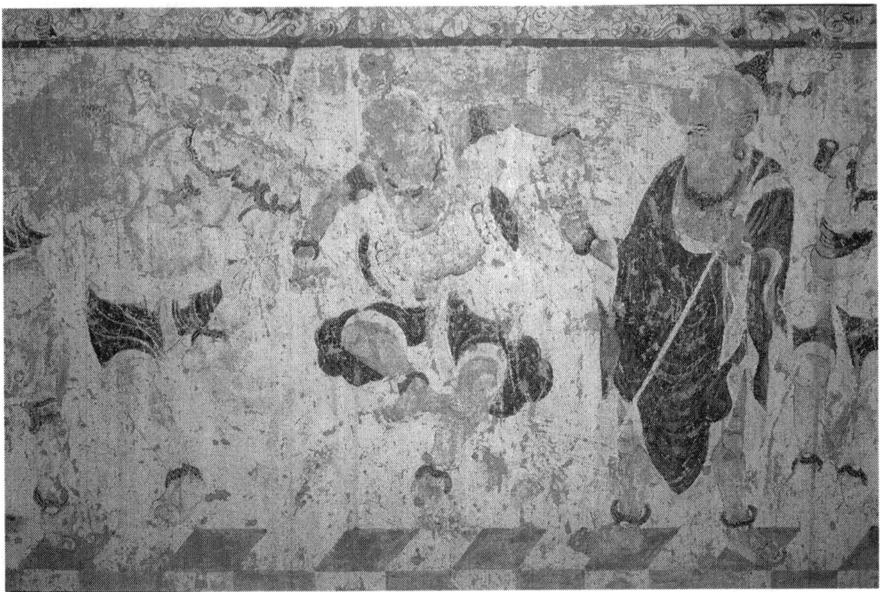

Figure 6.1. Mogao Cave 158, lower northern side of the altar, mural image of a percussion dancer. Permission to use image granted by Dunhuang Academy.

Gathering in small groups, they helped one another with the heavy, crystal-decorated headpieces that resemble the high-mounded hair with jewelry seen in murals in the Mogao Grottoes. Some were already standing in their stage dress and putting on gold fingernails, specially designed and made for this production. The long, metallic fingernails, when the young dancers placed and shook their hands together in specific positions, would create the visual effect of a shining gold circle, like the luminous ring often seen around a jewel or decorating the image of a divine being.

Stage 3, Scenario 3, entails one of the earliest local contexts within which the *Dunhuang bihua yuewu* was developed and taught in a classroom setting. I approached this example as one that helped me visualize the most original development setting of the genre. It was at the dimly lighted old auditorium and classrooms that Professor Gao had begun her lifelong teaching as the primary creator of the *Dunhuang bihua yuewu* genre. The setting itself, compared to the highly financed Beijing Dance Academy and even the new classroom building of the Dance College at the Northwestern Minzu University, showed challenges. The program was

*The Lotus Cup* (*Hehuabei* 荷花杯), which Professor Gao's daughter-in-law had been teaching the students for the annual national dance competition. Students were concerned mostly with their grades and futures, whereas local dance teachers were more concerned about the future of the dance programs they had developed and the prospect of winning at the national dance competition.

## Case Study 2: *Lotus Aloft*

Kinesthetic semiotics is a popular research approach for dance scholars. Semiotic symbols found in the religious art at Dunhuang, such as the lotus flower and the nine-colored deer, are among the Dunhuang meta-elements found in the *Dunhuang bihua yuewu*. *Lotus Aloft* is the 2015 pedagogical dance drama staged by Northwestern Minzu University under the direction of Professor Gao Jinrong.

### *The Original Context: The First Staged Performance*

The name *Lotus Aloft* is an English translation of 步步生蓮, a Chinese idiom that enacts the figurative symbolic motivation of a lotus flower in association with Buddhism. It may be traced to the fifth-century *Za baozang jing* 雜寶藏經 (Scripture on the Storehouse of Sundry Treasures, T.203), which contains the story of Lady Deer 鹿女. Representing beauty, purity, and youthfulness, the lotus flower in Buddhism is a floral semiotic symbol denoting the essence of enlightenment of those who have meditated and will meditate on the profound Law: the lotus supports the Buddha as the flower supports the world above the chaotic waters of the universe. Such virtues and characteristics embodied by the flower are founded in the creative poetic metaphors and phraseological units, whose figurative components reflect its cultural symbolism. Metaphors are simply "understanding and experiencing one kind of thing in terms of another" (Lakoff and Johnson 2003 5), and "every experience takes place within a vast background of cultural presuppositions" (57).

Lotus flowers—or perhaps better said, the various kinds of lotus patterns decorated in the Mogao Grottoes—are exquisite and highly representational. Scholars have divided the lotus pattern into several categories: the round-wheel lotus pattern that appeared in the Northern dynasties (397–581 CE) as a decorative pattern; the simple yet geometrically sophisticated

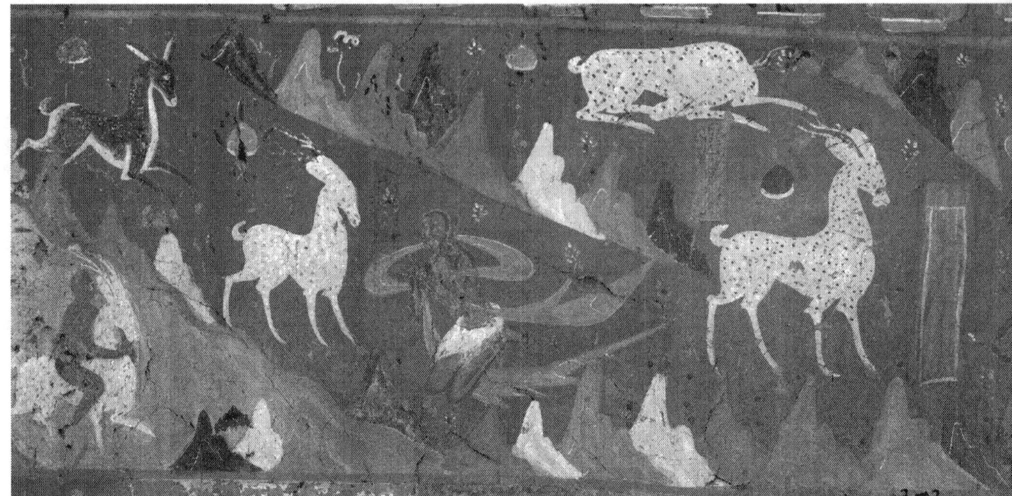

Figure 6.2. Cave 257's *Jātaka of the Nine-Colored Deer King* mural. Permission to use image granted by Dunhuang Academy.

flat-petal lotus from the Sui and Tang dynasties (581–907 CE), often paired with three rabbit patterns; the curly-petal lotus that appeared in the middle Tang dynasty (782–847 CE) and continued to be used in the Five Dynasties (907–979 CE); and the peach-shaped lotus from the early Tang dynasty (618–712 CE), which evolved into the Baoxiang flower pattern during the middle or high Tang dynasty (650–755 CE). The Baoxiang flower, an imaginary floral pattern, or floral semiotic, does not occur in nature. Because of the pattern's transformational nature, the Baoxiang flower resembles at the same time the lotus flower from India, the honeysuckle pattern found in the Western Regions of China, the peony pattern and the pomegranate patterns, and the curly-petaled lotus. Tens of thousands of lotus-flower patterns appear on the roofs of the Dunhuang Grottoes. Since the lotus flower represents purification and the growth of the inner self arising from the difficulties and trials of life, many Dunhuang murals show deities sitting or standing on a lotus flower or with lotus flowers blossoming around them. Thousands of images in the Mogao Grottoes show Buddhist practitioners sitting in the lotus meditation position; in fact, these images fill the background in nearly all the grottoes. In Hindu thought as interpreted in China, the lotus sitting position is a basic posture for awakening the dormant Kundalini energy (*qi*) at the base of the spine and moving the energy upward (J. Lin 2019).

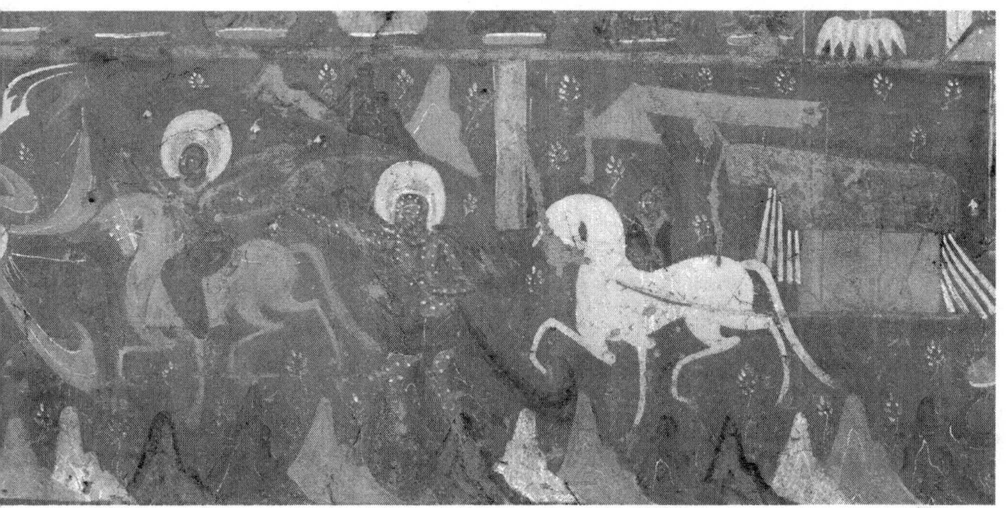



A staged dance, as the product of a cultural tradition, whether old or new, combines choreographic codes and conventions that appear in the form of choreographic elements, including movements, postures, gestures, facial expressions, proxemics (the use of space), costumes, and props, and technological elements, such as settings, sounds, and lighting.

Professor Gao Jinrong decided to create a pedagogic dance drama employing the lotus and the deer as primary elements, and the result was *Lotus Aloft*, an award-winning artwork. She wanted to give the Dunhuang dance unit at Northwestern Minzu University's College of Dance a systematically conceived teaching example. This unit was taught primarily by three of her former students, who used her training manual in the classroom to teach the basic techniques. The unit needed new teaching materials to provide more than simply technical training. *Lotus Aloft*, unlike *Flower Rain along the Silk Road* and *A Grand Dream of Dunhuang*, was meant to provide a context to help students understand the spirit of the *Dunhuang bihua yuewu* through storytelling. Each student who participated in it had a role in the story it would tell. Professor Gao was inspired by both the Lady Deer story from the *Scripture on the Storehouse of Sundry Treasures* and *Jātaka of the Nine-Colored Deer King*, a mural on the west wall of Mogao Cave 257, dated to the Northern Wei period. This is the only *jātaka* illustration at the

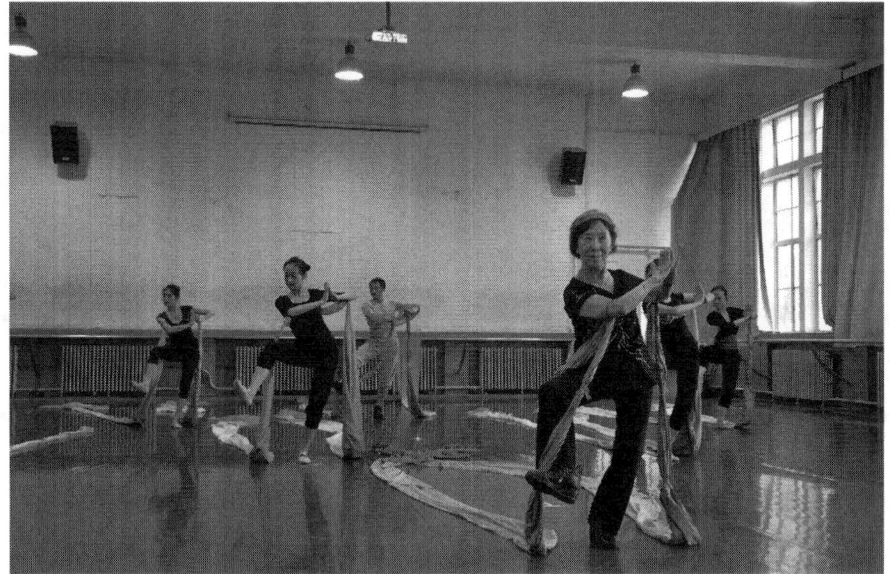

Figure 6.3. Professor Gao Jinrong producing *Lotus Aloft* at Northwest Minzu University in Lanzhou, Gansu Province. Photo credit: Lanlan Kuang, 2019.

Mogao Grottoes that uses an animal as the protagonist. A *jātaka* is a story of Śākyamuni's previous lives.

*The Nine-Colored Deer*, the tale behind the dance drama, was translated into Chinese by Zhiqian 支謙 (222–252) from the Wu Kingdom of the Three Kingdoms period. It promotes the idea that benevolence and good deeds will bring welcome rewards but that ungratefulness and evil deeds will bring severe punishment. This contrast is related to the Buddhist law of cause and effect underlying the doctrine of karma. The tale tells of a nine-colored deer that saves a man from drowning, but the man goes to the palace to disclose the whereabouts of the deer and leads the king to pursue the deer's antlers and pelt. The deer, showing no fear, appeals to the king by exposing the man's ingratitude. Deeply moved, the king issues an order to forbid his countrymen from hunting the deer. The ungrateful man suffers from sores all over his body.

The painter of the mural excels at depicting the inner world of the characters through details. The deer is portrayed, not kneeling before the king (as narrated in the tale), but standing tall and holding its head high. The image emphasizes the fearlessness of noble beings in the face of brutal force. The king's compassion and concern for the deer is expressed by his lowered head while he listens to the deer's appeal. *Lotus Aloft* combines both religious and narrative elements from Dunhuang, allowing the choreographers who collaborated with Professor Gao at Northwest Minzu University to introduce both male and female protagonists and employ group and solo dance movements. Most *Dunhuang bihua yuewu* dance programs highlight female dancers, but the choreographer took care to bring male dancers onstage. Finally, the presence of the deer allowed the choreographer to make an innovation in the genre by introducing animals as main characters.

## Case Study 3: Apsaras: From Celestial Beings<br>(*tianren* 天人) to *Feitian*

*China will launch its second lunar exploration probe by the end of 2010, boosting the country's effort to rise as a space power eventually capable of landing on the moon, official media said Friday. In 2003, China became only the third country, after the United States and Russia, to send a man into space aboard its own rocket.*

—"China Aims for Next Moon Orbit Shot This Year,"<br>Reuters (Beijing), September 9, 2010

In 2008, viewers around the globe watched on television the first spacewalk of a Chinese astronaut floating outside a vehicle orbiting the Earth. At the same time, audience members in a theater—Communist Party leaders, military generals, and engineers at the Jiuquan Space Center in Gansu Province—were watching *The Flying Apsaras*,[3] a *Dunhuang bihua yuewu* dance program. Staged by the Guangzhou Military Song and Dance Group (GZMSDG),[4] the performance was intended as a celebration of China's success in becoming a space power in the same league as the United States and Russia. Just as the name *The Flying Apsaras* suggests, the five female dancers—dressed in elegant yellow outfits of sleeveless tops, dress pants, and golden hairpieces, inspired by the images of flying deities that decorate the murals at the Mogao Grottoes—performed as if they were dancing in zero-gravity space on a specially designed, circulating round stage. An extraordinary moment awed the audience members when the performers' entire upper bodies stretched, bent, and moved effortlessly and fluently in different ninety-degree angles. They used their right legs, especially the tibia, as axes to accomplish what a normal person could not in normal gravity. After two months of intense practice, the dancers were able to remain still in extremely difficult positions for two measures of eight beats, lasting about ten seconds.

Ignoring that nine young female dancers had undergone extremely intense and harsh daily practices, which could well have injured the muscles and ligaments of the right leg, the result was truly beautiful and astonishing.[5] The five dancers flew just like the flying apsaras seen in the Mogao murals, accompanied by orchestral music that included a zither, a flute, and, most importantly, bronze bells. The use of such bells to recreate ancient sounds in a contemporarily composed symphonic work is not new. According to historical references, bells were an important part of the court music in China. Tan Dun 谭盾, an Oscar-winning composer who had presented the bronze bells at the 2005 China Festival held at the JFK Kennedy Center for the Performing Arts in Washington, DC, chose to incorporate the sounds of 2,400-year-old ancient bronze bells from the tomb of the Marquis Yi of Zheng (433 BCE), unearthed in 1978, for his compositions for the Beijing 2008 Olympic Games, the Paralympic Games, and the Sports Demonstration Symbol Music (Sheppard 2010; Witzleben 2002).

Zhang Qianyi 张千一, one of the most sought-after composers in China, composed music for the *Dunhuang bihua yuewu* program of *The Thousand-Handed and Thousand-Eyed Avalokiteśvara*, as well as for *The Flying Apsaras*. He had anticipated the effectiveness of using the sounds of bronze bells in a piece of music meant—borrowing Tan Dun's words in an interview—as a "meld of tradition and innovation . . . [to] represent the Chinese spirit, which must find a harmonious balance between ancient and modern."[6]

Each staged program of the *Dunhuang bihua yuewu* is unique, with its own inspiration and meaning(s) to deliver. In an interview, Liu Jin 刘晶, the first-generation female principal dancer of the theatrical dance drama *Dunhuang, My Dreamland* and the vice director of the GZMSDG, explained that *The Flying Apsaras* was inspired by the 2008 launch of China's lunar orbiter Chang'e 嫦娥, especially the spacewalk: "That is why we [the GZMSDG] performed it for the *lingdao* [Chinese Communist Party leaders] at the Jiuquan Space Center," she said, rather proudly but not without the self-control of one who has performed on multiple stages and has been promoted to a position that is the equivalent of a major in military rank.

In Chinese folklore and mythology, Chang'e is a goddess who flew to the moon (Yang and An 2008). The idea of staging a performance based on the gandharvas found decorating the murals at the Mogao Grottoes under the title *The Flying Apsaras* quickly gained approval from the GZMSDG leaders.[7] It was a combination of the historical and the modern, popular myth and actual event. Shortly after our interview, Liu mentioned casually that *The Flying Apsaras* would be staged in the Macao Special Administrative Region to celebrate the first decade of its return to Chinese control.

The significance of *The Flying Apsaras* is obvious. Reporters from Reuters and other news agencies who paid close attention to the performance, broadcast nationwide in China on China Central Television Station, the mainstream, state-administrated media channel, would have noticed that the same version had been staged as the final program on the China Lunar New Year's Celebration Show, broadcast annually from Beijing by CCTV. The finale, the last program in a New Year's show, is usually considered the most important one—"the one confining the axis" (*yazhouxi* 壓軸戲). The program won the Best Song and Dance Performance Award in the show, as decided by members of the Chinese CCTV audiences who voted using calls and text messages. The popularity of *The Flying Apsaras* even surpassed that of Jay Zhou (*Zhou Jielun* 周傑倫), a pop idol from Taiwan, who had been invited by CCTV to perform a song titled "Blue and White Porcelain Ware" (*Qinghua ci* 青花瓷), which uses historical and traditional elements to create an R&B-styled piece.[8] CCTV usually invites only a handful of entertainers from Hong Kong and Taiwan each year. An invitation to perform on the Lunar New Year's Show is an unspoken guarantee that the entertainers' works will encounter no marketing difficulties in mainland China and that the entertainers will likely be invited to participate in major productions by state-funded projects.

Xin Shimiao, coproducer of *The Flying Apsaras* and director of GZMSDG, later said in an interview that he had not expected the program to win against Zhou's performance. When asked how *The Flying Apsaras* differs from *The Thousand-Handed and Thousand-Eyed Avalokiteśvara*—another famous *Dunhuang bihua yuewu* program, first staged during the cultural ceremony at the 2004 Paralympic Games in Athens, Greece, which stunned the audience on CCTV's Lunar New Year's Celebration Show (discussed in detail below)—Xin pointed out: "*The Thousand-Handed and Thousand-Eyed Avalokiteśvara* is an excellent program; besides, the performers of *The Thousand-Handed and Thousand-Eyed Avalokiteśvara* were all handicapped dancers who are deaf and mute. The secret to the success of *The Flying Apsaras* is the stage probe: an iron stick to which the right leg of each dancer was attached. It was very effective" (translated by Kuang).

Examination of many versions of the *Dunhuang bihua yuewu* inspired by the flying deities of the Mogao murals shows that Xin's dance drama was groundbreaking in many ways; however, a potential consequence of this process was that dancers might injure their legs to the extent that they could no longer dance.

### *The Original Context: The First Staged Performance*

*The Flying Apsaras* has become one of the most frequently staged *Dunhuang bihua yuewu* programs. A literal translation of its title, *feitian*, is "flying 飛 heaven 天," considered a sinicized version of *deva* 天 *manusya* 人 from Sanskrit. The phrase *deva-manusya* first appeared in Chinese characters as 飛 天 in volume 2 of the *Luoyang Jialan Record*—"A Record of Buddhist Monasteries in Luoyang" (*Luoyangjialanji* 洛陽伽藍記), written by Yang Xuanzhi 杨街之 in the year 547. It describes the Buddhist monasteries in the city of Luoyang, Henan Province, during the earlier Northern Wei (516–529) dynasty. The court had moved its capital south to Luoyang in 494 and had built a nine-hundred-foot Buddhist pagoda, still a striking part of the urban landscape.

Another set of Buddhist supernatural figures are the gandharvas (*xiang yin shen* 香音神), one of the eight categories of deities that serve Dharma. According to Dunhuangologist and painter Duan Wenjie, those decorating the walls in the Mogao Grottoes are "a departure from the Indian Gandharvas who float with the support of coloured clouds" (1994: 81). Gandharvas and apsaras are always portrayed as musicians and dancers, flying as they entertain; nevertheless, they were painted variously in the Mogao murals, depending on the period of the cave's construction. As I discussed in earlier chapters, the techniques of painting, as well as the aesthetic principles that guided the changes in painting techniques in each dynasty, were transformed by new visualizations, contextualizations, or simply imaginations. Comparisons of images show that the creators of *The Flying Apsaras* drew their inspiration from the murals influenced by the so-called heartland style—the painting styles, techniques, and aesthetic principles that contributed to the sinicization of Buddhist arts in Dunhuang (Duan 1994). Multiple versions of *Dunhuang bihua yuewu* programs have been titled *The Flying Apsaras* or some variation thereof since the first staged version was created by Dai Ailian (戴爱莲, b. Trinidad, British West Indies, May 10, 1916, d. Beijing, February 9, 2006), a Chinese dancer, choreographer, and teacher of Professor Dong Xijiu, one of my most informative interviewees and chair emerita of the Department of Dance at the China Arts Academy.

Dai Ailian, known as "the mother of Chinese ballet" everywhere in China, was instrumental in introducing Western dance to China and in creating dances based on Chinese folk traditions. She studied ballet and modern dance in London. After she moved to Hong Kong in 1940, she began to use elements from traditional Chinese operas and learn the traditions of various ethnic groups.[9] In 1954, she was named principal of the newly founded Beijing Dancing School, and two works that she created, *Lotus Dance* and *The Flying Apsaras*, became international sensations; *The Flying Apsaras* won third place at the Fifth World Youth Conference in Warsaw, Poland, in 1955.

According to Professor Dong, Fei Xiaotong 费孝通—a renowned Chinese anthropologist who studied with Bronisław Malinowski at the London School of Economics—had told her that Dai Ailian had been the first to collect information on and study the dances of non-Han nationalities and to stage them, in the late 1940s (Dong Xijiu 2005: 350). In March 1946, one of the most critical times before the founding of the People's Republic of China, Dai staged the Frontier Music and Dance Show in Chongqing, now one of the PRC's four directly controlled municipalities (the other three are Beijing, Shanghai, and Tianjin) and the only such municipality in western China. The show went on for five days and was a huge success—which led to the founding of the Folk Song and Dance Club (*minjiangewushe* 民間歌舞社) at Beijing University in 1947 (Dong Xijiu 2005: 130–131).

Dai Ailian's *Flying Apsaras* was a program that consisted of two dancers with long dresses and long ribbons. In an interview, Professor Dong pointed out that Dai had learned from Mei Lanfang, the Peking opera master, who today is considered a national treasure. She borrowed from Mei the use of long sleeves seen in Peking opera performances. Her first contact with non-Han minority dances from the Northwest was a dance based on a Uighur folk song melody, "Dance of the Youth," which she learned from Ye Luxi in 1943.[10]

In 1917, Mei Lanfang had staged a Peking opera program that *The Flying Apsaras* later resembled; it was called *Celestial Goddess Sprinkling Flowers from Heaven* (*tiannü sanhua* 天女散花). Like *The Flying Apsaras*, it shows Buddhist influence. It represents the Buddhist story of a celestial goddess who sprinkles flowers on three Buddhas as they are preaching. Mei had studied the murals in the Mogao Grottoes before he created this Peking opera program, which Japanese audiences later named Mei Dance (*mei wu* 梅舞) after him. In Dai Ailian's version of *The Flying Apsaras*, long ribbons replaced the long sleeves of the Peking opera performance; whereas the long sleeves in the Peking opera performance were moved by hands and wrists, the ribbons were designed to be held with a wooden stick at each end so the dancers could swing them easily to create the impression of lightness in midair.

Dai's recreation of the flying apsaras was inspired by, and based primarily on, the copies of the Mogao murals she had seen in the home of the renowned painter Zhang Daqian 張大千 in 1945. Not unlike Chang Shuhong 常書鴻, the Dunhuang Academy's first director, who spent his life at Dunhuang after returning from Paris, Zhang was a prominent Chinese painter who spent years at the Mogao Grottoes, studying and copying the murals there before he finally went abroad on tours in India, Japan, the United States, France, and Brazil. As a leading figure in artistic movements in China during the 1950s, he left many commentaries regarding the Dunhuang murals and insisted over and over that "Dunhuang art are [*sic*] not imitations [of Indian art] but creations of China's own artists" after his investigation of the caves in India in 1950 (Li Yongqiao 1998).

Today, *The Flying Apsaras* is continuously staged as one of the more representative programs of a multiethnic and cosmopolitan China. The history behind this *Dunhuang bihua yuewu* program adds richness to its delivery of layered meanings in various historical and social contexts.

## Notes

1. "A thousand eyes observe, / A thousand ears hear all; / A thousand hands help and support / Living beings everywhere" (Epstein 2003: 284).

2. See *Staging the Cosmopolitan Nation: The Re-creation of the* Dunhuang Yuewu, *a Multicultural Music, Dance, and Theatrical Drama from China*, directed by Lanlan Kuang (2012), for program demonstrations. Multimedia components for *Staging Tianxia*, such as active maps, working color metagraphs, audiovisual files, and documentary film clips, can be found athttps://lanlankuangofficial.pub/. .

3. The translation of this program, *The Flying Apsaras*, is based on the nature of the image of the dancers; different types of flying deities are found in murals in the Mogao Grottoes. Apsaras are female deities without musical instruments.

4. The formal name is "Guangzhou Military District Song and Dance Group [*Guangzhou zhanshi gewu tuan*] under the Commend of Guangzhou Military District Political Department Soldiers' Arts Group" 廣州軍區政治部戰士文工團.

5. Five dancers performed onstage, but nine had prepared for this role because choreographers like to train extra performers as backups.

6. G. Schirmer and Associated Music Publishers, "Tan Dun at the Beijing Olympic Games," Wise Music Classical, September 9, 2008, https://www.wisemusicclassical.com/news/1443/Tan-Dun-at-the-Olympics-in-Beijing/. See also Melvin 2008.

7. The conception of apsaras in Buddhist art at Dunhuang is believed to have originated from that of gandharvas and kannaras in Indian Buddhist art.

8. For more details on Jay Zhou's work on the use of historical elements in the creative process of an R&B-styled hip-hop piece or a rap song, see Kuang 2004.

9. See Emily Wilcox (2020) on Dai Ailian's choreographic works.

10. Ye Luxi was a performer in a group from Shanghai. The group traveled to the Xinjiang Autonomous Region in today's northwest China during the reign of Sheng Shicai (1897–1970), the warlord who ruled Xinjiang from 1933 to 1944.

# 7

## BEING-IN-THE-FIELD

### Staged Dunhuang Arts and Intertextual Representations

When *Shun* was the son of Heaven, he plucked the five-stringed zither,
sang "the Airs of the South" and thereupon the whole world was governed
(舜為天子, 彈五弦之琴, 歌《南風》之詩, 而天下治)

Thus when the affairs of one state are embodied in the
experience of a person this is called a *feng* (air 風).

*Huainanzi*, 20.825 ("Tai zu" 泰族)

THIS CHAPTER INVESTIGATES THE INTERTEXTUAL STAGING processes
that emerged in the production of two documentaries: *Staging the Cosmopolitan Nation: Re-creating the Dunhuang Bihua Yuewu* (2012), an ethnomusicological documentary I produced as part of my Fulbright-IIE project, and "The Chapter on Dunhuang, Gansu Province" (《中國影像方志》甘肅敦煌篇), a forty-minute episode that Yang Qian 楊乾 produced for *Local Records of China* (2019), a documentary series produced by the China Central Television Station (CCTV).[1] A more accurate translation of the CCTV series would be *Filmed Gazetteers of China*. China has a long history of state-sponsored local gazetteers, or *difangzhi* 地方誌 productions. This practice started as early as the Yuan dynasty and was transmitted to historical Korea, Vietnam, and Japan. (Bol 2022; Chen et al. 2023). A main source of information on the topography, history, and local knowledge, the contemporary documentary series serves similar purposes under the sponsorship of China's most authoritative state media agency.

Close readings of materials presented in this chapter, such as pre- and postproduction film scripts, recorded interviews, and editorial notes of the two documentary projects, not only provide a better understanding of issues concerning ethnographic fieldwork methods, mediated representations, and documentary as transcription but help address critical research questions to be examined within the framework of the historical *tianxia* and the modern-day Chinascape: What aspects of staged Dunhuang arts performances do scholars, performers, and government agencies and officials promote, in what contexts, and why? Do the cultural agents of present-day China discursively or in practice model themselves on the successes of artists from the Han, Sui, and the Tang dynasties, when the arts were integrated into imperial state policies for governing multiethnic populations?

## *Being* and the Media of Representation

This chapter needs to be contextualized in relation to Martin Heidegger's (1962) argument on Being and time and Julia Kristeva (1980)'s notion of intertextuality. One could perhaps argue that as historical beings, we can comprehend intellectual inquiries only when we come to be. The staged Dunhuang arts are revealed to us through their intertextuality as a form of embodied expressive arts and as a practice of remembrance, representing the *field of Being*—a term used by Heidegger to avoid the assumption that we are dealing with a definite object with a fixed and gendered disposition. Within the context of these theories, by analyzing and representing the intertextuality of the documentary projects, we can better understand how staged Dunhuang expressive arts reveal themselves to us.

### *Heidegger's Theory*

Martin Heidegger's theory of Being signifies the "to-be" of things as he overthrows the empty abstraction of Being as a static object of the understanding. It provides a context for my scheme for the documentary, which considers Being to be a medium of representation. In *Being and Time* (1962), Heidegger argues for a preconceptual understanding of Being: understanding is "to be projecting towards a potentiality-for-Being for the sake of which any Dasein exists" (385).[2] For example, sounds and symbols exist only because we exist within language: before we utter sounds, we already exist within a mutual context of understanding, which signifies what in the end is nothing but Being itself (Barrett 1962: 222–224). Heidegger argues: "Whenever something is interpreted as something, the interpretation will be founded essentially upon projecting, foresight and preconception. An interpretation is never a presuppositionless apprehending of something presented to us" (1962: 91–92). Dilthey, Gadamer, and other hermeneutic philosophers share Heidegger's theory. Both Dilthey and Gadamer emphasize that no understanding can be entirely presuppositionless (Thompson 1996: 91–92).

This understanding is temporal, however, because it is grounded primarily in the thought that anticipating the future comes from the present: "Understanding temporalizes itself as an awaiting which makes present—an awaiting to whose ecstatical unity there must belong a corresponding 'having been'" (Heidegger 1962: 388). By suggesting the temporality of understanding, and later the temporality of Dasein, Heidegger characterizes us in terms of our belongingness and situatedness, our historicity and temporality. The Heideggerian argument on Being and time leads to two conclusions: a medium is a field of Being, and all presentation is representation.

#### MEDIUM

Heidegger's theory of Dasein provides the context for understanding the notion of Being in a multimedia representation such as a documentary film. Human existence is about being in a meaningful context. Nevertheless, no one meaning is shared without a preconceptualized understanding. Heidegger conceptualizes Dasein as understanding and considers the development of Dasein as understanding an "interpretation": "Understanding is the existential Being of Dasein's own potentiality-for-Being; and it is so in such a way that this Being discloses in itself what its Being is capable of" (1962: 184). He suggests "assertion" as a derivative mode of interpretation. He defines it as "a pointing-out which gives something a definite character and which communicates"; just as Dasein projects its Being as an understanding of possibilities, interpretation projects the development of Dasein through being (188–203; Dreyfus 1991).

The field of Being, in this sense, may be described here as a medium, itself defined as an extension of the human sensory apparatus or a technology that facilitates communication (Real 1996: 7). Essentially, this means that one's mind works in association with intertextual information to communicate within a meaningful context. This process of association is supported by continuous flows of memories, which store images, sounds, texts, and so on, making logical and affective connections.

According to Heidegger, remembering is a notion of the historical Being: "Just as expecting is possible only because of awaiting, remembering is possible only on that of forgetting, and not vice versa; for in the mode of having-forgotten, one's having been 'discloses' primarily the horizon into which a Dasein lost in the 'superficiality' of its object of concern, can bring itself by remembering. The awaiting that forgets and makes present is an ecstatic unity in its own right, in accordance with which inauthentic understanding temporaries itself with regard to its temporality" (1962: 385–389).

Memories are shared and thus become meaningful through representation. More importantly, as media of representation, human beings keep memories alive and share them. The process of producing *Staging the Cosmopolitan Nation* allows everyone involved in the production and viewing processes to share the experience of staging Chinascape through *Dunhuang bihua yuewu* performances.

**MULTIMEDIA**

The term *multimedia* is continuously being redefined. Since the arrival of new technologies of communication in the past two centuries—including the telegraph, photography, telephones, audio recording, and cinema—multimedia has emerged as the "defining medium of the twenty-first century" (Packer and Jordan 2002: xvi). It incorporates traditionally independent media forms into a single system. It is "a medium that would appeal to all the senses simultaneously—a medium that would mimic and enhance the creative capacities of the human mind" (xvi).

Among examples of performing-arts-oriented multimedia are music videos, commercials, films, television, CD-ROMs, and performances of songs, opera, and ballet (Cook 2001: v). The term "musical multimedia" may refer to any performance that combines visual and audio elements for artistic expression (Cook 2001; Zbikowski 2002; Warren and Reid-Hresko 2022). As we become aware of how significantly the quality of our communication with machines affects the quality of our inner lives, multimedia may be conceptualized as a phenomenon that occurs when we are experiencing multiple forms of interactive communication as Dasein.

Other characteristics of multimedia are integration, hypermedia, immersion, and narrativity. *Staging the Cosmopolitan Nation* is an example of multimedia in that it integrates multisite fieldwork, musical sound recording, staged dance performance, and ethnographic film production. Integration occurs when artistic forms and technologies merge as a hybrid form of expression (Packer and Jordan 2002: xvi).

### REPRESENTATION

Representation such as *Staging the Cosmopolitan Nation* is itself a process by which meaning is constructed and arranged to communicate and interact; it serves our fundamental need to remember. It is a systematic and dynamic rearrangement of intertextual media. Communication based on historical precedents—preexisting meanings—is important: when isolated from one another, "individuals finally have nothing to say, and the art of implication [of preexisting meaning through media of representation] brings forth a process that places us within a creative cycle, a living environment of which we are always to coauthors" (Lévy 1999: 370).

The cited documentaries serve as examples of the rearranged medium of representation since a rearrangement in live performance is always done through interaction, as during a recording session. In the analysis of culture through the production of perspective progress and prospects, "the social arrangements used in making symbolic elements of culture affect the nature and contents of the elements of culture that are produced" (Peterson 1994: 163). The staged Dunhuang arts performances, as different individual representations in the documentaries, constitute structures that led to a call for reinterpreting and rearranging the expressive arts genre per se. Details shown in appendixes A, B, and C reveal the changes of focus that altered the perceptions of the staged representation of the genre.

### *Kristeva's Theory*

Julia Kristeva studies texts as semiotic arrangements of elements that possess a double meaning: a meaning in the text itself and a meaning in what she calls "the historical and social text" (quoted in Allen 2000: 37). This leads us to the problem of intertextuality throughout the staging processes of *Dunhuang bihua yuewu* programs. Bakhtin called attention to "how a single strip of talk (utterance, text, story, etc.) can juxtapose language drawn from, and invoking, alternative cultural, social and linguistic home environment, the interpenetration of multiple voices and forms of utterance by introducing the notion of the dialogic organization of language" (quoted in Bauman 1992: 125).

Kristeva takes this idea further, to develop a notion of intertextuality: "Horizontal axis (subject—addressee) and vertical axis (text—context) coincide, bringing to light an important fact: each word (text) is an intersection of words (texts) where at least one other word (text) can be read. . . . Any text is constructed as a mosaic of quotations; any text is the absorption and transformation of another" (1980: 66, quoted in Allen 2000: 39).

Communication between author and reader is thus partnered by a communication or intertextual relation between poetic words and their prior existence in earlier poetic texts. There is an ongoing dynamic textual production process—"a production that cannot be reduced to representation" (Kristeva 1980: 86, quoted in Allen 2000: 34)—in which each utterance and the text itself is a moment. How each text, through a textual arrangement of elements in a series of historical processes, is constructed and produced as an intertext ensures textual historicity.

Intertextuality, a replacement of intersubjectivity, reflects the ways in which a given text is related to other texts, in that every text absorbs and transforms every other text. This kind of rearrangement is an important aspect of Kristeva's theory: it "changes the place of [the] thing . . . what [Kristeva] displaces is the *already said*" (Barthes 1970: 19). Intertextuality can be seen in poetic texts: "The meaning of a poem can only be a poem, but *another poem—a poem not itself.* And not a poem chosen with total arbitrariness, but any central poem by an indisputable precursor, even if the ephebe *never read* that poem.[3] Source study is wholly irrelevant here; we are dealing with primal words, but antithetical meanings, and an ephebe's best misinterpretation may well be of poems he has never read" (Bloom 1973: 70). Intertextuality may apply to purely visual features or to auditory ones. Today, studies of intertextuality by scholars who explore relationships between texts and contexts are focused on virtually all cultural and artistic productions.

## Intertextuality in Audiovisual Research

Intertextuality is not at all a new idea for music research; more recently, J. Michael Allsen (1993), Robert Hatten (1985), Kevin Korsyn (1999), and others have used it in the analysis of musical works. Hatten, for example, uses style theory to explain intertextual references in music; he explores the way a composer's competence in particular musical styles and strategic utilization of those styles in particular musical pieces constitute "regulators of relevant intertextual relationships" (Allen 2000: 175; Hatten 1985: 69–82). More recently, Korsyn has suggested that theories from Bakhtin have been used to explain dialogic processes and intertextuality in musical works; through a Bakhtinian reading, Korsyn examines how intertextuality affects both sides of the text-context opposition and suggests a new way of looking at preexisting analyses of musical works. For example, he juxtaposes Roy Howat's historical narrative with Jean-Jacques Eigeldinger's analysis of the Chopin Preludes op. 28. He points out that Howat has created a continuous history linking Chopin and Debussy in his allegations of Chopin's influence on Debussy through a unified narrative—which assures a common tradition and which represents "intertextual promiscuity." His analysis intends to establish "an orientation within which both concepts [unity and heterogeneity] are available to the analyst" (Cook and Everist 2001: 3).

Intertextuality involving music in films and music videos is a key topic in research on contemporary media culture: "The opening of media analysis to literary, hermeneutic, and rhetorical forms of study has recovered a sense of depth in texts. Literary theories of 'narrativity' consider far more than the mere transmission of 'information.' Correlatively, an understanding of sign and code systems, genre, formula, convention, discourse, intertextuality, and context opens important and interesting dimensions within the exploration of media culture" (Real 1996: 120).

Similarly, interconnections can be found between Hollywood musicals of the 1930s and music videos of the 1980s. Highlighting their sharing of a similar structure shows that both bodies of art are self-reflective and thus related intertextually (Stockbridge 1988).

## Recontextualization: Transcription and Media

Modern communicative technologies such as printing, filming, and broadcasting are now commonly used as tools to preserve and represent heritage and tradition, as well as to conduct ethnographic research. Multimedia transcription and analysis are critical to the present ethnomusicological study (Stone and Stone 1981). The rise of literary and print culture has enabled explorations of international cultural resources and facilitated the creation of a large-scale domestic public sphere (Anderson 1993).

For my research, I examined the media employed to create and present *Dunhuang bihua yuewu*. To comprehend more fully the processes by which broadcasts on Chinese national television channels have shaped the creation of the genre, I incorporated media analysis into my research and writing. I examined multimedia educational sources such as Gao Jinrong's 1983 publication and DVD *Dunhuang wudao de jiben xunlian* 敦煌舞蹈的基本訓練 (*Basic Training of Dunhuang Dance*), and I have produced my own multimedia educational documentary.

*Producing "Staging the Cosmopolitan Nation:*
*Re-creating the Dunhuang Bihua Yuewu"*

The ethnomusicological documentary *Staging the Cosmopolitan Nation: Re-creating the Dunhuang Bihua Yuewu* was completed in the summer of 2012. This project draws on methods from preexisting multimedia forms, such as ethnographic films and music videos, to reveal the intertextuality of staged Dunhuang arts through the process of recollecting, recontextualizing, representing, and reflecting on the genre. Unlike CCTV's "The Chapter on Dunhuang, Gansu Province" episode, which records Dunhuang's local history and knowledge through film and presents the region as an integral region of the country, *Staging the Cosmopolitan Nation* is an ethnographic documentary focusing on staged Dunhuang arts and the implicated intertextual creative processes. It recontextualizes cultural forms, including historically specific situations in the Dunhuang arts staging process, by illustrating how the media of representation can reflect and reproduce concrete social relations and conditions. Its focus and outcome are particularly valuable to the study of cultural change and the interaction between the Dunhuang expressive arts and context as a historical process.

As a medium of cultural expression, *Staging the Cosmopolitan Nation* has created multiple processes for mediating and manipulating the audio and visual components of the staging history of *Dunhuang bihua yuewu* with the goal of going beyond the artistic elements to represent intertextual cultural processes more broadly. It demonstrates the complexity of the process of the circulating media representations of the expressive art genre. Highlighting issues of power, identity, and representation through interviews, this documentary has greatly facilitated my research on the staging process of *tianxia* through staged Dunhuang arts performances. It has enabled me to explore and become eventually a part of the phenomena of the

Dunhuang metasystem involved in recreating the historical memory and identity of China in contemporary moments of contestation and transformation and has helped address some research questions identified in the first part of this book. The postproduction script (included at the end of this chapter) is a copy that was shared among the production crew members in Gansu and Beijing. It presents the thought processes that took place during the postproduction stage of the film.

The nature of my study subject made it difficult to take notes while conducting research as a participant in the dance studio or engaging interviewees in a conversation often accompanied by demonstrations. Since I used the participant-observation method, I participated as a dancer of *Dunhuang bihua yuewu* to understand the application of the theory and practice of technique related to the genre. To study the multimedia aspects of the genre when observing a dance practice in a classroom or a theatrical performance before an audience, I documented multisensual elements, such as musical and stage sound, spatial arrangements, gestures, dancers' dress, headpieces, and so forth. I usually made visual and aural transcriptions simultaneously when a video camera was available.

As an experienced ethnographic film producer, I made audiovisual recordings myself and in collaboration with Chinese colleagues to document the contexts in which *Dunhuang bihua yuewu* is recontextualized. For instance, I led a production team from the Gansu Provincial Radio, Television, and Film Service to Professor Gao Jinrong's master class at the Northwestern Minzu University in November 2009 for a weeklong session filmed on location. During the session, I multitasked as director, interviewer, and dancer in the studio where students practice *Dunhuang bihua yuewu*. The process of recontextualization is continuous. It comprises the academic setting in the dance studio at the university, where the live *Dunhuang bihua yuewu* is approached as a scholarly research subject. It comprises the postproduction setting in the editing studio at the Gansu Provincial Radio, Television, and Film Service, where the filmed *Dunhuang bihua yuewu* is approached as raw material, collected as digitized data for future references (often materials for television documentaries) and sources for my documentary. The process of recontextualizing employs textual transcriptions produced and enacted through scholarly writings and presentations.

According to Randy Martin, "The importance of adopting media technology in ethnographic research has been highlighted by ethnomusicologists. In dance studies, while audio recording might replicate at least the

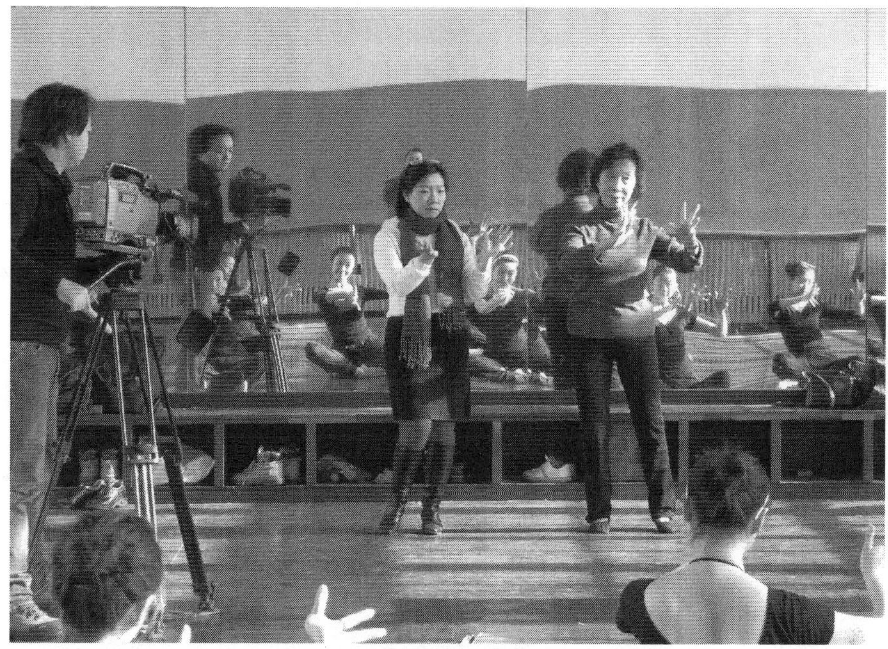

Figures 7.1 and 7.2 *A–B*. Images of the author multitasking as director, interviewer, and dancer during her Fulbright-IIE sponsored fieldwork, working with Professor Gao Jinrong (7.2*A*) and the production team (7.2*B*) at Northwest Minzu University. Photo credit: Kuang Jianren. © Lanlan Kuang, 2009.

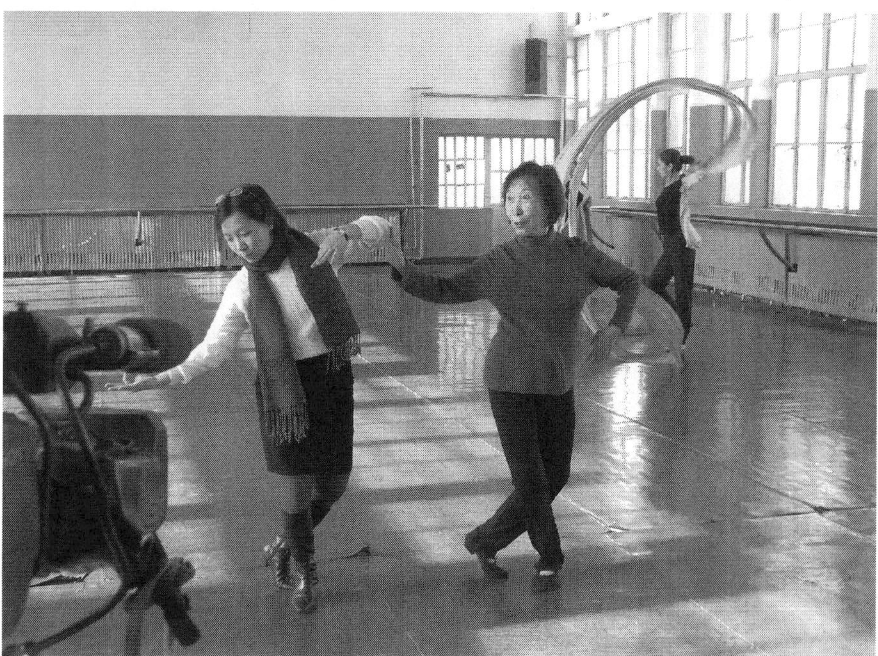

Figure 7.2*A*.

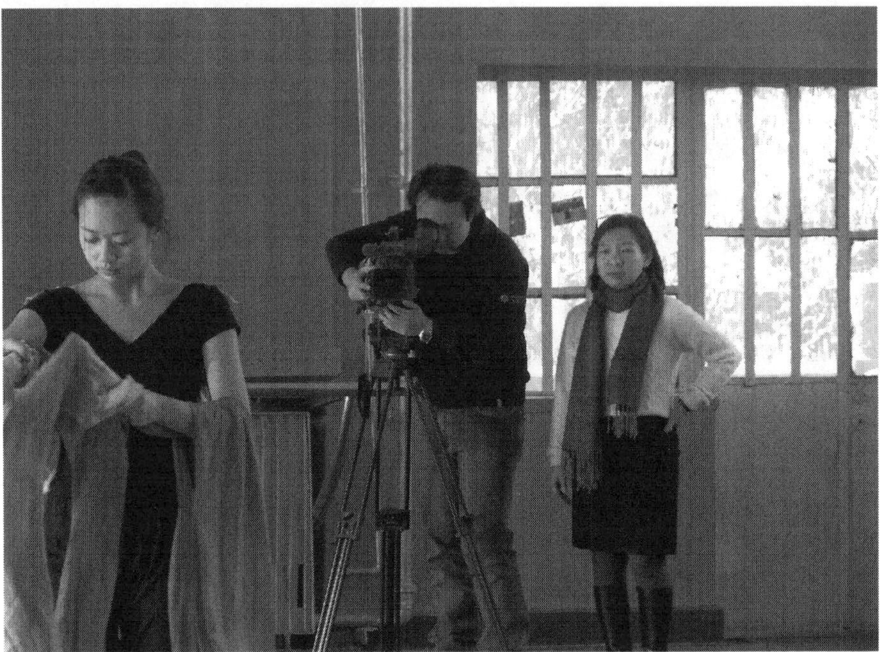

Figure 7.2*B*.

signifiers of a musical performance, video relies on a displacement of an activity that occurs within a three-dimensional space into some virtual equivalent. Videography re-inscribes dancing in another medium that can introduce an awareness of how, in the production of a document, a history is written" (quoted in Foster 1995: 108).

To transcribe is arguably to reinterpret and therefore to recontextualize. I found the process of transcribing the sources that constitute *Dunhuang bihua yuewu* both challenging and rewarding. I systematically collected video clips of *Dunhuang bihua yuewu* performances, practice sessions, interviews, and other related data, such as location shooting at geographic locations where the genre is performed and staged, and I produced a fifty-minute documentary film to illustrate the contexts in which it serves contemporary social and ideological functions.

### Translation and Misinterpretation

While transcribing performances of and interviews about *Dunhuang bihua yuewu*, I was constantly challenged by the process of translation, one of the commonest yet most difficult obstacles for ethnographers studying a group of people who use languages different from their own, as well as from those of their readers. I comprehend Mandarin Chinese as a native speaker, but most Dunhuang documents are manuscripts in other languages that differ substantially from the carved records found in other subfields of Chinese archaeology. The manuscripts consist of faded characters that are hard to read, ancient sayings that are difficult to understand, Buddhist terms that are not easy to translate, and writing styles that may cause confusion. Professor Zheng Binlin 郑炳林 from Lanzhou University's Dunhuang Research Institute has been most helpful in guiding me to the scholarly works about *Dunhuang bihua yuewu* that have been published in the Chinese academic journal *Dunhuang Research* (*Dunhuang yanjiu* 敦煌研究). In addition, although an ethnomusicologist with training in Chinese music theory and classical piano, I had to learn vocabularies and theories used in the fields of dance, traditional Chinese landscape painting, Chinese Buddhism, and ancient Chinese literature before I could begin discussing *Dunhuang bihua yuewu* on a scholarly level.

Before I started my fieldwork at Lanzhou University in 2008, I had begun to familiarize myself with necessary terms and materials while conducting preliminary research in the archives of the Dunhuang Academy at Dunhuang in 2005. Through conversations with scholars there, and at the Dunhuang Institute (Lanzhou University), the China Arts Academy (Beijing), the Northwestern Minzu University (Lanzhou), and other institutions, I assembled a glossary of terms and a considerable body of theoretical ideas that I knew would be essential for my research and writing. This was the beginning phase of my research. After a year of work in China, I spent another year in the libraries and archives in Bloomington and Beijing. I realized that to write on *Dunhuang bihua yuewu* theoretically, I would need to compile a glossary of terms and understand the ideas accumulated throughout the years I have spent on the genre. Since the pertinent terms and ideas have their origin in disciplines other than dance, I first had to interpret them in their original contexts before I could recontextualize them in reference to *Dunhuang bihua yuewu*.

### *Performances of Ethnographic Texts*

My research on staged Dunhuang arts centers on how ideas initiated at least in part for political and economic reasons are promoted through the arts and how ideas transmitted through the arts have affected sociocultural transformations. My work in China has already affected the process of staging Dunhuang expressive arts. My presence among Chinese scholars, government officials, and students as an academically trained researcher who had come to conduct ethnographic studies—an individual agent representing a certain institutional expectation from outside the local, regional, and even national system of cultural development—evidently contributed to the growth of the staged Dunhuang arts genre. In 2023, before I arrived, I had been notified by Director Zheng Binlin at the Dunhuang Research Institute that Lanzhou University's Department of the Arts had designated staged Dunhuang arts as a course to be taught within its official curriculum. I learned that Gao Jinrong had been promoted from visiting professor to full professor of dance at the Northwestern Minzu University. That the incorporation of both staged Dunhuang arts and their creator into the more prestigious academic curriculum and scholarly circles occurred during my presence as a researcher led me to reflect on my role as an individual agent in the process of recreating the genre. My name and research have been incorporated into daily discourse relating to it. I approach and interpret this phenomenon as the performativity of my own ethnographic research and text.

### Challenges of Writing

In the introduction to an ethnographic work on the social and cultural construction of a South Korean conglomerate, Roger Janelli listed some of the methodological dilemmas he faced as he tried to present an interpretation of the business, such as having to omit materials to maintain focus and trying to "address a theoretical debate concerning how the construction of cultural meanings articulates with the making of a political economy while . . . writing a descriptive ethnography of particular events and experiences" (1993: 13). Fredrick Lau also discussed the challenge to present ethnographic research: "It [ethnography] is basically an account of cultural phenomena seen through the eyes of the ethnographer in their social context. While being mindful of remaining objective, the ethnographer's subjectivity and self are implicitly or explicitly implicated in the portrayal of a culture, society, or community in situ. Like a selfie taker, an ethnographer must determine the structure of the narrative and the perspective, tone, color, texture, depth, and dimension of the story" (2023: 78–79). When writing on staged Dunhuang arts performances,

I faced similar dilemmas. While I tried to discuss the performativity of the genre in the construction of a cosmopolitan vision of the modern Chinese nation, I found myself trying to go back to the aesthetic principles and artistic processes through which it had been recreated to bring forth the idea of Chineseness, a concept that seems to me to need an approach beyond the rhetoric and discourse on nationalism. When I tried to reassemble and reconnect these focuses, this tug-of-war within my own research forced me to prolong my efforts after my fieldwork in China. The result became the core proposition of this study, which introduces the notion of a conceptual Chinascape and embodiments of the poetic suggestiveness that metaphorically and intertextually stages sensuous imageries from the past to enact representations of the past and visions of the present and perhaps even of the future.

## Notes

1. Multimedia components for *Staging* Tianxia, such as active maps, working color metagraphs, audiovisual files, and documentary film clips, can be found at https://lanlankuangofficial.pub/.

2. There are debates on how to interpret the Heideggerian notion of *Dasein* (Da-sein: there-being), which is loosely used in this book to highlight the existential quality of Being in the understanding of the a priori conditions of human beings. See Barrett (1962) for a discussion of Heidegger.

3. In Bloom's book *Anxiety of Influence* (1973), the ephebe is a poet who is just growing into his adversary role as an angel who is under the poetic influence of God—Wordsworth the ephebe of Milton, Roethke the ephebe of Yeats, and so on—and can never wholly escape his servitude.

# 8

# NATION BUILDING

## *Dunhuang Meta-elements in Peking Opera and Beyond*

聖人常無心，以百姓心為心。. . .
聖人在天下，歙歙焉，為天下渾其心，百姓皆注其耳目，聖人皆孩之。

**Sages do not hold any intentions but follow the people's intentions. . . .
Sages restrain their subjective will and prejudices to being in *tianxia*,
Sages maintain an unrestrained heart for *tianxia*.
People see and people listen, while sages bring them
all back to a state of childlike innocence.**

《道德經》四十九章
*Dao De Jing*, **Chapter 49**

THE RELATION BETWEEN THE CENTER AND THE PERIPHERY is mutually constitutive: one could not exist without the other, just as details entail the whole and an interior foundation is defined by its boundaries. The desire to maintain balance between the two always creates tension, not unlike the anxiety the present must endure from being caught between the past and the future: what is now present in the central stage would wish to remain under the spotlight, while those that have been situated in the wings would wish to be recognized (Bloom 1973). This tension or anxiety inspires and motivates the continuous recreation in and recontextualization of the arts. Expressive art forms, such as the *Dunhuang bihua yuewu* genre and other staged Dunhuang arts performances, guide a country and its people into imagining a national identity and a national history—by creating a culturally layered symbol for representing its population.

This chapter presents four cases, each showing strategies used for balancing the power between central and peripheral, old and new: two new versions of *Along the Silk Road* (*Silu huayu* 絲路花雨), a Dunhuang-themed Peking opera 京劇 highlighting the history of the Dunhuang Academy and the first generations of researchers in the grand backdrop of the founding of the modern Chinese nation in 1949; a Dunhuang-themed production adopted from an award-winning Japanese novel and staged in the form of Long opera 隴劇, a regional folk drama of Gansu Province, which I studied ethnographically in Lanzhou in 2023. These works demonstrate the Chinese government's promotion of the Dunhuang metaculture to serve in its state-building strategies.

## The New Version of *Along the Silk Road* (絲路花雨新版)

The Golden City Theatre (*Jincheng juyuan* 金城大劇院), named after the city of Lanzhou's historic name during the Han dynasty, was a landmark building in the center of the city. In December 2008, I learned from Li Qi 李琦, now dean of the School of Dance at Northwestern Minzu University, that a new version of *Along the Silk Road* was to be staged there, where it had first been performed, back in 1984. "You don't need to worry about a ticket," said Li Qi over the phone. "Wang Qiong 王瓊 will pick you up in front of the theater and guide you inside. She was the fifth-generation dancer of Ying Niang." Like He Yanyun, the first-generation dancer of this role, the lead female dancers of *Along the Silk Road* were addressed by titles as an honorific gesture, which implies the continuous importance of the original dance drama in the history of modern Chinese dance and theater. The character Ying Niang 英娘 and her solo "Playing the Pipa in Reverse Position" became so famous in China that it would be appropriate even to compare the role to Ophelia in Shakespeare's *Hamlet*. The new version serves to illustrate how popular and important *Along the Silk Road* has been among Chinese audiences, especially in the Northwest.

The dance drama was scheduled to be staged at eight o'clock on a Saturday night. The taxi driver in Lanzhou knowingly took a different route through the narrower streets when he learned that my destination was the Golden City Theatre. "It's the weekend. The main streets near the theater are blocked for the night market," he explained. I arrived at the theater early, around seven, with plans to interview Wang Qiong. Groups of people dressed in winter coats and boots came to attend the performance. In front of the building were huge, colorful banners that said "2008 Beijing Olympics Grand-Scale Cultural Activity—Gansu Dance Drama and Opera Ensemble Stages *Along the Silk Road*, a Splendid Classic of a National Dance Drama." Apparently, as I learned from various sources later, the project to renew *Along the Silk Road* was a mission specially assigned by the Propaganda Department of the Communist Party of China (*Zhonggong zhongyang xuanchuan bu* 中共中央宣傳部) and the State Cultural Bureau (*Wenhuabu* 文化部). It was part of the programs associated with the 2008 Olympics to promote Chinese culture. Usually known as the Central Propaganda Department (*Zhong xuan bu* 中宣部)—also in charge of media censorship—the department often worked with the cultural and educational bureaus to promote and guard ideology-related works.

In heavy stage makeup, with dramatically long fake eyelashes fanning the air, Wang Qiong came to greet me in front of the theater. She looked stunning, even before she changed into her stage costume. "There's no rush. My part won't appear until the third act," she explained. She no longer dances the role of Ying Niang, but she was to play the part of the Persian queen who would host Ying Niang in her palace during her exile in Persia. Framed photos taken from previously staged performances of *Along the Silk Road* and *A Grand Dream of Dunhuang* decorated the walls of the grand lobby of the theater. I noticed a photo of Li Qi wearing a light-blue costume, holding a clay waterpot with two hands on the top of her head, and swinging in an S shape. She was one of the lead dancers in *A Grand Dream of Dunhuang* when it premiered.

Wang Qiong noticed that I had been videotaping since I arrived at the theater and told me that I could film only in the grand hall and could not film the staged performance. Disappointed, I asked if I could film and interview her standing in front of another huge banner at the entrance, and she agreed. After a brief introduction of her experience as the fifth-generation dancer to stage Ying Niang, I asked what major changes had been made in the newest version of *Along the Silk Road*. She seemed to have spoken to many news reporters already and answered without hesitation. She pointed out that the director responsible for revising the choreography of the 2008 version was Xu Chenghua, a nationally ranked director from the Guangzhou Military Song and Dance Group (GZMSDG). In addition to reprising the signature *Dunhuang bihua yuewu*, the new version put more emphasis on the Indian dance, the Farsi bell dance, the Farsi banquet dance, the

Turkish dance, dances from Xinjiang Autonomous Region, and the "Dance on a Plate," in which the dancer would perform on a large plate held up by several supporting dancers, displaying a certain degree of acrobatic skill. This was a dance documented in historical references, just like the multi-ethnic dance suites from the Sui and Tang dynasties. The contemporarily created Chinese classical dance 中國古典舞, which draws its artistic elements from Yuan dynasty drama and Peking opera, has a more important role in the new version than it had in the original version.

Wang Qiong said: "One of the main differences between the original version and the new version of the dance drama *Along the Silk Road* is that the new version puts more emphasis on the lead male actor, Magic Brush Zhang, instead of Inus, the Persian merchant. The older version focused more on the lead female actress, Ying Niang, who was known for her solo dance *Playing the Pipa in Reverse Position*. The new version puts more emphasis on the Chinese classical dance style that Magic Brush Zhang performed" (2008 interview with Wang Qiong by Kuang, recorded and translated).

*Along the Silk Road* was originally staged to present mainly music and dance styles drawn from the Dunhuang materials, but the new version focused on both the *Dunhuang bihua yuewu* and Chinese classical dance by giving a Han ethnic artist and the male lead actor longer solo parts in each act. The music, too, was changed from the original version, which had more folk instruments and indigenous themes, to feature a full string orchestra, to which electronic sound effects were added. It would seem appropriate to change the music when lighting and other stage effects were also changed to suit the larger stages of theaters with advanced technologies in Beijing and Shanghai. Even the lead dancers were no longer from the local dance troupes.

The previous generations of dancers who had performed the roles of Ying Niang and her father, Magic Brush Zhang, had been technically trained graduates from northwestern institutions such as the Gansu Vocational School of the Arts, directed by Professor Gao Jinrong during the earlier years, but the two female lead dancers for Ying Niang—Sun Qiuyue and Zhao Qiao—were graduates of the China People's Liberation Army Arts Academy and the Beijing Dance Academy, respectively. Wang Zihan, the male lead dancer, was also a graduate of the Beijing Dance Academy. Unlike the previous generations of Ying Niang dancers, the current performers were not trained specially in the *Dunhuang bihua yuewu* genre but were more familiar with mainstream styles of Chinese classical dance. In other words, not only had a new team of choreographers and musicians from outside the region been brought in to revise the dance drama but the performers of the newer version had been recruited from around the country. These are among the changes that illustrate that the officials in the Propaganda Department and the Cultural Bureau had taken *Along the Silk Road* under their wing and were promoting the production as a national treasure by utilizing what they considered the best human and other resources available.

The 1979 version of *Along the Silk Road* was made into a film by the Xi'an Film Studio in 1982. Today, viewers of the 1979 version of *Along the Silk Road* can still review the dance drama on DVD. As a researcher of staged Dunhuang arts and especially the *Dunhuang bihua yuewu* genre, I had watched the original version numerous times before I encountered the 2008 version and had never failed to appreciate its originality. Nevertheless, that night, when I was sitting in the front row in the Golden City Theatre, I was not overly impressed by the new version. The costumes, props, stage settings, and other things were all bright and colorful, dazzling in the stage light. The solo dance program of Magic Brush Zhang and the signature dances from Ying Niang all showed the exceptional mastery of general dance technique, but their performances revealed a lack of in-depth training in the *Dunhuang bihua yuewu* genre. The orchestral version of the music sounded full in body, echoing inside the theater, but the clarity and style of the original score were gone. In summary, this case shows the ways in which a Dunhuang-themed dance was reconstructed for staging as a national treasure, the purposes it was intended to serve, and some of the changes made.

In the 2008 version of *Along the Silk Road*, the *Dunhuang bihua yuewu* was no longer the dominant dance genre, which was now labeled *classic national dance drama* (*jingdian minzu wuju* 經典民族舞劇); the adjective *national* here means "Chinese national."[1] Professor Dong, during our interviews, said, "On the grander scale, of course, it is of our Chinese nationality [*zhonghua minzu* 中華民族]." Here, too, instead of advertising *Along the Silk Road* as a multiethnic dance drama (*duo minzu wuju* 舞劇多民族), although it kept the multifaceted elements that constitute the work, the publicity materials simply referred to it as a national dance drama. In this case, during a staged performance, the center "stole the thunder" while quietly diminishing the periphery by expanding its own space and time.

## The Peking Opera Version of *Along the Silk Road* (絲路花雨京劇版)

If I had not been in Lanzhou for my research, I would probably never have learned about the Peking opera version of *Along the Silk Road*. The subject came up later, during my filming of the *Dunhuang bihua yuewu* documentary in Lanzhou. I cannot remember clearly now whether it happened while I was eating a bowl of steaming-hot, delicious Lanzhou beef noodles or merely craving it during one of the seemingly endless work sessions in the no-drink, no-food editorial room (*jifang* 機房) at the Gansu Radio, Film, and Television Service.

My excuse for almost overlooking the Peking opera version would probably be that my research was focusing on the *Dunhuang bihua yuewu*, not on Peking opera. As an expressive art form that was, and is, considered a national treasure and remains highly popular among Chinese elites in Beijing and major cities around the country, Peking opera was not as popular as other expressive art forms in the Northwest.[2] Unlike Peking opera, the regionally developed drama style Qinqiang 秦腔 has a larger following in the Northwest. Qinqiang, glossed literally as "tunes of Qin," is a style based on dialogues and melodies that originated in the region. Therefore, when the subject of the Peking opera version of *Along the Silk Road* came up in the editorial room, other editors laughed and said they would prefer Qinqiang over Peking opera because they thought Qinqiang was more pleasant to listen to.

The person who mentioned the Peking opera version of *Along the Silk Road* to me was a senior colleague of Liu Hongqi 劉泓岐, the young editing director from the Gansu Radio, Film, and Television Service, who had been assisting me as cinematographer for a documentary I was making. Liu, who was assigned to me as my contact person, worked as an assistant to Liu Shengping 劉省平, director of the Cultural and Film Channel of the Gansu Radio, Film, and Television Service. Liu Shengping was himself a seasoned producer and cinematographer of the Dunhuang arts and was well acquainted with many Dunhuangologists. Liu Hongqi, in contrast, was responsible for making arrangements to facilitate my filming: booking studios; arranging for me to get permission to use the archives at the Gansu Radio, Film, and Television Service; suggesting team members when it came to on-site filming; and so on. Thanks to their help, I spent many days at the computer screen in the editorial room, going through hundreds of films, documentaries, and recordings to extract useful information on the *Dunhuang bihua yuewu*.

It was during one of those days in the editorial room (during which the editors and producers do not usually sleep because of the busy booking schedule for the machines), while I was chatting with other editors and producers, that a senior editor, whose name I do not know, casually mentioned that there was a Peking opera version of *Along the Silk Road*. He asked me if I had heard of it. "How embarrassing! How could I not know about this after I've spent so much time studying the *Dunhuang bihua yuewu*!"—I said exactly that. The senior editor seemed pleased when he saw he had surprised me on the subject that I was researching, and he became enthusiastic when he noticed my interest in the details of the performance. I asked whether he knew the people responsible for staging the Peking opera version, and he immediately listed the names of people he thought would be important for me to meet, including Yang Chengwei 楊成偉, former director of the Gansu Provincial Peking Opera Group, and Ma Shaomin 馬少敏, at the time the lead female singer, portraying Ying Niang. I arranged not only to meet and interview both but also to film them in the studio for my documentary, and I even attended their premiere at the Mei Lanfang Theatre in Beijing in January 2009. I was eager to learn why, and how, the famous Dunhuang dance drama had been made into a Peking opera.[3]

## "Dunhuang, Silk Road, Multinational," Peking Opera Style

"We were instructed to create artistic productions according to the slogan 'Dunhuang, Silk Road, Multinational' [*Dunhuang, silu, duo minzu* 敦煌, 絲路, 多民族] by the Gansu Provincial Cultural Bureau during the annual conference in 2004," recalled Yang Chengwei, director of the Gansu Provincial Peking Opera Group. "What exactly does the slogan mean?" I asked, and he explained: "It means that we should follow these principles: use Dunhuang as the resource, the Silk Road as the connection, and multinationality to add flavor when we create new work." This slogan indeed had become the guiding principle for the Gansu Provincial Peking Opera Group when its members began to write the script for the Peking opera version of *Along the Silk Road*. It was clear that officials in the government of Gansu had learned from the success of the dance drama that they should encourage creative products to promote the cultural industry of the region; however, to create an equally successful work would be extremely difficult, especially for the Gansu Provincial Peking Opera Group. Therefore, Yang Chengwei and his team decided to create a Peking opera version of *Along the Silk Road*.

"The dance drama is extremely rich in its content and is a high-level artistic work. We thought, why can't we help make it even more popular, more successful, since it was already Gansu Province's 'business card'?" said Yang Zhiwei in an interview recorded in Lanzhou on November 24, 2008.

The idea gained support, and not only from the Gansu provincial government, which had been eager to promote its culture productions. It received a budget of 2 million renminbi (about $287,000 as of 2023) from the Propaganda Department of the Communist Party of China and the Cultural Bureau, as they expected the group to stage an excellent program. Nevertheless, to rewrite the "business card" of Gansu Province was challenging. *Along the Silk Road* was originally a dance drama, consisting mainly of well-organized programs of *Dunhuang bihua yuewu*. In a dance drama, actors tell stories through body language accompanied by expressive music composition. Although Peking opera also incorporates some dance and aerobic movements, its primary way of communication is through singing (*chang* 唱) and lyrical recitation (*nian* 念). To stage *Along the Silk Road* as a Peking opera program without losing its "Dunhuang, Silk Road, Multi-nationality" characteristics, performers must tell the story of Ying Niang, Magic Brush Zhang, and Inus without relying entirely on the *Dunhuang bihua yuewu* yet at the same time keep it an essential element in the work.

Yang Chengwei and his production team decided to revise the original script and added a character: Inus's young son, Zhang En: "Because dance has the advantage of expressing [sentiments], with a relatively simple plot, the relationships among characters do not need to be very complex to achieve emotional conflicts. Things are different with opera. A good opera must have a relatively complex plot and setting to create an interesting relationship among characters. Without a good dramatic plot, there will be no good operatic performances. Therefore, we added a key figure" (Yang, Chengwei, video recording, Lanzhou, November 24, 2008).

In the Peking opera version of *Along the Silk Road*, Zhang En would be adopted briefly by Magic Brush Zhang and fall in love with Ying Niang. The plot consisted of exile to the foreign land, revenge, and a love story that gave the Peking opera version just enough tension for a good vocal performance. "By adding the key figure of Zhang En, and through the love relationship between Zhang En and Ying Niang, this version showed even more in-depth the close connection between the families," added Yang.

The work of writing a script for the dance drama *Along the Silk Road* began in 2005, and the production team rewrote it more than eighteen times before they had a script they could perform. The Gansu Provincial Peking Opera Group originally belonged to the Political Bureau of the First Field Operation Army and was established in 1949. Its members were graduates from the China Drama Academy and the Gansu Drama Academy. Yang Chengwei stressed the group's dedication to following the "tradition of Peking opera," even if its productions were created according to the "Dunhuang, Silk Road, Multinationality" slogan:

> We have been engaged in the creation of Peking opera from the Western Region (*xibu jingju* 西部京劇). Constituted of creative ideas from the Western Region and constructed in Peking opera style, this is what makes Peking opera different from the Western Region. This does not mean we have to depart from the traditional Peking opera art form. That is impossible! We are a Peking opera group; it [our work] must always be based on and develop from our tradition. We must be able to incorporate into our work unique elements from the Western Region, so the people from within this region could appreciate it. It [our work] also is the cultural product of this province, a good utilization of the local, geographic resource. Because this opera group dwells in the Great Northwest (*daxibei* 大西北), there is something special about its survival. For instance, one of the differences is that in comparison to other well-developed provincial capital cities (*fada shenghui* 發達省會), there is a very small group of Peking opera audiences, relatively speaking; therefore, we must present our geographical characteristics. (Yang Chengwei, video recording, Lanzhou, November 24, 2008)

## Dunhuang Meta-elements in Peking Opera and Beyond

In 2022, Professor Xie Bailiang 謝柏梁 from the National Academy of Chinese Theatre Arts (中國戲曲學院) reached out to me in regard to a collaborative project to develop a theoretical foundation for analyzing the Dunhuang expressive arts. A renowned literary scholar and art critic known for his specialty in traditional Chinese drama and comparative studies of dramatic tragedies, Professor Xie is collaborating with Gao Ming of Gansu Provincial Peking Opera Theater Company as the coproducer of *A Love Story from Dunhuang*. Unlike the well-known Dunhuang expressive art programs that highlight the historical past and multiculturalism of the frontier metropolis, such as *Along the Silk Road* and *A Grand Dream of Dunhuang*, Xie's *A Love Story from Dunhuang* is a Peking opera based on the history of Dunhuang Academy. It introduces the life of generations of Dunhuang scholars who stayed in Dunhuang for the sake of heritage research and conservation, and it shifts its focus from the past to the present by portraying characters who are still actively engaging in the conservation and research of Dunhuangology.

Most importantly, Dunhuang in the new Peking opera piece becomes a critical part of China's nation-building rhetoric, but it focuses on the Dunhuang meta-elements that are beyond its multiculturalism. It presents a Dunhuang-themed Chinascape that is discovered, safeguarded, and developed by scholars whose self-imposed intellectual search has drawn them to live and work in peripheral northwest China. The center of the state, in this case the administrative and cultural center of the nation, becomes increasingly desirable because of its unattainability.

## Dunhuang Meta-elements in Northwest Folk Drama—Long Opera 隴劇

During my sabbatical research in Lanzhou, Gansu Province, in March 2023, I had the invaluable opportunity to investigate the reproduction of *Dunhuang*, a Long-opera-style drama staged by the Gansu Provincial Long Opera Group 甘肅省隴劇院. This Dunhuang-themed folk drama came into being twenty years ago, but it was awarded one of the China State Intangible Cultural Heritage Protection Finance Projects and restaged by the Gansu Provincial Long Opera Group.

To understand the nature of this production, we must understand the current development of Gansu's regional arts. The present-day operatic drama from Gansu 甘肅 Province and the surrounding regions is known as Long opera, or *Longju* 隴劇, known formerly as the Narrative Tune from the East of Long Region (*Longdong daoqing* 隴東道情). With a long history in which it once prevailed in the eastern part of Gansu, the lesser-known local drama genre *Longju* gave birth to Xiqin qiang 西秦腔 (the Tune from Western Qin), folk songs and dances found in the neighboring Shanxi 陝西 Province, and it eventually evolved into Qinqiang 秦腔 (Zhao Xiaohuan 2022: 217–218).

My interviews with Director Wang Cun 王存 in his office at the Gansu Provincial Long Opera Group's building started with his self-introduction as a professional Western opera 西洋歌劇 singer transferred to oversee the endangered Long Opera Group and the genre in general: "My background is in Western opera. I was asked by the upper administration to come and direct the Long Opera Group because of my achievements directing the Western Opera Group" (Wang Cun, audio recording, Lanzhou, May 2023).

Unlike Peking opera or *kunqu* opera, both selected by UNESCO as world heritages and staged frequently with state funding, China's regional, local, and folk drama, collectively known as *defang xiqu* 地方戲曲, relies more heavily on revenues from performing tours in the countryside and sponsorship from local businesses. Support from the state government was minor to almost nonexistent. Stressing the challenges overcome after joining the Gansu Provincial Long Opera Group, Director Wang led me to the Long Opera Group's small but new theater building, where a long stele with a single line of red inscribed text—"National Intangible Cultural Heritage" 國家非物質文化遺產—stands in the center of the lobby. Beneath the stele is a small gallery of photos introducing the history of *Longju*. As a national-level intangible cultural heritage, according to Wang, the group now has more funding opportunities, such as applying for state funding with projects developed according to the themes set by the state Bureau for Culture and Tourism. While governmental funding opportunities often involve compliance with state objectives, financial support from the state Bureau for Culture and Tourism nevertheless advances the conservation, preservation, and representation of many local and regional cultural heritages by enforcing certain grant requirements. For instance, a pedagogical design must be presented and implemented. In the case of preserving *Longju* performances, for instance, one of Director Wang's primary goals is to educate a younger generation of *Longju* performers. "It is very difficult to attract talents and even more difficult to keep talents in a regional group. We need to be able to train our own performers at Gansu Long Opera Group" (Wang Cun, audio recording, Lanzhou, May 2023). Sponsored by the state as a national project, the staging of *Longju Dunhuang* with a new generation of *Longju* talents became the perfect solution to address the pedagogical needs.

On May 29 and 30, 2023, Gansu Provincial Longju Opera Group premiered *Longju Dunhuang* 隴劇《敦煌》at the People's Theatre in Lanzhou. The operatic drama in *Longju* style had been adapted by the playwright Wang Yuanping from the award-winning novel by Japanese author Inoue Yasushi (日语: 井上 靖/いのうえ やすし) of the same name (but spelled *Tun-huang* 《敦煌》 in Wade-Giles transliteration). Yasushi became the first winner of Japan's Mainichi Art Prize for *Tun-huang* in 1959. Set in China's Song dynasty, when the Song emperor Taizu's court alternated between warfare and diplomacy with the ethnic Khitans of the Liao dynasty in the northeast and the Tanguts of the Western Xia in the northwest, *Tun-huang* tells the story of Chao Hsing-te. This multilingual Chinese Han ethnic scholar became interested in the now-extinct Tangut language of the Western Xia dynasty after his chance encounter with a Uighur princess on his way to take the civil-service exam for becoming a scholar-official for the court. The novel paints a vivid picture of multiethnic and multicultural activities along the Silk Road, in war and in peace.

The staged Dunhuang-themed *Longju* drama highlighted the importance of Dunhuang as a cultural center, created, shared, and protected by a diverse group of people dwelling in the region and traveling along the routes. The sad love story of Chao and the Uighur princess, who bore the name Gelisa in the staged *Longju* Dunhuang drama, is interwoven with their joint effort to save the cultural heritage hidden in the Mogao Grottoes from warfare and corruption. In the official report on the premiere of the *Longju*-style Dunhuang drama, the Gansu Provincial Department of Culture and Tourism wrote:

> It follows the fate of the Uighur princess Gelisa as the main thread and depicts a magnificent picture of the descendants of the Chinese people protecting Chinese culture in the baptism of blood and fire. The drama, with its ups and downs, presents the unprejudiced nature of the Dunhuang culture, which is "to appreciate other forms of beauty with openness. The world will be blessed with harmony and unity only if beauty represents itself with diversity and integrity" 美人之美, 美美與共 [from Chinese anthropologist Fei Xiaotong], the peace-making ideologies that "military forces are to be used only for the maintenance of peace and order" 止戈為武 [from *The Spring and Autumn Annals of Zuo's Biography / Xuan Gong Year Twelve* 左傳宣公十二年] and "harmonizing with all nations" 協和萬邦 [from *Book of Documents* Shangshu 尚書], the Eastern wisdom of "harmony is precious" 和为贵 and "harmony but difference" 和而不同 [from *Analects / Chapter Zilu* 論語子路篇] as well as the spirit of "striving for self-improvement" 自強不息 and the sacrifice spirit of "sacrificing life for righteousness" 捨生取義, showcasing the patriotism, national righteousness, and cultural roots. (Translated and annotated by Kuang)[4]

Among several concepts associated with the staged Dunhuang arts performance cited in the above passage, Fei Xiaotong's key phrase—"to appreciate other forms of beauty with openness. The world will be blessed with harmony and unity only if beauty represents itself with diversity and integrity" 美人之美, 美美與共—appears frequently in China's official statements on cultural and ethnic affairs and is not limited to those in the Northwest: these popular Chinese idiomatic expressions could be interpreted as dealing with culture and ethnic affairs everywhere in China. The peacemaking ideologies and "Eastern wisdoms" from the classics are used in rhetoric as political philosophy for forging diplomatic ties on an international scale, including those focusing on promoting President Xi Jinping's "Community of Common Destiny" 人類命運共同體 ideal and Belt and Road Initiatives.[5]

Finally, the sacrificial spirit, also highlighted in *A Love Story from Dunhuang*, appeals to patriotic sentiment on the individual level.

A great amount of scholarly attention has been given to the ethnic minority groups in China as well as to the conservation, preservation, and representations of their identities, cultures, and what today is called intangible cultural heritages (Rees 2000; Tuohy 2001; Wilcox 2019). This study, in addition to conducting and placing within the larger framework of a modern Chinese nation the multifaceted staged Dunhuang arts as the central subjects of research, examines the ongoing challenges and development of the frame itself—China's nation building and its internal image construction—by looking at the contemporary governing of pluralistic cultural factors. The staged Dunhuang arts and *Dunhuang bihua yuewu* case examples presented in this book tackle both the art form itself and the slippery concept of Chineseness that emerges through these staged performances. Furthermore, as we recognize the Dunhuang meta-elements within diverse staged performances—including multimedia formats like documentaries, online games, and commercial films—we gain insights from the decisions made at local, regional, and folk levels of these productions. These choices not only reflect the country's policy priorities but also illuminate its cultural development tendency and subsequently, the country's grand design, or the *shi* trajectory 勢, aligning with the state's overarching vision.

## Notes

1. As stated in earlier chapters, different translations and wordings in the research materials allow *nationality* in all translated Chinese phrases to imply ethnicity. English-language writers often make distinctions among the various meaning of *minzu* 民族 and of *nationality* (which means different things in English as well). Conceiving of ethnicity as nationality has affected the construction of a multiethnic Chinese nation. Some of the Chinese institutes now use *minzu*, the *pinyin*, of instead of *nationality*, the romanized translation; for instance, Northwest *Minzu* University 西北民族大學 was once translated as Northwest University for the Nationalities.

2. In a study on the popularity of Hubei *chuju* opera in the countryside, Brian DeMare (2012) points out that Peking opera and spoken drama—both used by the Kuomintang (KMT), the Nationalist Party of China (NPC) government, to promote patriotism and raise funds for patriotic causes while it simultaneously banned "vulgar" *chuju*—were favored only by urban elites.

3. For a demonstration of "Playing Pipa in Reverse Position" in the Peking opera version of *Along the Silk Road* and an interview with Wang Chengwei and Ma Shaomin, see *Staging the Cosmopolitan Nation: The Re-creation of the* Dunhuang Yuewu, *a Multicultural Music,*

*Dance, and Theatrical Drama from China*, directed by Lanlan Kuang (2012). Multimedia components for *Staging* Tianxia, such as active maps, working color metagraphs, audiovisual files, and documentary film clips, can be found at https://lanlankuangofficial.pub/.

4. In "Zi Lu" of *The Analects* (《论语·子路》), the Master said: "The superior man is affable, but not adulatory; the mean man is adulatory, but not affable" (君子和而不同, 小人同而不和). For a complete report, see Zhou Wei, "*Longju Dunhuang* Premiered at the Gansu Provincial Longju Theater," Gansu Provincial Department of Culture and Tourism, June 1, 2023, https://www.mct.gov.cn/whzx/qgwhxxlb/gs/202306/t20230601_944163.htm.

5. One of the most relevant sample references is the article by Hu (2018) on the Belt and Road Initiative for *Journal of China and International Relations*, in which the idea that "harmony is precious" 和为贵 is discussed on page 8. For sample reference on "harmonizing with all nations" 協和萬邦 and Xi's "Community of Common Destiny" 人類命運共同體, see Kern 2017; Shu and Zhu 2018.

# 9

## CODA

### China's New Cosmopolitan Heritage

The ancients who wished to manifest the luminous virtue
throughout *tianxia*, first governed well their states.
Wishing to govern well their states, they first regulated their families.
Wishing to regulate their household, they first cultivated themselves.
Wishing to cultivate themselves, they first rectified their hearts.
Wishing to rectify their hearts, they first sought to be sincere in their intentions.
Wishing to be sincere in their intentions, they first extended perfect their
knowledge through investigations. . . .
From the Son of Heaven down to the commoners, all are united
in considering self-cultivation as the original.

**Da Xue (the Way of Great Learning 133)[1]**

古之欲明明德於天下者, 先治其國;
欲治其國者, 先齊其家; 欲齊其家者, 先修其身;
欲修其身者, 先正其心; 欲正其心者, 先誠其意,
欲誠其意者, 先致其知, 致知在格物. . . .

自天子以及庶人, 壹是皆以修身為本。[2]

IN MARCH 2013, DURING VISITS TO KAZAKHSTAN AND Indonesia, Chinese president Xi Jinping introduced the initiatives of the Silk Road Economic Belt and the Twenty-First-Century Maritime Silk Road. These initiatives are together called the Belt and Road Initiative. The China State Council 中華人民共和國國務院, the chief administrative authority of the People's Republic of China, lists in detail the policies and implementation plans for the initiative on its official website.

In April 2013, the China Institute in New York launched a yearlong celebration, starting with "Dunhuang: Buddhist Art and the Gateway of the Silk Road," with a recreation of one of the caves and a selection of artifacts from the site. In March 2015, the National Development and Reform Commission, China's top economic planning agency, released an action plan outlining key details of the Belt and Road Initiative. Xi Jinping has made the program a centerpiece of both his foreign and domestic economic policies. One of Xi's central economic strategies is to promote cultural industry that can enhance trade along the Silk Road.

In March 2016, encouraged by the initiative's cultural policies, *The Silk Princess* premiered in Xi'an; it was staged at the National Center for the Performing Arts in Beijing the following July. *A Grand Dream of Dunhuang* and *Along the Silk Road* had been inspired by the Buddhist art found in Dunhuang, but *The Silk Princess*, based on a story about a princess bringing silk and silkworm-breeding skills to western China in the Tang dynasty (618–907), has a different origin. The story was portrayed in a woodblock print from the Tang dynasty discovered by Sir Marc Aurel Stein, a British archaeologist, during his expedition to Xinjiang (now Xinjiang Uighur Autonomous Region) in the early twentieth century and in a temple mural discovered during a 2002 Chinese-Japanese expedition in the Dandanwulike region.

In January 2016, the Shaanxi Provincial Song and Dance Troupe staged *The Silk Road*, a new theatrical dance drama. Unlike *A Grand Dream of Dunhuang*, it "centers around the 'road' and the deepening relationship merchants and travelers developed with it as they traveled along its course," said Director Yang Wei during an interview with the author. According to her, the show uses seven archetypes—a traveler, a guard, a messenger, and so on—to present stories that took place along this historic route. Unbounded by space or time, each of these archetypes embodies the foreign-travel experience of a different group of individuals, in a manner that may well be related to the social actors of globalized culture and transnationalism today.

On May 14, 2017, global leaders gathered in Beijing to attend a two-day inaugural summit on China's Belt and Road Initiative. This venture, implementing a trillion-dollar economic and diplomatic program, boosts what it calls the New Silk Road and represents official Chinese thinking with respect to globalization. China's emergence as a global leader, however, began long before the summit. In addition to creating vast new road and rail networks, energy projects, and other infrastructure across many parts of Eurasia, Africa, and even western Europe, China spends an estimated $10 billion annually on a plan to boost its soft power around the world. Expanding China's presence abroad is one of the government's desired strategies, and the Silk Road–themed theatrical dance dramas, and the Dunhuang expressive art forms in general, seem to many its most delightful form of soft power for attracting scholarly and media attention.

In 2022, for the first time, Chinese president Xi Jinping adopted the term *intangible cultural heritage* in a speech, underlining "the systematic protection of intangible cultural heritage and better promoting Chinese culture around the world."[3] This is a notable phenomenon. The Chinese scholarly community is highly attentive to any changes in key words and in general language that could lead to changes in state policies. The Chinese language is conceived to be isomorphic with the world that it describes; language is unified with the world, socially or otherwise. Hence, changes in language are believed to lead to similar changes in reality, and vice versa (Bao 1990). Some of the scholars with whom I interacted during my most recent research trip in China brought to my attention the "official adaptation of the term [*intangible cultural heritage*]," as they described it. Their reading is supported by China's increasing push for preserving and promoting its cultural heritages.

The choice of words and language reveals political-cultural significations and intertextual interferences in the Dunhuang arts. By the end of 2022, the Dunhuang Academy had finished compiling a digital data collection on 278 caves, processing the images in 164 of them, and making three-dimensional reconstructions of 145 painted sculptures and seven ruins, while delivering a panoramic tour program for 162 caves. Zhao Shengliang 趙聲良, Communist Party director of the Dunhuang Academy, stated that "the academy has strengthened cultural exchanges with more countries and regions, especially those along the Belt and Road."[4] Consequently, in 2023, celebrating the tenth anniversary of the Belt and Road Initiative, China's Belt and Road Portal—a state-run information portal supervised jointly by the National Development and Reform Commission and Xinhua News Agency and cohosted by the Xinhua-affiliated China Economic Information Service and the State Information Center—launched a newly revised Chinese and English interface. This portal, supported by "big data and artificial intelligence technologies," is ready to "better serve the needs of domestic and overseas users").[5]

This book, on staged Dunhuang expressive arts, tackles central issues of representation—the ways that performance arts are enlisted in representing the nation in sites ranging from local theaters in northwest China to large-scale international events. The stylistic choices made by the increasingly diversified global agents who have participated in mounting productions of the staged Dunhuang arts are often guided by the nature of the event and the effects the different organizing institutions would like to generate. Each of the case studies presented in this book was constructed within and created for a specific context. A single program may be staged for different audiences at different events.

The case studies of *The Thousand-Handed and Thousand-Eyed Avalokiteśvara*, *Lotus Aloft*, and *The Flying Apsaras* in chapter 6 and the documentary scripts in the appendices provide data on my research on the individual agents involved in, and state policies on, the arts. In the context of staging Dunhuang arts, contemporary cultural agents in China, both in discourse and practice, increasingly pattern their endeavors after the successes of artists from the Han, Sui, and Tang dynasties, when the arts were highly cultivated and actively promoted to showcase the country's sociocultural richness and political progress. Simultaneously, these historical epochs saw the incorporation of the arts into local, regional, and state policies aimed at governing diverse ethnic populations. The categorization and institutionalization process associated with the *Dunhuang bihua yuewu* as a Chinese classical dance genre presented in this study is a perfect example of such an administrative strategy. Another example I have presented is the comparison of the musical suites recorded in historical references, such as the *New Book of Tang*, and performed in the contemporarily staged Dunhuang arts. Comparative study shows that the staging and administration of musical suites representing ethnic groups have always been a state affair. Collecting these suites and staging them at rituals and state events demonstrates a pattern of cultural interpretation and administration of the state, historically and contemporarily.

The research that inspired this book started more than twenty years ago, in 2002. The staging of the Dunhuang expressive arts around the globe continues. It is interesting not only to study the intellectual history of the staged Dunhuang arts but also to become part of this history as I continue to study, publish, and interact with key personnel involved in the processes. Key concepts of the emerging Chinascape, such as *tianxia*, Dunhuang meta-elements, and cosmopolitanism, continue to evolve, given China's rise within the existing international system.[6] They are being developed into various forms, including musical compositions, theatrical dance dramas, and digital exhibitions such as the Smithsonian's "Pure Land: Inside the Mogao Grottoes at Dunhuang" and the Getty's "Cave Temples of Dunhuang: Buddhist Art on China's Silk Road."

On December 24, 2022, *Venice and Dunhuang above Desert and Sea*, a four-episode documentary reconnecting two ancient centers of culture, commerce, and trade, premiered on China's Central Television channels. As one of the most recently produced Dunhuang expressive arts projects, this documentary signals the continuity of cultural exchange and scholarly collaboration between China's Dunhuang Academy and Italy's Ca' Foscari University of Venice since 2017.[7] It represents aspirations for renewing China's Silk Road legacy through academic and cultural exchanges. This documentary does not focus on the multifaceted Dunhuang expressive arts alone; detailed accounts by Italian explorer Marco Polo (ca. 1254–1324) set the stage for spotlighting Dunhuang's strategic role on the Silk Road and for staging a conceptual landscape that participates in the continuous construction of a Chinascape (*Zhongguo jingguan* 中國景觀). Andreas Miranda, an Austro-Belgian multi-instrumentalist composer based in Berlin, instead of employing Zhang Qianyi or other composers from China who have worked on Dunhuang-themed projects, composed *The Lotus of Desert*, theme music for the documentary, after he visited Dunhuang in 2018. He also composed a piece titled *Apsara* (2020), which was used in an episode of *If Treasures Could Talk* (2020), a state-sponsored documentary on the nation's heritage conservation and preservation. Increasingly frequent invitations to global talents from China's state-sponsored staged Dunhuang arts projects signal the state's goal of continuing to build and develop new visions of Chinascapes beyond its border, embodied by cultural actors and friendly institutions.

## Finale

As I argue in the introduction, the development of the staged Dunhuang expressive arts as an integral part of contemporary China's advancement is a concealed trajectory of power, which deserves close examination in association with the *tianxia* concept. In 2023, Zhao Tingyang gave a talk titled "A Tianxia System as A Possible World for the Future" at the Aristotle-Confucius Symposium in Athens, Greece. In it, he proposed more specifically the need for "an alternative concept of the political as the art of changing hostility into hospitality," namely, the Tianxia system he reinvented on the basis of the original *tianxia* concept. Citing core Chinese classics such as *The Spring and Autumn Annals* 春秋 and *The Book of Documents* 尚書, Zhao (2023) spoke of *tianxia* as "the 3,000 years old concept of a world system . . . which defines an all-inclusive world of 'no outside' with 'great harmony' of all peoples or 'compatibility of all nations.'"[8] He stressed the need for a new alternative worldview: "If politics cannot stop hostility, it is no politics, nothing more than war. And war proves the failure of politics rather than the continuation of politics[,] as Carl von Clausewitz thinks."

In December 2023, as tension continued to rise in the international arena, audiences learned that the release day of *Heroes of Dunhuang* 敦煌英雄 (*Dunhuang ying xiong*), a film based on the history of the Guiyi Circuit 歸義軍 (see chap. 2) in the Dunhuang-Hexi Corridor territory, had been postponed. This film highlights how Zhang Yichao 張義潮 (799–872), a Han ethnic general and a resident of Dunhuang, and the Return-to-Allegiance Army rebel against the Tibetan regime, which ruled over Dunhuang from the second half of the eighth century to the mid-nineth century. Consequently, the film's Chinese-language synopsis uses two phrases that are often seen in narratives concerning pre-1997 Hong Kong and Taiwan to introduce the plot, in which the Guiyi jun reverted the Dunhuang-Hexi region to allegiance to the Tang Dynasty (618–907) empire: "not forgetting/abandoning" 不忘 (*buwang*) and "returned home" 回歸 (*huigui*).[9]

The delayed release day of *Heroes of Dunhuang* may in this case be interpreted metaphorically as deviating the trajectory of power and creating a neutral space for creativity and negotiations—"blank-retention" (*liubai* 留白). In the Chinese arts, the deliberate application of blank space on paper constitutes a profoundly artistic and skillful technique, grounded in considerable artistic, aesthetic, and moral prowess. This trajectory move is comparable to the "edge-hidden" (*cangfeng* 藏鋒) technique of withholding the tip or the edge of the brush in the middle part of the stroke in Chinese calligraphy and painting. In contrast to the "edge-exposure" (*lofeng* 露鋒) technique that exhibits force in each stroke by revealing the tip or the edge of the brush without any reservations, the "edge-hidden" technique embodies self-reflection and self-control. In this approach, the brush's tip or edge remains concealed within the middle part of the stroke. The "edge-hidden" technique therefore has been regarded as the rightful and proper way of using the brush because it reflects the quality of a noble character (*junzi* 君

子): modesty, humbleness, and inconspicuousness. In contemporary China, the interplay of sociopolitical choices and aesthetic principles, which has its roots in the era of master artists and calligraphers like Dong Zhongshu 董仲舒, 179–104 BCE), Cai Yong (蔡邕, 133–192 CE), Wang Xizhi (王羲之, 321–379 CE), Wu Daozi (吳道子, 689–759 CE), and Yan Zhenqing (顏真卿, 709–785 CE), continues to be a significant aspect of cultural expression. Once aestheticized through staged performances, such as that of the staged Dunhuang arts performances, the historical and topological landscape of Dunhuang becomes a performed narrative, embodying a national heritage that invites not only intertextual but also intercontextual interpretations.

Staging a nation's heritage abroad in contemporary theaters invites a new vision of homeland, borders, transnationalism, and the idea of "all under heaven." Later scenes in the dance drama *A Grand Dream of Dunhuang* portray through multiethnic music and dances the dynamic interactions among merchants, cultural and religious envoys, warriors, and politicians making their own journey from abroad to China. This theatrical dance drama presents a historically inspired, reimagined vision of both home and abroad to its audiences as they watch the young painter travel along the Silk Road and across the Gobi Desert to arrive at his own ideal, artistic "homeland," the Dunhuang Mogao Caves. Since his journey is ultimately a spiritual one, the conceptualization of traveling abroad could be perceived as a journey home. This sentiment is reminiscent of the poetic expression in *Bie Dong Da* (Saying Farewell to Dong Da 別董大) by High Tang poet Gao Shi 高適 (ca. 704–c. 765), a famous frontier poem long associated with the Chinese way of seeing the world in a relational manner: "Do not fret that on the road ahead there will be no friends, / for who is there in *tianxia* who does not know you?" (莫愁前路無知己，天下誰人不識君?).[10]

"Saying Farewell to Dong Da"
Ten miles of yellow clouds in twilight of the white sun:
The north wind blows the flying geese and the snowflakes all as one.
Do not fear that the road before you won't hold those who understand you.
Where in *tianxia*, sir, could you go and not be known?

別董大
千里黃雲白日曛
北風吹雁雪紛紛
莫愁前路無知己
天下誰人不識君

We find a similar sentiment interpreted intercontextually and expressed "scientifically" in Tuan Yi-fu's writing on cultural geography and an understanding of the earth as home: "A final observation. No matter how reductive and abstract may be an individual's line of research, geographers are never comfortable with the single vision of Newton or an economist. The reason is simple: if in every instance geographers insist on precision and quantifiability at the expense of a roundedness of view and resonance, they can never hope to understand the earth as home" (1991b: 106).

## Notes

1. The quoted passage in the *Great Learning* is translated by James Legge (1976) and is adopted by Donald Sturgeon in the Chinese Text Project: http://ctext.org.

2. See also Legge 1976: 411–412.

3. China's state media outlets have been reporting Xi's increasing focus on intangible cultural heritage. See Xinhua News, "Xi Stresses Systematic Protection of Intangible Cultural Heritage," December 12, 2022.

4. Xinhua News, "Xi Focus-Closeup: Protection Comes First for Cultural Heritage," June 12, 2023, *China Daily*, https://www.chinadaily.com.cn/a/202306/12/WS648663c1a 31033ad3f7bba54.html.

5. For details, see Shi Chunjiao and Zhang Wenyu, "China's Official Website for BRI Launches New Chinese, English Stations," Belt and Road Portal, edited by Yu Huichen, last modified July 20, 2023, https://eng.yidaiyilu.gov.cn/p/0J5T4KDL.html.

6. Mencius was one of the ancient philosophers who paid much attention to achieving peace in the ancient *tianxia* context: "If the world is to become peaceful at this time, who else but me should take the responsibility?" (Mencius 3B.13). In other words, instead of suggesting that everyone should become a ruler, Mencius suggests that a person should not escape responsibility for world peace and harmony (7A.9).

The late Sinologist Yu Yinshi 余英時 (1930–2021) argued that the tradition of caring for the world is the Chinese intellectuals' tradition. He pointed out that China's intellectualism, or the ideal of "following the Way of inquiry and learning" (*Dao wenxue*) that took center stage in late imperial thought, was set back only during the Song–Ming era, when anti-intellectualism, the ideal of "honoring one's heaven-endowed moral nature" (*zun dexing*), predominated (Yu 1975: 105–136). He quoted *Daxue* on the importance of continuing intellectualism or the Way of inquiry and learning for achieving the Dao of *tianxia*, or the right principles for governing *tianxia* because "*tianxia* will always be in a state of 'without Dao' or 'not fully submit to Dao'" (天下永遠是處在'無道'或不盡合於 '道'的狀態) (114, Kuang's translation). "Confucius's teaching says 'When right principles prevail in *tianxia*, there will be no disputes among the common people' (天下有道，則庶人不議)[.] In other words, 'There will be disputes among the common people when the incorrect principles prevail in *tianxia*' (天下無道則庶人議)." Yu's argument is pragmatic, certainly one that would appeal to elites, who he said are among the common people.

7. Ca' Foscari University of Venice and Dunhuang Academy signed a collaborative agreement in 2017 and jointly hosted *Jewel of the Silk Road: Buddhist Art of Dunhuang*, an exhibition in Venice in 2018.

8. For a complete transcript of Zhao Tingyang's 2023 speech at the Aristotle-Confucius Symposium in Athens, Greece, see http://philosophy.cass.cn/kygz/xszm/xfzx/202307/t20230713_5667651.html.

9. The handover of Hong Kong from the United Kingdom to the People's Republic of China occurred on July 1, 1997, bringing an end to 156 years of British rule. To see a few examples of the Chinese language synopsis, visit https://www.themoviedb.org/movie/1089598?language=zh-CN and http://culture.taiwan.cn/cul/202311/t20231108_12580059.htm. For an English-language synopsis, see https://www.imdb.com/title/tt28131387/.

10. *Dong Da* 董大 was the style name of Dong Tinglan 董庭蘭 (ca. 695–765), a famous Tang dynasty *qin* master, born in Long Xi 隴西 (now Gansu Province). I give two different translations of the poem in this section on purpose: they both serve the poet's hope to encourage faith and understanding in humanity.

# APPENDIXES

## Appendix A

*Postproduction Script for* Staging the Cosmopolitan Nation,
*an Ethnographic Documentary*[1]

**Staging the Cosmopolitan Nation: The Re-creation of the *Dunhuang yuewu***
**A Multicultural Music, Dance, and Theatrical Drama from China**
A documentary film (50 minutes)
Produced and Directed by Kuang, Lanlan
2008, 2009
All right reserved

**Trailer   1 minute**
    0:00:00–0:01:22

**Section I   Prologue—With What Eyes: The Multi-visualization of China**
5 minutes   (0:01:23–0:06:02)
a. This section puts forward inquiries on the multiple visions of China that are embedded, in terms of historical memory and eventful temporality in the contemporary and global discourse of cosmopolitanism and nationalism;
b. The *Dunhuang yuewu* is introduced as one of the many contemporary visions created based on archaeological sources and staged to represent a historically cosmopolitan, yet modern, Chinese nation;
c. General introductory history of the Northwest China, including its multi-faceted nature as a borderland region, its unique development as a strategic point on the ancient Silk Road, and its association with the Central Plateau of China sets the greater context for the birth of the *Dunhuang yuewu*.

**Section II   Staging the Visual—the Creation of the *Dunhuang yuewu* (Part One)**
4 minutes   (0:06:03–0:10:04)
a. This section combines interview, classroom and on-stage performances to introduce the process of creating the *Dunhuang yuewu* based on two albums of selected pictographic images used by Professor Gao Jinrong;
b. The visual source, which is "the re-creation of the past itself," makes note on the participation of different groups (or communities) of people involved historically in the modern creation of the *Dunhuang yuewu*. Specifically, in addition to choreographers, scholars (scholar-officials) and painters.

**Section III   Dunhuang—the Frontier Metropolis on the Silk Road (Part One)**
4 minutes    (0:10:05–0:14:08)

   a. This section traces the visual, archaeological source for the *Dunhuang yuewu* back to Dunhuang, the geo- and topo- graphical site on the ancient Silk Road and the Hexi Corridor; it highlights Dunhuang's important role as a frontier metropolis hosting traveling merchants, non-Han nationalists, during the Chinese Han, Wei, Jing, and Tang dynasties;

   b. Interviews with two prominent Dunhuang scholars in this section focus on the cultural exchanges on the Silk Road and the non-Han nationalities live in the region whose expressive arts has been embedded in the Chinese literary and artistic repertoire, such as the "Whirling Dance of the Hu" in Tang poetry.

**Section IV    Dunhuang—the Frontier Metropolis on the Silk Road (Part Two)**
3–4 minutes   (0:14:11–0:17:28)

   a. This section takes note on the performative and rhetorical processes by which non-Han cultural elements were recorded and localized in Dunhuang through the forms of dance and music on Buddhist [ritual] archaeological materials.

   b. Interview with Professor Zheng Binglin describes how Dunhuang is a crucial and unique representation of such cultural phenomenon in the geopolitical history of imperial China since the Han dynasty because it processes both the "frontier" or "borderland" characteristic as well as the "metropolis" or "cosmopolitan" characteristic.

**Section V   Staging the Visual—the Creation of the *Dunhuang yuewu* (Part Two)**
4 minutes    (0:17:28–0:21:57)

   a. Interview with Professor Dong Xijiu opens this section, which entails the becoming of the first Dunhuang inspired dance drama in the 1970s as it is since considered one of the benchmark and ground-breaking productions representative of the new Chinese nation since the Chinese Cultural Revolution;

   b. This section, through interviews, also explores how the Dunhuang inspired staged performances is rhetorically embedded in the whole (vs. local, regional, or a single group of nationality) modern Chinese national history through scholarly or "authentic" recognition, as they are at the beginning state-sponsored artistic productions;

   c. It is also through the performative process—modern theatrical dance drama with the *Dunhuang yuewu* elements that the modern choreographers recognize and define the groups/communities of people mentioned in Section II b, namely, the non-Han nationalities, the foreign merchants, the political and religious envoys, and painters into the contemporary Chinese national discourse.

**Section VI   Visualization of the Cosmopolitan Tang in Dunhuang Arts**
9 minutes    (0:21:58–0:30:55)

   a. How is Dunhuang and its artistic production a unique representation of China? This section focuses on the interplay between artistic developments in the Dunhuang region during the Han-Tang period and those in the Central Plateau. Through this lens, audiences gain insight into the visual representation of China within Dunhuang arts;;

b. While the general contents found in the Dunhuang Mogao murals reflect highly developed artistic techniques and styles due to frequent communication between a "centre" and a "peripheral," more specifically, the music and dance performances found in the arts (and not only the Dunhuang Mogao murals) confirm this cultural exchange phenomenon among the multi-ethnic groups;

c. This section focuses on the cosmopolitan nature of the Tang dynasty from the perspective of painting, dance, music, poetry, aesthetic philosophy and politics; it is to which the modern creation of the *Dunhuang yuewu* draws its essence from—a creative style which is at once open to Other and reflexive of Self.

## Section VII  Staging the Visual—the Creation of the *Dunhuang yuewu* (Part Three)

7 minutes     (0:30:56–0:37:55)

a. Why is the *Dunhuang yuewu* considered as a genre of classical Chinese dance? Is it because it is inspired by elements from a "cosmopolitan" past? This section explores the formation of Chinese Classical Dance as a theoretical concept at the time of the founding of the modern Chinese nation, and Professor Dong Xijiu talks about its association with the *Dunhuang yuewu*.

b. This section also shows the multifaceted elements—in addition to those from the ancient Dunhuang murals, that are found in the *Dunhuang yuewu* and how this modern creation plays an important role in the process of "renewal" of other forms in the Chinese expressive culture, including Peking Opera, Kun qu Opera.

c. Current development of the *Dunhuang yuewu*, including the history of its institutionalization into the Chinese dance curriculum, and the challenges exist during this process due to the "central" and "regional" conflict. This idea will be revisit[ed] and represent[ed] by the final performance include in this documentary.

## Section VIII  Staging the Visual—the Creation of the *Dunhuang yuewu* (Part Four)

8 minutes     (0:37:56–0:45:21)

a. This section begins with staged demonstrations of the *Dunhuang yuewu* by the Beijing Dance Academy students as well as those from the Gansu Vocational School of the Arts;

b. Professor Gao discusses, demonstrates, and teaches Kuang the three core elements of the *Dunhuang yuewu*;

c. Professor Zheng Binglin highlights the general and contextual aesthetic and political philosophy that maybe observed in the *Dunhuang yuewu* based on the Dunhuang mural arts as it is the source of the modern creation;

d. Discussion on the natures of audience and arts patrons.

**Section IX   Coda—the Colors in Between: Seeing One Nation in Multiplicity**
5 minutes     (0:45:22–0:50:00)
   a. How important is it to perceive the *Dunhuang yuewu* and its source—the arts
      from Dunhuang and elsewhere, in different contexts? This section with the
      narration in background explains the necessity to place the *Dunhuang yuewu*
      as well as its source, Dunhuang arts, in context beyond China's national stage;
   b. A selection of *Dunhuang yuewu* performances staged in different contexts
      and events in China showing the different forms the *Dunhuang yuewu* is
      represented to achieve different goals and for different groups of audience;
   c. Conclusion.

## *Sample Script with Narratives (Abridged) for*
## Staging the Cosmopolitan Nation

**Time code may be different depending on what kind of software is used to play the DVD.**

| Time | Outline | Abridged Subtitle Is Given to Support the Outline Sections |
|------|---------|------------------------------------------------------------|
| 00:00 | Thriller | |
| 00:08 | English film title: Staging the Cosmopolitan Nation: the Re-creation of the *Dunhuang yuewu*, a multicultural music, dance, and theatrical drama from Northwest China | |
| 00:10 | Chinese film title: 敦煌乐舞: 中国民族文化多元化之呈现<br><br>Producer and Director title: Kuang Lanlan 制片, 导演 邝蓝岚 | |
| 00:12 | **Section I**<br><br>This introductory section puts forward questions concerning the multiple "visions" that China as a modern nation bestows by its Self and Others (including those that are identified as Chinese nationalities, such as the ethnic minorities and those that are identified foreign).<br><br>History and its temporality are laid out in terms of time and space, also in the form of questions and are linked with ideas such as "imagined," "field," and "scopes."<br><br>These questions and terms intended to bring out the core question of China's contemporary national identity since its founding in 1949 and prepared for audiences a display of the *Dunhuang yuewu* as one of its many state-sponsoring created representations. | With what eyes does a nation like China see itself? With what eyes does a nation like China want to be seen? Through the eyes of one? The eyes of many? Or, of both?<br><br>And to see clearly the specifics and the infinite, to see that complex, delicate, and ever-changing interdependent relationship between the two,<br><br>How long must a nation like China travel back in time for a view extensive enough to reveal the numerous particulars that are imagined and re-imagined?<br><br>How far must a nation like China travel back in space for a field open enough to render the layered scopes that are created and re-created to present, however temporarily, a vision of a historically modern, cosmopolitan Chinese nation on the contemporary world stage? |
| | **End of Section I** | |
| 01:40 | **Section II**<br><br>This section opens with a staged performance of the *Dunhuang yuewu* and introduces it as "a modern and contemporary representation of cosmopolitanism." | The idea of "cosmopolitanism" is an ancient one, perhaps as old as its staged modern and contemporary Chinese representation, the *Dunhuang yuewu*. |

*Sample Script with Narratives (continued)*

| Time | Outline | Abridged Subtitle Is Given to Support the Outline Sections |
|---|---|---|
| | The film further delves into the nature of Dunhuang *yuewu* and its intricate features, particularly its connection to Buddhism. Subsequently, it explores the highly developed Buddhist arts uncovered through archaeological excavations at the Dunhuang Mogao and Yulin Grottoes. | The *Dunhuang yuewu* is a genre of multiethnic, multicultural music, dance, and theatrical drama historically derived from and discursively located in Northwest China. It is inspired by the performative images, narratives, and musical tunes depicted in the historical wall paintings, murals, and tablature discovered in the Dunhuang Mogao and Yulin Grottoes. The Mogao caves were declared a World Heritage Site by the United Nations Educational, Scientific, and Cultural Organization (UNESCO) in 1986 for their murals and wall paintings, spanning 1,000 years of Buddhist art, as Buddhism was introduced to China through the city Dunhuang, along the ancient Silk Road. |
| | Map with layering effects to show the material, cultural, and religious interactions along the Silk Route connecting China's Tang dynasty capital city Chang'an, Dunhuang, and India. The topographic recreation in this section is to hint on the notions of "contact zone," "center," "peripherals" and their independent and coherent influence on the Buddhist arts from Dunhuang Mogao Grottoes, and thus, the modern re-creation of the *Dunhuang yuewu*. | Originating from the ancient city Chang'an, present-day Xi'an in China's northwestern Shaanxi Province, and passing through the city Dunhuang, the Silk Road reaches as far as the shores of the Mediterranean, establishing invaluable sociocultural connections with metropolitan centers of imperial China and simultaneously transmitting the geopolitical concept of as well as the name "China" far beyond its Northwestern peripherals.<br><br>And yet, the peripheral often becomes the center, just as details eventually entail the whole, and interior foundation defines by its boundaries. |

*Sample Script with Narratives (continued)*

| Time | Outline | Abridged Subtitle Is Given to Support the Outline Sections |
|---|---|---|
|  | This section also briefly introduces a general history of the imperial China, especially the condition of the humanities arts during that time. This historical background allows further discussion on the aesthetic development of the Chinese performing arts, and specifically, the multifaceted *Dunhuang yuewu*. | Throughout the time of imperial China, the peripheral Northwest has been an utterly important region as it was the borderland area which delineated the geopolitical and cultural economic status of the Middle Kingdom, especially during the Han, Sui, and Tang dynasties. . . . It is also where battles were fought, powers were gained, and where the once prestigious scholar-officials from metropolitan centers of China were banished to, bringing with them cultural models from the Central Plateau that are to be transmitted elsewhere, beyond the shifting boundaries of ancient imperial China. It was there, on the vast land of Northwest, that civilizations clashed, learned, and thrived and the multicultural *Dunhuang yuewu* was first staged for its domestic and eventually, international audiences. |

**End of Section II**

# Appendix B

## *Postproduction Script for* Staging the Cosmopolitan Nation

| Shots for Edit | Narrative and Text for Subtitles |
| --- | --- |
| Footprints in the sky. Fireworks over the Beijing National Stadium (Bird's Nest), a venue of the 2008 Summer Olympics. | With what eyes does a nation like China see itself? With what eyes does a nation like China want to be seen? Through the eyes of one? The eyes of many? Or, of both? And to see clearly the specifics and the infinite, to see that complex, delicate, and ever-changing interdependent relationship between the two. How long must a nation like China travel back in time for a view extensive enough to reveal the numerous particulars that are imagined and reimagined?<br><br>—Show quoted text—<br><br>How far must a nation like China travel back in space for a field open enough to render the layered scopes that are created and recreated to present, however temporarily, a vision of a historically modern, cosmopolitan Chinese nation on the contemporary world stage? |
| *Thousand Hands Buddha Shiva* performed at (FACD) | The idea of cosmopolitanism is an ancient one, perhaps as old as its staged modern and contemporary Chinese representation, the *Dunhuang yuewu.* |
| Laying effect: ADI Yuan Dynasty, Yulin Grottoes, Cave 3 southern wall "transformation pictures of Buddhist script" (*jinbian*) lower section Twin dancers face each other | The *Dunhuang yuewu* is a genre of multiethnic, multicultural music, dance, and theatrical drama historically derived from and discursively located in Northwest China. It is inspired by the performative images, narratives, and musical tunes depicted in the historical wall paintings, statues, and tablature discovered in the Dunhuang Mogao and Yulin Grottoes. The Mogao Caves were declared a World Heritage Site by the United Nations Educational, Scientific, and Cultural Organization (UNESCO) in 1986 for their statues and wall paintings, spanning 1,000 years of Buddhist art, as Buddhism was introduced to China through the city of Dunhuang, along the ancient Silk Road. |

*Postproduction Script (continued)*

| Shots for Edit | Narrative and Text for Subtitles |
| --- | --- |
| Map of Tang Dynasty showing the main Silk Route connecting Chang'an, Dunhuang, and India. | Originating from the ancient city Chang'an, present-day Xi'an in China's northwestern Shaanxi Province, and passing through Dunhuang, the Silk Road reaches as far as the shores of the Mediterranean, establishing invaluable sociocultural connections with metropolitan centers of imperial China and simultaneously transmitting the geopolitical concept of, as well as the name, *China* far beyond its northwestern periphery. <br><br> And yet, the periphery often becomes the center, just as details eventually entail the whole, and a landscape is defined by its boundaries. |
| Monumental images from northwest China. Example: Relic of ancient Great Wall built during the Han Dynasty | Throughout the time of imperial China, the peripheral Northwest has been an important region, as it was the borderland area which delineated the geopolitical and cultural economic status of the Middle Kingdom, especially during the Han, Sui, and Tang dynasties. The Sui dynasty is marked by the reunification of southern and northern China, and the Tang dynasty is the period most often cited in relation to the idea of cosmopolitanism historically in China. The Han dynasty is China's first successful imperial state; it inherited the centralized organization from the short-lived Qin dynasty (221–207 BCE) and initiated some of the earliest encounters with the powers beyond China proper. <br><br> The Northwest region of China is where cultural models were first carried into the ancient imperial kingdom, with imported goods along the Silk Road. <br><br> It is also where battles were fought, powers were gained, and the once prestigious scholar-officials from metropolitan centers of China were banished to, bringing with them cultural models from the central plateau that were to be transmitted elsewhere, beyond the shifting boundaries of ancient imperial China. <br><br> It was there, on the vast land of Northwest, that civilizations clashed, learned, and thrived and the multicultural *Dunhuang yuewu* was first staged for its domestic and eventually, international audiences. |
| Close shot: Cover of "Ancient Dance Movement Pictographic Images" | These static, inked pictographic images, a recreation of a past themselves, are the tangible sources of the modern and contemporarily staged *Dunhuang yuewu*, which is perhaps the most representative of a sociohistorical phenomenon of cultural exchange and integration that took place in Northwest China. This hand-printed collection of "Images of Ancient Dance Movements" contains 123 pictographic images selected from archaeological materials found in China's northwestern Dunhuang region, namely, the performative images depicted in the historical wall-paintings and statues discovered in the Dunhuang Mogao and Yulin Grottoes, which span a period of one thousand years. |

*Postproduction Script (continued)*

| Shots for Edit | Narrative and Text for Subtitles |
| --- | --- |
| Kuang and Gao are looking at the collection of images. | Kuang (Voice):<br>Musicians, artists, choreographers, and playwrights often utilize historical materials in attempts to construct connections between the past and the present.<br><br>Ms. Gao Jinrong, Professor of Dance at China's Northwestern Minzu University and former President of Gansu Provincial School of the Arts, is known as the creator of the *Dunhuang wu*, meaning *Dunhuang dance*. She recreated, based primarily on this three-volume collection of "Ancient Dance Movement Pictographic Images," the first systematic training course of the Dunhuang dance, which laid the foundation for the development of the *Dunhuang yuewu* as a unique and independent dance genre on the contemporary stage. |
| *Guwu xinzi* data<br>14:04<br>Fade to Northwest Minzu University shots<br>Layer with original image sources from "Ancient Dance Movement Pictographic Images"<br><br>Cave 85 S Wall<br>39:41 Full shot | Kuang (Voice):<br><br>In the late 1970s, Professor Gao Jinrong, then President of Gansu Vocational School of the Arts, began to develop what she called the Dunhuang wall-painting dance. She was inspired and encouraged by *Flower Rain on the Silk Road*, one of the benchmark modern theatrical dance dramas from China. Her effort to recreate a genre of dance based on pictorial images from Dunhuang's wall-paintings was timely and well-acclaimed. The term *Dunhuang yuewu* was coined by modern Chinese dance scholars soon after she systematically developed a training course to teach this genre of dance. Now a faculty member at Gansu's Northwestern University for Nationalities, she has taught her course in various institutions in China, and abroad in Taiwan and the United States. |
| Image of Dunhuang scholars at Dunhuang<br>15:59–60 cut to<br>16:16 cut to<br>116:30 cut to<br>16:48–50 | The *Dunhuang yuewu* tends to draw primarily on performative images from the cosmopolitan Sui dynasty (581–618 CE) and the Tang dynasty (618–907 CE), while patterns established in the first (and earlier) imperial Han dynasty (206 BCE–220 CE) are also evident.<br>These performative images, narratives, and musical tunes are depicted in the historical wall paintings, statues, and tablature discovered in the Dunhuang Mogao and Yulin Grottoes in Gansu Province.<br>These historical materials embody the negotiation and contestation between monolithic and pluralistic value systems in China—processes that continue to this day. |

*Postproduction Script* (*continued*)

| Shots for Edit | Narrative and Text for Subtitles |
|---|---|
| Congling Mountain Dunhuang Mogao Grottoes Dunhuang Yulin Grottoes Camels carrying merchandise and walking in the desert | Today, the city of Dunhuang is situated in the common boundary of Gansu Province, Qinghai Province, and the Xinjiang Uighur Autonomous Region, a strategic point along the Silk Road in northwestern China and a crossroads of trade, as well as a locus for religious, cultural, and intellectual influences. Dunhuang's geopolitical location during the Han, Sui, and Tang dynasties enabled it to establish close cultural connections with metropolitan centers of China and adopt cultural models from peripheral kingdoms and beyond, as these were carried with imported goods along the Silk Road. |
| Tang Dynasty ceramic of Central Asian merchants and their camels. | Kuang (Voice): The name of "Silk Road" was first given to this route by a German geographer in the 1870s. At first, the function of the trade route was to transport silk and other fine, delicate, elegant, and portable goods, representing the civilization of ancient China, which enjoyed advanced agriculture and a well-developed handicraft industry. |
| Singers and dancers from Xinjiang Uighur Autonomous Region | Kuang: Present-day Northwest China was called the Western Region (*xiyu*), referring to the areas west of the Yumenguan Pass, including present Xinjiang and parts of Central Asia. Northwest China is densely populated by ethnic minorities. Ancestors of people living in this region created a brilliant civilization by merging the cultures of the nationalities of Han, Tibetan, Uighur, and Qiang. Yet why was Dunhuang, but not any other city in Northwest China, considered the most representative place of this historical multiculturalism? |
| Sarira casket from Subashi. Wood covered with hemp and painted. 6th–7th centuries. Otani Collection. Tokyo National Museum. | Kuang (Voice): Since ancient times, languages, names, rituals, and customs could all be associated with dances. Some dance performances were described in historical texts, such as the *New History of Tang*; some, however, were painted on archaeological materials, such as this Sarira casket from Subashi, a lost kingdom near Qiuci, present-day Kucha of Xinjiang Autonomous Region. According to Chinese dance scholar Dong Xijiu, the dance performance painted on this casket is Sumuzhe (苏目遮 or 飒磨遮). Not only is the name of this Buddhist ritual from the Western Region translated from Tocharian, or Kuchean to Chinese, but the dance performance was described in Tang dynasty poetry, and its name, Sumuzhe, became a particular Song dynasty lyric poem title for poets to compose, with its set rhythm, rhyme, and tempo. Beautifully decorated with performative images, this casket suggests the introduction of Buddhism and its art into Chinese culture through the Western Region. |

*Postproduction Script (continued)*

| Shots for Edit | Narrative and Text for Subtitles |
|---|---|
| Cut to murals from interview with Ji Xianlin 13:24 Still shot | Kuang (Voice): The evolving process and tangible samples for the localization of foreign cultures, religions, art, and especially Buddhism and Buddhism art, are all completely recorded and preserved along the Silk Road. Eventually, they reach Dunhuang. |
| Desert overlay with images of Buddhist caves and monks Interview of Zheng Binlin. | Kuang: The Silk Road functioned as the main road for migration and communication before the Western Han dynasty (206 BCE–25 CE). It is said that in the fourth century a Buddhist monk had a vision of a thousand Buddhas and began to carve grottoes into the sandstone cliff and fill them with Buddhist images. They were abandoned and forgotten around the 11th century, until Aurel Stein and other archaeologists arrived. |
| Interview of Ji Xianlin | Kuang (Voice): During the period of Wei-Jin (220–420), Buddhism was introduced along the Silk Road on a large scale due to continuous communication among the political powers of Europe, Africa, Southern Asia, and Western Asia and those along the Hexi Corridor with China's Central Plain region. |
| *Flower Rain on the Silk Road* | Kuang (Voice): The modern dance drama *Flower Rain on the Silk Road* is perhaps the first to portray China as an open, cosmopolitan state since the founding of the People's Republic of China in 1949. |
| Historical photos of Chinese leaders at Dunhuang. | Kuang: In the late 1970s, China began to recover from the turmoil caused by the infamous Cultural Revolution. China's post-Mao leaders began to reformulate their foreign policies. China has sought to foster international relations and enhance its social and economic development. Like the governments of many other multiethnic states, the Chinese government works to strengthen internal cohesion. It was at this time, to restrengthen China's culture and reestablish a heritage and a tradition agreeable to the people and acceptable by the post–Cultural Revolution Chinese government, that the China State Cultural Bureau commissioned scholars and artists to study the historical materials and recreate new artistic products, including the theatrical dance drama *Flower Rain on the Silk Road*, and later, the *Dunhuang yuewu*. Chinese dance scholars then institutionalized the *Dunhuang yuewu* as a genre within the also newly established tradition of Chinese classical dance, thereby making the genre a dynamic expressive resource embedded historically, performatively, and rhetorically in China's contemporary national discourse and available for further reconfiguration. |

*Postproduction Script (continued)*

| Shots for Edit | Narrative and Text for Subtitles |
| --- | --- |
| Data shots on painters | There is no doubt that the artistic technique, style, and compositional characteristics we observed in the Dunhuang wall-paintings and statues greatly affected the creation of the *Dunhuang yuewu*. In fact, the presence of artist-workers from Dunhuang was incorporated into the plot of modern *Dunhuang yuewu* dance dramas, such as *Flower Rain on the Silk Road*, and the more recently produced *Grand Dream of Dunhuang*.<br>Kuang (Voice):<br>By analyzing and comparing the artistic achievements in the Dunhuang region, we see that Buddhist art in Dunhuang should be understood as reflecting the overall painting techniques, patterns, skills, and accomplishments in China since the Wei-Jin period.<br><br>What does this artistic and historical fact tell us about the association between artist-workers from Dunhuang and the modern recreation of the *Dunhuang yuewu*?<br><br>Narrator: What is the role of painters in Dunhuang music and dance? |
| 24:16<br>Cut to | From "Go and see the characteristics of each period"<br>To "So by the Sui and Tang dynasties" |
| 24:46<br>Layer with Tang dynasty murals | Kuang:<br>Images from each dynastic period from ancient imperial China are perhaps one of the best representations of sociocultural and even political economic features of that time.<br><br>According to Professor Gao Jinrong and Professor Dong Xijiu, the *Dunhuang yuewu* tends to draw primarily on performative images from the cosmopolitan Sui dynasty (581–618 CE) and the Tang dynasty (618–907 CE); therefore, special features of aesthetic values from those dynastic periods are evident in contemporarily staged *Dunhuang yuewu*.<br><br>China's Sui dynasty is marked by the reunification of southern and northern China after almost 300 years of disjunction, and the Tang dynasty is the period most often cited in relation to the idea of cosmopolitanism historically in China. |

*Postproduction Script (continued)*

| Shots for Edit | Narrative and Text for Subtitles |
|---|---|
|  | The rise of so-called banquet music during the Tang symbolizes the prosperity of the empire and love for cultural affairs. According to historical references, the ten musical suites before the structural transformation during Emperor Tàizōng Lǐ Shìmín's reign are: *Suite Qīnshāng* 清商, *Suite from Western Liang* (*Xīliáng* 西凉), *Suite from India* (*Tiānlán* 天竺), *Suite from Goryeo* (*Gālì* 高麗), *The Whirling Dance Suite of Foreign Barbarians [from Uzbekistan]* (*Húxuán* 胡旋), *Suite from Kösän* (*Qiucí* 龟兹), *Suite from Bukhara* (*Ānguó* 安國), *Suite from Kashgar* (*Shūlè* 疏勒), *Suite from Samarkant* (*Kāngguó* 康國), and *Suite Wénchāng* 文康. Together, they represent the imperial culture of the Tang dynasty since it was founded by Lǐ Shìmín's father, Táng Emperor Gāozǔ Lǐ Yuān 李渊. China's colonization of Gāochāng (*Qočo* 高昌) in East Turkestan in 640 during Tàizōng Lǐ Shìmín's reign. This event is recorded in the chapter on music in *The Old Book of Táng* (*Jiù Táng shū* 舊唐書). Interactions and communications occurred with Gāochāng (*Qočo* 高昌) since the West Wei dynasty, and thus there were performances from Qočo. Emperor Tàizōng conquered Gāochāng, collected its music, composed *Yanyue* in addition, and dismissed the musical piece *Libi*. Presently whoever composes according to *ling* [would follow the structures] only by these ten suites. Even if [they would] not compose by *ling*, as long as the melody and parts are recognizable, *Yuefu* would place them [by the *ling* of these ten suites] still. This structural transformation of *The Ten Musical Suites* demanded by Emperor Tàizōng Lǐ Shìmín is particularly important in demonstrating (1) the emperor's musical aestheticism described in historical references, which emphasize the feeling of the human subject and the social function of music, and (2) the foreign policy of the Tang court regarding trade, diplomacy, and war with the frontier minorities—the barbarians from the surrounding foursquare borders of China (*sìyí* 四夷). Here, music is viewed as an embodiment of power; hierarchies that are formed through both peaceful and violent encounters between cultures and civilizations. In 640, Emperor Lǐ Shìmín conquered the Eastern Turkic Khanate (Hotan, kanate) and forged the Tang state into an overwhelming imperial power that the Turks could neither manipulate nor ultimately withstand. It is at this time that Lǐ Shìmín personally ordered *The Ten Musical Suites* to be reconstructed. We can see detailed descriptions of the *Suites from Qočo* (Gāochāng 高昌) in *The Old Book of Táng* (*Jiù Táng shū* 舊唐書): |

| Shots for Edit | Narrative and Text for Subtitles |
| --- | --- |
|  | Suites from Qočo (Gāochāng 高昌), two dancers, [dressed in] white jackets with embroidered sleeves, red leather boots, red leather belts, red headbands. For music [they] use one *dala* drum, one set of waisted drums, one *jilou* dram, one *jie* drum, two vertical notched flutes, two horizontal flutes, two *bili*, two four-stringed pipa (from China), two five-stringed pipa (from Central Eurasia), one bronze bell, and one angular harp. Angular harps are not extinct. |
|  | The instruments used to perform the Suite from Gāochāng (Qočo 高昌) are characteristic of the Eastern Turks. During the Tang dynasty, one of the most important changes in musical structure was the introduction of foreign instruments, which musicians began to incorporate, mainly from central Eurasia, into pieces composed for traditional Chinese instruments. Percussion instruments are among the most adoptable, and dances are believed to have become a main part of performances due to the selection of instruments. |
| 26.18 Cut other shots without black<br><br>Collaborate with narration<br><br>Version C 29:59 Xi'an Location Map | The Tang dynasty is the period most often cited in relation to the idea of cosmopolitanism historically in China. The eighth century was the most creative period of Chinese history in painting, poetry, and prose. Perhaps the reason for this is at least partially found in the immersive cultural exchange and infusion that took place during the chaos of the preceding centuries. |
| Cut 31:34 Xi'an Quick Panorama<br><br>Cut 36:00 Dunhuang Documents<br><br>Cut 31:56 Monks in Xi'an | Li Bai and Wang Wei were both born in the Northwest, where cultural and social exchange and mixture were most active and the human spirit became free and creative. This century gave us Li Po and Tu Fu and a good number of other first-class poets, Li Bai, Wang Wei, and Wu Daozi in painting, Chang Hsu in the "running style" and Yen Chench'ing in the formal style of calligraphy, and Han Yu in prose. |
| Version A Monk in Xi'an Translation Field (New Silk Road)<br><br>Cut 32:25<br><br>32:40 Long River sunset yen<br><br>33:00 Dunhuang Map<br><br>Afterwards, it's Wang Wei's music until 34:19<br><br>Dunhuang music and dance scenes<br><br>Layer on dance scores | Wang Wei introduced the spirit and technique of Chinese poetry into minute artistry, with its impressionism, its lyricism, its emphasis on atmosphere, and its pantheism. He was the consummate master of the short imagistic landscape poem, which came to typify classical Chinese poetry. He developed a landscape poetry of resounding tranquility, wherein deep understanding goes far beyond the words on the page—a poetic that can be traced to his assiduous practice of Ch'an (Zen) Buddhism. But despite this philosophical depth, many of his best poems are not difficult but are incredibly concise, composed of only twenty words, and they often invoke the tiniest of images: a bird's cry, a splinter of light on moss, an egret's wingbeat. Such imagistic clarity is related to the fact that Wang was one of China's greatest landscape painters. A famous poetic sentence by Wang Wei paints the scenery of Northwest China with words in a montage: |

*Postproduction Script (continued)*

| Shots for Edit | Narrative and Text for Subtitles |
| --- | --- |
| | Vast desert, stands out a vertical smoke toward the sky, |
| | Long river backgrounds a round sunset in the west. |
| | At Weicheng morning rain has dampened light dust, |
| | By the hostel, the willows are all fresh and green. |
| | I urge my friend to drink a last cup of wine. |
| | West of Yang Pass, there will be no friends. |
| | Wei City morning rain dampens the light dust, |
| | by this inn, green, newly green willows. |
| | I urge you to drink another cup of wine; |
| | West of Yang Pass are no old friends. |
| | It was in the Tang poetries modern and contemporary that scholars, painters, and chorographers found their inspiration of the modern and contemporarily staged *Dunhuang yuewu.* |
| | 那么这是否说明，敦煌乐舞并不能够反映历史朝代特征呢？ |
| | What is the meaning of time reflected in a modern recreation of ancient dance movements based on archaeological material such as the Dunhuang wall paintings? What is the relationship between the staged time and historical time? |
| | How do we select, or is it possible for us to select, a time, which we stage for our present audiences? |
| | What is the meaning of space represented in a modern theatrical dance drama based on the contents found in layers of historical wall paintings and documents from the ancient caves in Dunhuang? |
| | Zheng: |
| | The [Dunhuang] wall paintings are reflections of history |
| | Narrator: So is it because of this that Dunhuang dance is considered a genre of Chinese classical dance? |
| | Dong: "What is our classical dance?" |
| | 采访：5：14"我们的古典舞是什么呢？"切 |
| | Version B 45:31–47:23 |
| | Interview with Gao Zai Beiwu |
| | Narrator: Aesthetic and Audience Needs of That Era |
| | Who are the audience? Who has hope of seeing their own image? |
| Interview of Zheng Binlin. | Zheng: "In my opinion, |
| | 实际上我想， |
| | you should examine this with the Dunhuang wall-paintings. |
| | 你这块应该把敦煌壁画的体现来看。 |
| | You see, in the Dunhuang wall-paintings, |
| | 你看，要敦煌壁画里头， |
| | no matter what kind of wall-paintings, |
| | 不论什么样子的壁画， |

*Postproduction Script* (*continued*)

| Shots for Edit | Narrative and Text for Subtitles |
| --- | --- |
| | To present the eastern paradise or Pure Land of the Buddha Bhaishajua,<br>只要体现东方净土<br>or the western paradise or Pure Land of the Buddha Amitābha<br>或者西方净土,<br>or to present any Pure Land, in addition to a pond of Lotus Flower<br>那么体现净土，除了那荷花池以外，<br>There is scenery of performance.<br>上头呢就是一个表演场面。<br>What was being performed in these performative scenes?<br>表演场面里头表演的，啥东西？<br>On each of the two sides, instrumental performances."<br>两边是乐器，吹拉弹唱，<br>Kuang: "The performance is for the Buddhist gods."<br>邝：[可]它是表演给那个佛神看的<br>Zheng: "It is in essence performing for the audience.<br>郑：它实际上是表演给观众看的。<br>Because at such an important religious ritual,<br>因为大的法会，<br>it is mostly for the entertainment of the mass public.<br>它实际上以大部分的殉众，<br>In the center, there is dance [performance].<br>它中间部分啊，它有舞蹈。<br>The dance performances, we can predict,<br>舞蹈呢，咱们可以推测，<br>the 'Whirling Dance of the Hu,' or the 'Whirling in the Air Dance of the Hu'<br>胡旋舞或者胡腾舞，<br>let us put aside for now<br>那至于胡旋舞和胡腾舞它们之间的区别在哪<br>the difference between the two dances.<br>一般供养人拿到 一起看，<br>What are the inconsistencies that you will see?<br>In other words,<br>实际上就是，<br>emphasize the common and shared features,<br>突出了它的共性，<br>and diminish the individualities.<br>掩盖了它的个性。<br><br>那么共性越突出，<br>When similarities are emphasized,<br>人与人就没区别了。<br>There is no difference between peoples.<br>所以你能看到那个供养人， |

*Postproduction Script (continued)*

| Shots for Edit | Narrative and Text for Subtitles |
| --- | --- |
| | Therefore, the sponsors you see [their images], |
| | 不论是回鹘的， |
| | Whether if [they are] Uighur, |
| | 还是于阗的, Hétián, Yutian） |
| | Or Khotanian Ho·tan） |
| | 还是汉族的， |
| | Or Han |
| | 还是粟特的， |
| | Or Sogdian |
| | 都是一样的。 |
| | 佛的像貌跟菩萨的像貌， |
| | The image of Buddha and Bodhisattva |
| | 更人性化了。 |
| | 比如说菩萨这一块儿， |
| | For instance, take the image of Bodhisattva, |
| | 它原先是男性化， |
| | it was masculine |
| | 他有胡子有啥东西，很威严。 |
| | with a beard, and appeared to be very majestic. |
| | 但后来它就女性化了， |
| | Yet later it became very feminine, |
| | 它完全女性化， |
| | completely feminine |
| | 越来越女性化， |
| | just like a female." |
| | Kuang (Voice): |
| | Musical performance, some and most with dance performance. |
| | Is it possible to conclude that the *Dunhuang yuewu* is the secularized dance of Buddhism? |
| | 旁白: How have our views changed? Have they changed? Who is the audience? |
| | Kuang (Voice): |
| | In 1987, a time when reform was one of the most common terms in China's sociopolitical vocabulary, China began participating in international cultural and educational organizations, and the Mogao Grottoes were declared a World Heritage Site by the United Nations Educational, Scientific, and Cultural Organization. Today, the performative images from Dunhuang that inspire the musical instruments, dance movements, theatrical themes, and architectural models of the *Dunhuang yuewu* are frequently used to represent cultural and ethnic pluralism of China. |
| | China cannot grow without the rest of the world |
| | 中国发展，它离不开世界， |
| | Nor can the world prosper without China. |
| | 世界发展，它离不开中国。 |

| **Shots for Edit** | **Narrative and Text for Subtitles** |
| --- | --- |
|  | Kuang: |

To quote Nietzsche, "After Buddha was dead, they still showed his shadow in a cave for centuries—a tremendous, gruesome shadow. God is dead; but given the way people are, there may still for millennia be caves in which they show his shadow.—And we—we must still defeat his shadow as well!"[1]

Within the context created through the contemporarily staged *Dunhuang bihua yuewu*, the Buddha or its shadow are presented at a discourse, a narrative written beyond the language of one language through multi-semantic symbols; its openness rests upon the multi-symbolic narration that it represents.

By means of the documents that we now possess, it is possible to follow the great lines of the history and the evolution of Buddhist art from the moment when, at the beginning of the Christian era, it borrowed Hellenistic formulae from the Gandhára to the time when, in the fifth century and onwards to the eighth, it became transformed under the ever-expanding influence of China.

Today, the *Dunhuang yuewu* is staged, taught, and broadcast within a variety of contexts ranging from sites in Northwest China to metropolitan centers on the coasts and abroad.

Through discursively mediated practices, it becomes a presupposition and a constitutive force for a Chinese culture and participates in the construction of potential Chinascapes of historical and transnational mobility and the repositioning of large-scale group identities that are hypothetically conscious of the concept and signifiers of Chineseness. Each of these scapes is manifested in situated contexts of performance that offer potential for the reconceptualization of musical meaning and identity.

In 2008, the *Dunhuang yuewu* was staged during the opening ceremony of the Olympic Games in Beijing—a phenomenon that invites the study of the contesting and constitutive forces underlying the construction of the concept of Chineseness and its impact on the imagination of Chinese place, culture, and identity around the globe. Yet why are we seeing, here and now, the emergence of this multiethnic, multicultural, cosmopolitan vision of China?
What was presented to nearly 2 billion people worldwide on the date of August 8th, 2008?
Was the opening ceremony of the Beijing Olympics, a $300 million spectacle that featured 15,000 performers, nearly 11,000 athletes from 204 countries, merely "a dazzling display"?

*Postproduction Script (continued)*

| Shots for Edit | Narrative and Text for Subtitles |
| --- | --- |
| | The term *cosmopolitanism* is being interpreted and reinterpreted differently according to various specific contexts and gains new meanings over time. It came onstage as China and its image as a rapidly emerging modern nation is continuously shaping and being shaped by domestic and foreign influences in and from the past and the present. |
| | What we see is what *Dunhuang yuewu* represented: a poetic cosmopolitanism that has been marginalized in the contemporary Chinese cognitive schema—a nation that has constantly been sentenced and sentenced itself into exile, depending on its interaction with foreign influences and internal conflicts, with a people becoming diasporic within their own land due to the shifting changes in its context, a people nostalgic of an openness or nothingness that could allow the manifestation of newness—only the one that renders the ten thousand things of this world in such a way that they empty the self as they shimmer with the clarity of their own self-sufficient identity. |
| | Within this searching process, the *Dunhuang yuewu* was born, bearing with it the historical mark of a country looking outward. "With what eyes"—in a fragment left by Sappho, the ancient Greek poet, from many centuries ago, these words—rather than a question that has remained open for centuries, they were sung to a retrospective, poetic gaze, which allows us to imagine and then reimagine with the traces of a past that has not entirely passed. With what eyes, then, shall we see what is being staged and not imagine and reimagine China on the contemporary world stage? Buddha, in his earliest stage, had no form, nor an image—not until he was created and recognized. |
| | Perhaps Wang Wei's famous line, "the color of the mountain is between being and nonbeing," allows us to stand in-between—to see how light and silhouette, conflict and harmony, rehearse and perform for each other in time and space, and as one which shapes itself, in and of itself. |

[1] I quoted Friedrich Nietzsche's famous line in my documentary's narration (2001: 109).

# Appendix C

*Film Script for the Section on Dance in* The Chapter on Dunhuang, Gansu Province, *Episode 366*
*(Written by Yang Qian; Translated by Lanlan Kuang)*

**Interviewees for the Dance Section:**
**Gao Jinrong, and Shi Min, one of the lead dancers for the role of Ying Niang who is currently in Shanghai**

| Location | Shots and Movement | Narration | Interview Outline |
|---|---|---|---|
| Location to be confirmed | 1. Video from "Silk Road Flower Rain" on May 23, 1979<br>2. Capture the character of Ying Niang in the video | The static murals transformed into flowing music and dance, reviving the bustling scene of the prosperous era.<br>On May 23, 1979, the dance drama *Along the Silk Road*, created by the Gansu Provincial Song and Dance Troupe, was premiered. | |
| Location to be confirmed | He Yanyun Interview | He Yanyun: Dancing with a pipa in his hand, his arms pinned behind his back, sometimes "lightly twirling and slowly closing," sometimes "suddenly pouring rain." He had to repeatedly search for the S-shaped rhythm countless times, often resulting in stiff neck and back, and arm cramps. | |
| Lanzhou | Shooting the "bouncing pipa" shape at Lanzhou Dance Academy<br><br>Partial close-up | This "rebound pipa" ultimately became a legendary dance posture in the history of Chinese dance. Its prototype comes from a Bodhisattva with a pipa in Cave 112 of the Mogao Grottoes. In this dance drama, which tells the glorious history of Dunhuang, the creators bring many dance movements and shapes from the Dunhuang murals, marking the first time that Dunhuang dance moves have jumped from murals to the world. | |

*Film Script for the Section on Dance* (*continued*)

| Location | Shots and Movement | Narration | Interview Outline |
|---|---|---|---|
| Gansu Provincial Art School | 1. Choose a distinctive road or corridor with Dunhuang photos in the school for shooting.<br>2. During the rehearsal in the classroom, Professor Gao Jinrong is explaining to the students the three curved shapes in Dunhuang dance movements. | When *Along the Silk Road* first emerged, Gao Jinrong, the principal of Gansu Provincial Art School, was deeply attracted by the dance posture with the characteristic of three bends. She came to Dunhuang to personally experience its musical charm from the murals. | |
| Professor Gao's Office Or at home | 1. Mr. Wu Manying's paintings of Dunhuang Dance Figure | Gao Jinrong: I am very lucky to have obtained the keys to over 200 caves, and I can go in and see each one. Master Chang Shuhong (Dunhuang Academy's first Director) also gave me a copy of the Dunhuang dance pose by Mr. Wu Manying, and I hung it in my office, constantly pondering every detail of the movements. | |
| Gansu Provincial Art School | 1. Professor Gao Jinrong watches students' dance rehearsal<br>2. The natural light in the classroom gradually disappears, and a more stagelike effect can be seen.<br>3. Passing through the actors in the dance, filming Professor Gao Jinrong's expression in slow motion<br>4. Close-up of Professor Gao Jinrong | Gao Jinrong, who has devoted her life to dance creation and teaching, understands that these dance movements have distinct characteristics and are different from all existing dance genres. She summarized various dance movements in murals, grasped the dynamic connections, and determined to extract and explore a new genre. | |

| Gansu Provincial Art School | 1. Person interviews<br>2. Still in the environment of the rehearsal room, dimming the surrounding environment, creating a sense of stage with lighting, and filming dancers.<br>3. Partial close-up of eyes, fingers, arms, toes, etc. | The expression is rich in eyes, the posture of the hands is slender and diverse in fingers, the arms and wrists are soft and curved with classical beauty, the toes are sometimes raised and sometimes curved, the overall posture is sinking, and the props are generally made of long silk waist-drum pipa. It originated from Dunhuang, and I named it *Dunhuang wu* (Dunhuang dance). |
| Source material | Mural<br>Cross editing with dance movements | After a long period of polishing, Gao Jinrong established the style of Dunhuang dance, mainly featuring Tang style, with both Buddhist and Western style, and absorbed the footwork and movements of local dance. |
| Professor Gao's Office Or at home | 1. Professor Gao Jinrong is reading old materials and dancing design drawings at home<br>2. A group of shots of Professor Gao Jinrong viewing murals at the Lanzhou Dunhuang Digital Exhibition Hall | In 1981, Gao Jinrong began to enroll Dunhuang dance classes specializing in this dance at Gansu Provincial Art School, using the outline of *Dunhuang Dance Basic Practice*, a textbook he had compiled. At the end of this year, various research experts from the Dunhuang Research Institute saw the Dunhuang dance performance created by him and his students, which stunned four people for a moment. |
| Professor Gao's Office Or at home | Professor Gao Jinrong Interview | Gao Jinrong: Everyone says that this is Dunhuang dance. |

*Film Script for the Section on Dance* (continued)

| Location | Shots and Movement | Narration | Interview Outline |
| --- | --- | --- | --- |
| Professor Gao's Office Or at home | 1. Collection of materials from that year<br>2. Scenery shot of Gansu Provincial Art School and the Empty Mirror of Dunhuang Dance Teaching and Research Office<br>3. Scenery shot for Students' Dance Practice | On August 12, 1982, an article in the *Guangming Daily* titled "Revival of Millennium Ancient Dance, Reproduction of Mural Fairy Posture" made Dunhuang dance famous everywhere, and countless artists and dancers came to observe it. Under the careful arrangement of Gao Jinrong, Dunhuang dance plays such as *Thousand Handed Guanyin*, *Miaoyin Rebound*, and *Huanteng Jile* have achieved success. Gao Jinrong trained batch after batch of students at Gansu Provincial Art School. Dunhuang dance also began to take root and sprout everywhere. | Data collection<br>1. The old newspaper that reported on Dunhuang dance back then<br>2. Photos of Gao Jinrong in Dunhuang back then<br>3. Dance videos. |
| Beijing Dance Academy | 1. Shi Min's Character Mirror at Beijing Dance Academy<br>2. Shi Min solo dances the role of Ying Niang onstage, while Professor Gao Jinrong watches from the stage.<br>3. Leave a beam of chasing light on stage. Pay attention to filming the relationship shots and close-up of the two teachers.<br>4. Remember to leave blank space on the stage for the mid-panoramic shot of Shi Min's solo dance, and overlay old video materials in the later stage. | In 2007, the Beijing Dance Academy offered a course on Dunhuang dance, and her proposer was Shi Min, who had played the third generation of Ying Niang in *Silk Road Flower Rain*. She has always been committed to learning and researching Dunhuang dance and wants to impart her insights into Dunhuang culture to more people. | |

| Lanzhou | Shi Min Interview | Shi Min: Dunhuang dance comes from the human civilization on the Silk Road, and is also an art presentation after cultural integration. I want students to pursue the beauty from the Buddhist world from the bottom of their hearts and experience the artistic atmosphere of that splendid culture. | Did you learn that for the first time, you added a male character to Dunhuang dance? Could you please explain how you designed and encountered any difficulties in the process of reference materials? Dunhuang art is a fusion of diverse cultures; how can it be seen from the movements of Dunhuang dance? Can you explain your understanding of Dunhuang mural art by combining dance with the special copying of murals using your body? |
| --- | --- | --- | --- |
| Beijing | 1. Record of Shi Min Teaching Students at Beijing Dance Academy | In early 2010, the Classical Dance Department of Beijing Dance Academy officially established the Dunhuang Dance Teaching and Research Office. In the long-term work plan, the balanced development of Dunhuang dance has become the core content of the research work of the teaching and research office. | You are also the actress of the dance drama *Silk Road Flower Rain*. How did you feel when you first got this role? Has someone played it before you, and is it stressful for you? On the other hand, you have shaped this character; what does this character bring to you? |
| Lanzhou | Documentary: Shi Min and Gao Jinrong attended the 2019 *Along the Silk Road Colloquium* | Documentary: Shi Min and Gao Jinrong participated in the 2019 *Along the Silk Road Colloquium* | |

*Film Script for the Section on Dance* (*continued*)

| Location | Shots and Movement | Narration | Interview Outline |
| --- | --- | --- | --- |
| | 1. Cross editing of a set of empty mirrors from domestic and foreign cities and Dunhuang dance dramas | The art of dance has been revived from Dunhuang murals, and the ancient Silk Road culture has taken on a wider world in such a colorful form. | In 2010, the Dunhuang Teaching and Research Office of Beijing Dance Academy was established. You have always wanted the world to tell your own story. I think the establishment of the teaching and research office will be helpful for your wishes. How do you understand what you mean by "your own story"?<br>The creation of Dunhuang dance art is an exploration of Dunhuang cultural and historical resources. How can Dunhuang dance exist in the future and provide a more creative display of Dunhuang art? |

[1] Multimedia components for *Staging* Tianxia, such as maps, working color metagraphs, audiovisual files, and documentary film clips, can be found at https://lanlankuangofficial.pub/.

# REFERENCES


Allen, Graham. 2000. *Intertextuality*. London: Routledge.

Allsen, J. Michael. 1993. "Intertextuality and Compositional Process in Two Cantilena Motets by Hugo de Lantins." *Journal of Musicology* 11, no. 2 (Spring): 174–202.

Alons, Ana Maria. 1994. "The Politics of Space, Time and Substance: State Formation, Nationalism and Ethnicity." *Annual Review of Anthropology* 23:379–405.

Anagnost, Ann. 1997. *National Past-Times: Narrative, Representation, and Power in Modern China (Body, Commodity, Text)*. Durham, NC: Duke University Press.

Anderson, Benedict. 1993. *Imagined Communities: Reflections on the Origin and Spread of Nationalism*. London: Verso.

Appadurai, Arjun. 1990. "Disjuncture and Difference in the Global Cultural Economy." *Public Culture* 2 (2): 1–24.

———. 2002. "Introduction." In *China off Center: Mapping the Margins of the Middle Kingdom*, edited by Susan D. Blum and Lionel M. Jensen, xiii–xvi. Honolulu: University of Hawai'i Press.

———. 2003. *Modernity at Large: Cultural Dimensions of Globalization*. Minneapolis: University of Minnesota Press.

Aylesworth, Gary. 2010. "Postmodernism." In *The Stanford Encyclopedia of Philosophy*, edited by Edward N. Zalta. Stanford University, winter 2010 edition. http://plato.stanford.edu /archives/win2010/entries/postmodernism.

Baert, Patrick. 1998. "Foucault's History of the Present as Self-Referential Knowledge Acquisition." *Philosophy and Social Criticism* 24:111–126.

Bai, Juyi 白居易. 1980. "Pipa xing 琵琶行." In *Bai Juyi xuanji* 白居易選集 [A selection of Bai Juyi's writings], 177. Shanghai: Guji chubanshe.

Bakhtin, Mikhail Mikhaïlovich. 1982. *The Dialogic Imagination: Four Essays*. Austin: University of Texas Press.

———. 1995. "Supplement: The Problem of Content, Material, and Form in Verbal Art." In *Art and Answerability: Early Philosophical Essays by M. M. Bakhtin*, 208. Austin: University of Texas Press.

Ban Gu 班固. 1962. *Han shu.* 漢書. Beijing: Zhonghua shuju.

Bao, Zhiming. 1990. "Language and World View in Ancient China." *Philosophy East and West*, 40 (2): 195–219.

Barrett, William. 1962. *Irrational Man: A Study in Existential Philosophy*. New York: Anchor.

Barthes, Roland. 1970. "L'Étrangère." *La Quinzaine littéraire*, May 1–15, 19–20.

Barz, Gregory F., and Timothy J. Cooley. 1997. *Shadows in the Field: New Perspectives for Fieldwork in Ethnomusicology*. New York: Oxford University Press.

Baudrillard, Jean. 2000. *The Vital Illusion*. Edited by Julia Witwer. New York: Columbia University Press.

———. 2001. *Impossible Exchange*. Translated by Chris Turner. London: Verso.

Bauman, Richard. 1992. "Contextualization, Tradition, and the Dialogue of Genres: Icelandic Legends of the *kraftaskáld*." In *Rethinking Context: Language as an*

*Interactive Phenomenon*, edited by Alessandro Duranti and Charles Goodwin, 125–145. Cambridge: Cambridge University Press.

———. 2001a. "Tradition, Anthropology of." In *International Encyclopedia of the Social and Behavioral Sciences*, edited by Neil J. Smelser and Paul B. Baltes, 23:15819–15824. London: Elsevier.

———. 2001b. "Verbal Art as Performance." In *Linguistic Anthropology: A Reader*, edited by Alessandro Duranti, 290–311. Malden, MA: Blackwell.

———. 2004. *A World of Others' Words: Cross-Cultural Perspectives on Intertextuality*. Hoboken, NJ: Wiley-Blackwell.

Bauman, Richard, and Charles L. Briggs. 1990. "Poetics and Performance as Critical Perspectives on Language and Social Life." *Annual Review of Anthropology* 19:59–88.

———. 2003. *Modernizing Discourse: Language Ideologies and the Politics of Inequality*. Cambridge: Cambridge University Press.

Beck, Ulrich. 2006. *Cosmopolitan Vision*. Cambridge: Polity.

Berlin, Isaiah. 1979. *Against the Current: Essays in the History of Ideas*. Edited by Henry Hardy. London: Hogarth Press.

———. 2000. *The Proper Study of Mankind: An Anthology of Essays*. Edited by Henry Hardy and Roger Hausheer. New York: Farrar, Straus and Giroux.

Bi, Nan. 2022. "Chinese Elements Highlighted at Olympic Closing Ceremony." *China Daily HK*, February 22. https://www.chinadailyhk.com/article/260792.

Bielawski, Ludwik, and Ludwik Wiewiorkowski. 1985. "History in Ethnomusicology." *Yearbook for Traditional Music* 17:8–15.

Blacking, John. 1995. *Music, Culture, and Experience: Selected Papers of John Blacking*, edited by Reginald Byron. Chicago: University of Chicago Press.

Bloch, Marc. 1964. *The Historian's Craft: Reflections on the Nature and Uses of History and the Techniques and Methods of Those Who Write It*. Translated by Peter Putnam. New York: Vintage.

Bloom, Harold. 1973. *The Anxiety of Influence: A Theory of Poetry*. Oxford: Oxford University Press.

Blum, Susan D., and Lionel M. Jensen, eds. 2002. *China Off Center: Mapping the Margins of the Middle Kingdom*. Honolulu: University of Hawai'i Press.

Bohlman, Philip V. 1991. "Representation and Cultural Critique in the History of Ethnomusicology." In *Comparative Musicology and Anthropology of Music: Essays on the History of Ethnomusicology*, edited by Bruno Nettl and Philip V. Bohlman, 131–151. Chicago: University of Chicago Press.

———. 1999. "Ontologies of Music." In *Rethinking Music*, edited by Nicholas Cook and Mark Everist, 17–34. Oxford: Oxford University Press.

———. 2002a. "Europe and North America." In *The World's Music: General Perspective and Research Tool*. Vol. 10 of *Garland Encyclopedia of World Music*, edited by Ruth M. Stone, 157–168. New York: Routledge.

———. 2002b. "World Music at the 'End of History.'" *Ethnomusicology* 46:1–32.

Bokenkamp, Stephen R. 2004. "The Silkworm and the Bodhi Tree: The Lingbao Attempt to Replace Buddhism in China and Our Attempt to Place Lingbao Daoism." In *Religion and Chinese Society: Ancient and Medieval China*, edited by John Lagerwey, 1:317–339. Hong Kong: Chinese University of Hong Kong Press.

Bol, Peter K. 1994. *"This Culture of Ours": Intellectual Transitions in T'ang and Sung China*. Stanford, CA: Stanford University Press.

———. 2022. "On the Spatio-temporal Analysis of Religious Institutions." In *The Formation of Regional Religious Systems in Greater China*, edited by Jiang Wu, 58–70. New York: Routledge.

Bourdieu, Pierre. 1991. *Language and Symbolic Power*. Edited by John B. Thompson. Translated by Gino Raymond and Matthew Adamson. Malden, MA: Polity.

Breuilly, John. 2007. "Nationalism and Historians: Some Reflections; The Formation of National(ist) Historiographical Discourse." In *Nationalism, Historiography and the (Re) Construction of the Past*, edited by Claire Norton, 1–28. Washington, DC: New Academia.

Briggs, Charles L. 1993. "Generic versus Metapragmatic Dimensions of Warao Narratives: Who Regiments Performance." In *Reflexive Language: Reported Speech and Metapragmatics*, edited by John A. Lucy, 179–212. Cambridge, MA: Cambridge University Press.

Brook, Timothy. 1993. "Rethinking Syncretism: The Unity of the Three Teachings and Their Joint Worship in Late Imperial China." *Journal of Chinese Religions* 21 (Fall): 13–44.

Brown, Michael F. 2004. *Who Owns Native Culture?* Cambridge, MA: Harvard University Press.

Brown, Wendy. 1995. *States of Injury: Power and Freedom in Late Modernity*. Princeton, NJ: Princeton University Press.

Buchli, Victor, and Gavin Lucas. 2001. *Archaeologies of the Contemporary Past*. London: Routledge.

Bulag, Uradyn E. 2012. "Seeing Like a Minority: Political Tourism and the Struggle for Recognition in China." *Journal of Current Chinese Affairs* 41 (4): 133–158.

———. 2023. "Introduction: Ethnic Politics, War and the Future of Multinational States." *Inner Asia* 25 (1): 1–6.

Bush, Susan. 1998. "The Double Screen: Medium and Representation in Chinese Painting." *China Review International* 5:271–277.

Butler, Judith. 1993. *Bodies That Matter: On the Discursive Limits of Sex*. New York: Routledge.

Butler, Lawrence. 2005. "Silk Road Buddhist Cave Art in American Collections: Recovering the Context." *East–West Connections: Review of Asian Studies* 5:61–74.

Cai, Yuandi. 2010. "Textual Research on a Fragment of Dunhuang Manuscript: Bi Shi Lun (The Law of Brush Strokes)." *Dunhuang Research* 121 (3): 111–114.

———. 2012. "Xinyu shuwucang Dunhuang wupujuan yu jiaolu bing yanjiu. 杏雨書屋藏敦煌舞譜卷子校錄並研究" [Transcription and study of the Xinyushuwu Collection of Dunhuang Dance Notation]. *Dunhuang Research* 敦煌研究 131:100–105.

Cai, Zhongde. 1995. *Zhongguo Yinyue Meixueshi* 中國音樂美學史 [A history of Chinese musical aesthetics]. Beijing: Renmin Yinyue Chubanshe.

Cai, Zong-qi. 2001. *Configurations of Comparative Poetics: Three Perspectives on Western and Chinese Literary Criticism*. Honolulu: University of Hawai'i Press.

———, ed. 2004. *Chinese Aesthetics: The Ordering of Literature, the Arts, and the Universe in the Six Dynasties*. Honolulu: University of Hawai'i Press.

———. 2010. "Evolving Practices of *Guan* and Liu Xie's Theory of Literary Interpretation." In *Interpretation and Literature in Early Medieval China*, edited by Alan K. L. Chan and Yuet-keung Lo, 103–132. SUNY Series in Chinese Philosophy and Culture. Albany: State University of New York Press.

Calame, Claude. 2009. *Poetic and Performative Memory in Ancient Greece: Heroic Reference and Ritual Gestures in Time and Space*. Translated by Harlan Patton. Cambridge, MA: Harvard University Press.

Calhoun, Craig. 2007. *Nations Matter: Culture, History, and the Cosmopolitan Dream.* London: Routledge.

Callahan, William A. 2007. "Tianxia, Empire, and the World: Soft Power and China's Foreign Policy Discourse in the 21st Century." British Inter-university China Center Working Paper Series, no. 1.

———. 2008. "Chinese Visions of World Order: Post-hegemonic or a New Hegemony?" *International Studies Review* 10:749–761.

Cao, Yin 曹寅, et al., comps. 1960. *Quan Tang shi* 全唐詩. Beijing: Zhonghua shuju.

Caparini, Marina, ed. 2004. *Media in Security and Governance: The Role of the News Media in Security Oversight and Accountability.* Baden-Baden: Nomos.

Cartelli, Mary Anne. 2013. *The Five-Colored Clouds of Mount Wutai: Poems from Dunhuang.* Leiden: Brill.

Castells, Manuel. 2010. *The Power of Identity.* Oxford: Wiley Blackwell.

Chai, Jianhong. 2007. *Dunhuang xue yu Dunhuang wenhua* 敦煌學與敦煌文 [Dunhuang studies and Dunhuang culture]. Shanghai: Shanghai guji chuanbshe.

Chang, Chang. 2011. *Decorative Designs from China Dunhuang Murals.* Hong Kong: Hong Kong University Press.

Chen, Huaiyu, and Q. Edward Wang. 2020. "Dunhuang on the Silk Road: A Hub of Eurasian Cultural Exchange—Introduction." *Chinese Studies in History* 53 (3): 187–191.

Chen, Kenneth K. S. 1973. *The Chinese Transformation of Buddhism.* Princeton, NJ: Princeton University Press.

Chen, S. P., C. Yeh, S. Wang, and Qun Che. 2023. "Treating a Genre as a Database: A Digital Research Methodology for Studying Chinese Local Gazetteers." *International Journal of Digital Humanities* 4:171–193.

Chen, Yingshi. 2005. *Dunhuang yuepu jieyi bianzheng* 敦煌樂譜解疑辯證 [Analysis of the Dunhuang music score notation]. Shanghai: Shanghai Yinyue Xueyuan Chubanshe.

Chen, Yushu, and Huang Bing. 2022. "The Influence of Daoist Astrology on the Chinese Visual Representation of Tejaprabha Buddha." *Religions* 13 (1016): 1–18.

Cheng, François. 2017. *Chinese Poetic Writing.* New York: New York Review Books.

Cheown, Eric Teo Chu. 1969. "China as the Center of Asian Economic Integration." *China Brief* 4 (15): 3–5.

Chhabra, Deepak, Robert Healy, and Erin Sills. 2003. "Staged Authenticity and Heritage Tourism." *Annals of Tourism Research* 30:702–719.

Ching, Julia. 1997. "Son of Heaven: Sacral Kingship in Ancient China." *T'oung Pao* 83:3–41.

Chow, Rey. 1998. "Introduction: On Chineseness as a Theoretical Problem." *Boundary 2* 25 (3): 1–24.

———. 2001. *Modern Chinese Literary and Cultural Studies in the Age of Theory: Reimagining a Field (Asia-Pacific: Culture, Politics, and Society).* Durham, NC: Duke University Press.

———. 2005. *The Age of the World Target: Self-referentiality in War, Theory, and Comparative Work (Next Wave Provocations).* Durham, NC: Duke University Press.

Chuang, Penli. 1972. "A Historical and Comparative Study of Hsün, the Chinese Ocarina." *Bulletin of the Institute of Ethnology, Academia Sinica* 33:177–253.

Clifford, James. 1983. "On Ethnographic Authority." *Representations* 2: 118–146.

———. 1986a. "Introduction: Partial Truths." *Writing Culture: The Poetics and Politics of Ethnography*, edited by James Clifford and George E. Marcus, 1–26. Berkeley: University of California Press.

———. 1986b. "On Ethnographic Allegory." *Writing Culture: The Poetics and Politics of Ethnography*, edited by James Clifford and George E. Marcus, 98–121. Berkeley: University of California Press.

Clifford, James, and George E. Marcus, eds. 1986. *Writing Culture: The Poetics and Politics of Ethnography*. Berkeley: University of California.

Cody, Gabrielle H., and Evert Sprinchorn, eds. 2007. *The Columbia Encyclopedia of Modern Drama*. Columbia University Press, 2007.

Cook, Nicholas. 2001. *Analysing Musical Multimedia*. Oxford: Oxford University Press.

Cook, Nicholas, and Mark Everist, eds. 2001. *Rethinking Music*. New York: Oxford University Press.

Currie, Gabriela, and Lars Christensen. 2022. *Eurasian Musical Journeys: Five Tales*. Elements in the Global Middle Ages. Cambridge: Cambridge University Press.

Dai, Jinhua, and Judy T. H. Chen. 1997. "Imagined Nostalgia." *Boundary* 24:143–161.

Daniel, Yvonne Payne. 1996. "Tourism Dance Performances: Authenticity and Creativity." *Annals of Tourism Research* 23:780–797.

Davis, Sara L. M. 2005. *Song and Silence: Ethnic Revival on China's Southwest Borders*. New York: Columbia University Press.

Dear, Michael J., and Steven Flusty, eds. 2002. *The Spaces of Postmodernity: Readings in Human Geography*. Oxford: Blackwell.

DeLisle, Jacques. 2022. "Beijing's Olympic Moments, 2008 and 2022: How China and the Meaning of the Games Have, and Have Not, Changed." *Foreign Policy Research Institute*, February 3. https://policycommons.net/artifacts/2232816/beijings-olympic-moments-2008-and-2022/2990747/.

DeMare, Brian. 2012. "Local Actors and National Politics: Rural Amateur Drama Troupes and Mass Campaigns in Hubei Province, 1949–1953." *Modern Chinese Literature and Culture* 24 (2): 129–178.

Demas, Martha, Neville Agnew, Jinshi Fan, and Shin Maekawa. 2015. *Strategies for Sustainable Tourism at the Mogao Grottoes of Dunhuang, China*. Cham: Springer International.

Demiéville, Paul, and Jao Tsung-i. 1971. *Airs de Touen-houang=Touen-houang k'iu: Textes à chanter des VIII$^e$–X$^e$ siècles manuscrits reproduits en fac-similé*, Mission Paul Pelliot. Documents conservés à la Bibliothèque nationale 2. Paris: Éditions du Centre national de la recherche scientifique.

Demirduzen, Cagla, and Cameron G Thies. 2022. "A Role Theory Approach to Grand Strategy: Horizontal Role Contestation and Consensus in the Case of China." *Journal of Global Security Studies* 7 (1): ogab018.

Deng, Xiaoping. 1984. "Building a Socialism with a Specifically Chinese Character." *Deng Xiaoping Works*, June 30. https://www.marxists.org/reference/archive/deng-xiaoping/1984/36.htm.

———. 1985. *Build Socialism with Chinese Characteristics*. Beijing: Foreign Languages.

Denton, Kirk A. 2005. "Museums, Memorial Sites and Exhibitionary Culture in the People's Republic of China." *China Quarterly* 183:566–586.

DeWoskin, Kenneth. 2001. "Chinese Philosophy and Aesthetics." In *East Asia: China, Japan, and Korea*. Vol. 7 of *Garland Encyclopedia of World Music*, edited by Robert C. Provine, Yosihiko Tokumaru, and J. Lawrence Witzleben, 97–104. New York: Garland.

Diamond, Elin. 1996. Introduction to *Performance and Cultural Politics*, edited by Eli Diamond, 1–12. London: Routledge.

Ding, Zijiang. 2010. "An Aesthetical Examination of Traditional Chinese Illustration." *Academic Perspective: Chinese Scholars Association—Southern California* 6:52–64.

Dirlik, Arif. 2011. "Guoxue / National Learning in the Age of Global Modernity." *China Perspectives* 1:90–91.

Doi, Mary Masayo. 2002. *Gesture, Gender, Nation: Dance and Social Change in Uzbekistan.* Westport, CT: Bergin and Garvey.

Dong, Gao 董誥, et al., comps. 1983. *Quan Tang Wen* 全唐文. Beijing: Zhonghua Huju 中華書局.

Dong, Xijiu. 1984. *Zhongguo wudao shi: Song, Liao, Jin, Xixia, Yuan bufen* 中國舞蹈史：宋，遼，西夏，元部分 [History of Chinese dance: Dynastic periods of Song, Liao, Jin, Xixia, and Yuan). Beijing: Wenhua Yishu Chubanshe.

———. 1989a. *Dunhuang bihua he tangdai wudao.* 敦煌壁畫和唐代舞蹈 [Dunhuang wall painting and Tang dynasty dances]. Lanzhou: Lanzhou daxue chubanshe.

———. 1989b. *Dunhuang bihua zhong de wudao yishu: "Sichou zhi lu shang de yue wu yishu"* 敦煌畫中的舞蹈藝術：“絲綢之路上的樂舞質疑” [Art of dance in the Dunhuang wall painting: "Inquiry of music and dance along the Silk Road"]. Lanzhou: Lanzhou Daxue Chubanshe.

———. 1995. *Sichou Zhilu* 絲綢之路 [The Silk Road]. Beijing: Xinhua Chubanshe.

———. 1998. *Yue wu zhi* 樂舞誌 [Record of music and dance]. Shanghai: Shanghai Renmin Chubanshe.

———. 1999. *Jiekai "Dunhuang wupu" zhimi* 解開 “敦煌舞譜”之謎 [The revelation of the mystery of "Dunhuang dance notation"]. Lanzhou: Gansu Wenhua Chubanshe.

———. 2005. *Binfen wudao wenhua zhilu: Dong Xijiu wudao shilun ji* 繽紛舞蹈文化之路董錫玖舞蹈史論集 [The colorful road of dance culture: A collection of articles on dance history by Dong Xijiu]. Dunhuang: Dunhuang Wenyi Chubanshe.

Dong, Xijiu, and Liu Junxiang, eds. 1997. *Zhongguo wudao yishushi tujian* 中國舞蹈藝術史圖解 [A pictorial analysis of the history of Chinese dance]. Changsha: Hunan Jiaoyu Chubanshe.

Dong, Xijiu, Mark Stevenson, Jixing Xu, and Ying Zhu, eds. 2001. *Dance and Communication in Chinese Culture.* Melbourne: Victoria University.

Dong, Xijiu, and Zhu Ying. 2007. *Wudao shilun yanjiu fangfa chutan* 舞蹈史論研究方法初探 [An inquiry into dance historiography research methods]. Beijing: Wenhua Yishu Chubanshe.

Dreyfus, Hubert L. 1991. *Being-in-the-World : A Commentary on Heidegger's* Being and Time, Division I. Cambridge, MA: MIT Press.

Drompp, Michael R. 2005. *Tang China and the Collapse of the Uighur Empire.* Leiden: Brill.

Du, Jiwen. 2006. *Fojiao Shi* 佛教史 [History of Buddhism]. Jiangsu: Jiangsu Renmin Chubanshe.

Du, Yaxiong. 2001. "National Minorities in the Northwest." In *East Asia: China, Japan, and Korea.* Vol. 7 of *Garland Encyclopedia of World Music*, edited by Robert C. Provine, Yoshihiko Tokumaru, and J. Lawrence Witzleben, 455–466. New York: Garland.

Du, You 杜佑. 1935. *Tongdian* 通典. Shanghai: Shangwu.

Duan, Wenjie. 1994. *Dunhuang Art through the Eyes of Duan Wenjie.* Translated and edited by Tan Chung. New Delhi: Indira Gandhi National Centre for the Arts.

———. 1997. "The History of Conservation of Mogao Grottoes." In *International Symposium on the Conservation and Restoration of Cultural Property: The Conservation of*

*Dunhuang Mogao Grottoes and the Related Studies*, edited by Kuchitsu Nobuaki, 1–8. Tokyo: Tokyo National Research Institute of Cultural Properties.

Duara, Prasenjit. 1996. *Rescuing History from the Nation: Questioning Narratives of Modern China*. Chicago: University of Chicago Press.

———. 2002. Introduction to *China Off Center: Mapping the Margins of the Middle Kingdom*, edited by Susan D. Blum and Lionel M. Jensen, xiii–xvi. Honolulu: University of Hawai'i Press.

Dunhuang yanjiuyuan 敦煌研究院, ed. 1982–1987. *Zhongguo shiku: Dunhuang Mogaoku* 中國石窟·敦煌莫高窟 [Grottoes of China: Dunhuang Mogao Grottoes]. Beijing: Wenwu chubanshe.

———. 1996. *Dunhuang Mogaoku neirong zonglu* 敦煌莫高窟內容總錄 [General record of Dunhuang Mogao Grottoes contents). Beijing: Wenwu chubanshe.

Durham, M. G., and D. M. Kellner. 2001. "Adventures in Media and Cultural Studies: Introducing the KeyWorks." In *Media and Cultural Studies: Keyworks*, edited by M. G. Durham and D. M. Kellner, 1–30. Oxford: Blackwell.

Ebrey, Patricia Buckley, and Peter N. Gregory, eds. 1993. *Religion and Society in T'ang and Sung China*. Honolulu: University of Hawai'i Press.

Egan, Ronald, ed. and trans. 1998. *Limited Views: Essays on Ideas and Letters by Qian Zhongshu*. Cambridge, MA: Harvard University Asia Center.

Eliot, T. S. 1920. *The Sacred Wood: Essays on Poetry and Criticism*. London: Methuen.

Elliott, Gregory. 1996. *A Dictionary of Cultural and Critical Theory*. Edited by Michael Payne. Malden, MA: Blackwell.

Emerson, Robert M., Rachel I. Fretz, and Linda L. Shaw. 1995. *Writing Ethnographic Fieldnotes*. Chicago: University of Chicago Press.

Eminov, Sandra. 1975. "Folklore and Nationalism in Modern China." *Journal of the Folklore Institute* 12:257–277.

Eno, Robert. 1987. Review of *Philosophy and Tradition: The Interpretation of China's Philosophic Past: Fun Yu-lan, 1939–1949*, by Michel C. Masson. *Journal of the American Oriental Society* 107:159–162.

———. 1990. *The Confucian Creation of Heaven: Philosophy and the Defense of Ritual Mastery*. Albany: State University of New York Press.

Epstein, Ronald B. 2003. *Buddhism A to Z*. Edited by Buddhist Text Translation Society Editorial Committee. Burlingame, CA: Buddhist Text Translation Society.

Erlmann, Veit, ed. 2020. *Hearing Cultures: Essays on Sound, Listening and Modernity*. London: Routledge.

Fan, Jie. 2004. "Western Development Policy: Changes, Effects and Evaluation." In *Developing China's West: A Critical Path to Balanced National Development*, edited by Y. M. Yeung and Shen Jianfa, 79–106. Hong Kong: Chinese University of Hong Kong.

Fan, Ye 范曄. 1971. *Hou hanshu* 後漢書. Beijing: Zhonghua Shuju.

Fang, Xuanling 房玄齡 et al., comps. 1974. *Jinshu* 晉書. Beijing: Zhonghua Shuju.

Featherstone, Mike. 2002. "Cosmopolis: An Introduction." *Theory, Culture & Society* 19:1–17.

Feld, Steven, and Don Brenneis. 2004. "Doing Anthropology in Sound." *American Ethnologist* 31 (4): 461–474.

Feng, Chongyi. 2022. "Frontier Politics in the Family Empire and Party Empire: The Position of Hainan in the Chinese State." *Eurasian Geography and Economics*, May 3, 2022. https://doi.org/10.1080/15387216.2022.2071312.

Ferguson, Niall. 2010. "Complexity and Collapse: Empires on the Edge of Chaos." *Foreign Affairs*, March/April 2010. http://www.foreignaffairs.com/articles/65987/niallferguson/complexity-and-collapse.

Ferrarotti, Franco. 2002. "What Is Cultural Property? An Overview." Speech presented at Columbia University.

Fong, Wen C. 1992. *Beyond Representation: Chinese Painting and Calligraphy, 8th–14th Century*. New York: Metropolitan Museum of Art.

———. 2003. "Why Chinese Painting Is History." *Art Bulletin* 85 (2): 258–280.

Foster, Susan L., ed. 1995. *Choreographing History (Unnatural Acts: Theorizing the Performative)*. Bloomington: Indiana University Press.

Foucault, Michel. 1969. *The Archaeology of Knowledge: And the Discourse on Language*. Paris: Editions Gallimard.

———. 1977. "Nietzsche, Genealogy, History." In *Language, Counter-Memory, Practice*, edited by D. F. Bouchard, 140–164. Ithaca, NY: Cornell University Press.

———. 1990. *Politics, Philosophy, Culture: Interviews and Other Writings, 1977–1984*. Edited by L. D. Kritzman. London: Routledge.

———. 1991. *The Order of Things: An Archaeology of the Human Sciences*. London: Routledge.

Fraser, Sarah Elizabeth. 2004. *Performing the Visual: The Practice of Buddhist Wall Painting in China and Central Asia, 618–960*. Stanford, CA: Stanford University Press.

Fung, Youlan. 1983. *A History of Chinese Philosophy*. Vol. 1. Princeton, NJ: Princeton University Press.

Gao, Dexiang. 2008. *Dunhuang gudai yuewu* 敦煌古代樂舞 [Dunhuang dance and music in the classical time]. Beijing: Renmin Yinyue Chubanshe.

Gao, Jinrong. 1983. *Dunhuang wudao de jiben xunlian* 敦煌舞蹈的基本訓練 [Basic training of Dunhuang dance]. Beijing: Wudao Luncong.

———. 1993. *Dunhuang wudao* 敦煌舞蹈 [Dunhuang dance]. Lanzhou: Dunhuang Wenyi Chubanshe.

———. 2000. *Dunhuang shiku wuyue yishu* 敦煌石窟舞蹈藝術 [The art of Dunhuang Grottoes dance and music]. Lanzhou: Gansu Renmin Chubanshe.

———. 2002. *Dunhuang wu jiaocheng* 敦煌舞教程 [Dunhuang dance Tutorial]. Shanghai: Shanghai Yinyue Chubanshe

Geertz, Clifford. 1973. *The Interpretation of Cultures: Selected Essays*. New York: Basic Books.

———. 1988. *Works and Lives: The Anthropologist as Author*. Stanford, CA: Stanford University Press.

———. 2008. "Thick Description: Toward an Interpretive Theory of Culture." In *The Cultural Geography Reader*, 41–51. London: Routledge.

Gibbs, Levi S. 2018. *Song King: Connecting People, Places, and Past in Contemporary China*. Honolulu: University of Hawai'i Press.

Gill, Bates. 2006. "Meeting the Challenges and Opportunities of China's Rise: Expanding and Improving Interaction between the American and Chinese Policy Communities." Washington, DC: Centre for Strategic & International Studies.

Gill, Bates, and Yanzhong Huang. 2006. "Sources and Limits of Chinese 'Soft Power.'" *Survival* 48 (2): 7–36.

Gladhart, Amalia. 2000. *Leper in Blue: Coercive Performance and the Contemporary Latin American Theater*. Chapel Hill: University of North Carolina Press.

Gladney, Dru C. 1991. *Muslim Chinese: Ethnic Nationalism in the People's Republic*. Cambridge, MA: Council on East Asian Studies, Harvard University.

Goffman, Erving. 1974. *Frame Analysis: An Essay on the Organization of Experience.* New York: Harper and Row.

Gould, Richard A. 1974. "Some Current Problems in Ethnoarchaeology." In *Ethnoarchaeology*, edited by C. B. Donnan and C. W. Clewlow Jr., 29–48. Archaeological Survey Monograph 4. Los Angeles: University of California, Institute of Archaeology.

Graham, Brian. 2002. "Heritage as Knowledge: Capital or Culture?" *Urban Studies* 39: 1003–1017.

Gries, Peter Hays. 2005. *China's New Nationalism: Pride, Politics, and Diplomacy.* Berkeley: University of California Press.

Gu, Mingdong. 2003. "Aesthetic Suggestiveness in Chinese Thought: A Symphony of Metaphysics and Aesthetics." *Philosophy East and West* 53:490–513.

———. 2005. "Mimetic Theory in Chinese Literary Thought." *New Literary History* 36: 403–424.

Guo, Maoqian. 1979. *Yuefu Shiji* 樂府詩集. Beijing: Zhonghua.

Guss, David M. 2000. *The Festive State: Race, Ethnicity, and Nationalism as Cultural Performance.* Berkeley: University of California Press.

Gutting, Gary, and Johanna Oksala. 2022. "Michel Foucault." In *The Stanford Encyclopedia of Philosophy*, edited by Edward N. Zalta and Uri Nodelman. Stanford University, fall 2022 edition. https://plato.stanford.edu/archives/fall2022/entries/foucault/.

Guy, Nancy. 2002. "'Republic of China National Anthem' on Taiwan: One Anthem, One Performance, Multiple Realities." *Ethnomusicology* 46:96–119.

———. 2005. *Peking Opera and Politics in Taiwan.* Chicago: University of Illinois Press.

Hafstein, Valdimar. 2018. *Making Intangible Heritage: El Condor Pasa and Other Stories from UNESCO.* Bloomington: Indiana University Press.

Hahn, Tomie. 2007. *Sensational Knowledge: Embodying Culture through Japanese Dance.* Middletown, CT: Wesleyan University Press.

Hall, Stuart. 1996. *Stuart Hall: Critical Dialogues in Cultural Studies.* Edited by David Morley and Kuan-Hsing Chen. London: Routledge.

Han, Kuohuang, and Judith Gray. 1979. "The Modern Chinese Orchestra." *Asian Music* 11:1–43.

Harris, Rachel. 2006. *Singing the Village: Music, Memory and Ritual among the Sibe of Xinjiang.* London: Oxford University Press.

Hatten, Robert. 1985. "The Place of Intertextuality in Music Studies." *American Journal of Semiotics* 3 (4): 69–82.

Hayashi, Kenzō 林謙三. 1936. *Sui Tang Yan Yue Diao Yan Jiu.* Chu ban. Shanghai: Shang wu yin shu guan.

Hebdige, Dick. 2006. "From Culture to Hegemony." In *Media and Cultural Studies: Keyworks*, 198–216. Rev. ed. Oxford: Blackwell.

Heidegger, Martin. 1962. *Being and Time.* Oxford: Blackwell.

Hemel, Hans Mommaas, and Cas Smithuijsen, eds. 1996. *Trading Culture: GATT, European Cultural Policies, and the Transatlantic Market.* Amsterdam: Boekman Foundation.

Henry, Sara Lynn. 2008. "Grace Bakst Wapner's Scholar's Garden: An East–West Aesthetic Dialogue." *Hyperion: On the Future of Aesthetics* 3 (4): 29–38.

Herzfeld, Michael. 1985. *Ours Once More: Folklore, Ideology, and the Making of Modern Greece.* Austin: University of Texas Press.

———. 1991. *A Place in History.* Princeton, NJ: Princeton University Press.

———. 2004. *Cultural Intimacy: Social Poetics in the Nation-State*. New York: Routledge.

Hillman, Ben. 2003. "Paradise under Construction: Minorities, Myths and Modernity in Northwest Yunnan." *Asian Ethnicity* 4:175–188.

Hilton, James. 1933. *Lost Horizon*. New York: Macmillan.

Hockx, Michel, and Julia Strauss. 2005. *Culture in the Contemporary PRC*. Cambridge: Cambridge University Press.

Hu, Jian. 2018. "'*Yidaiyilu*' *de jiazhi yanjiu*" "一帶一路"的價值研究 [Study on the value of the "Belt and Road" initiative]. Edited by Ashley Kim Stewart. *Journal of China and International Relations* 6 (2): 1–108.

Huang, Hetao. 1995. *Chan yu Zhongguo yishu jingshen de shanbian* 禪與中國藝術精神的嬗變 [Zen and the development of Chinese artistic spirits]. Beijing: Shangwu Yinshuguan Guoji Youxian Gongsi.

Hucker, Charles O. 1985. *A Dictionary of Official Titles in Imperial China*. Stanford, CA: Stanford University Press.

Ingram, Paul, Jeffrey Robinson, and Marc L. Busch. 2005. "The Intergovernmental Network of World Trade: IGO Connectedness, Governance and Embeddedness." *American Journal of Sociology* 111:824–858.

Ishiguro, Setsuko. 2004. "The Flying Deities Project: An Attempt Performing East Asian Ancient Dance in Zero Gravity Environments." In *Body as Medium of Meaning*, edited by Suhaylā Shahshahānī, 72–86. Münster: Lit Verlag International Union of Anthropological and Ethnological Sciences.

Ives, Kelly. 1997. "An Introduction to Julia Kristeva." In *Julia Kristeva: Art, Love, Melancholy, Philosophy, Semiotics and Psychoanalysis*. New York: Crescent Moon.

Jackson, Jason Baird. 2014. "Seminole Histories of the Calusa: Dance, Narrative, and Historical Consciousness." *Native South* 7:122–142.

Jackson, Julie. 2005. "Theatrical Space and Place in the Presentational Aesthetic of Director Frank Joseph Galati." *Theatre Topics* 15 (2): 131–148.

Jackson, Michael. 1995. *At Home in the World*. Durham, NC: Duke University Press.

Jacobs, Justin. 2008. "How Chinese Turkestan Became Chinese: Visualizing Zhang Zhizhong's *Tianshan Pictorial* and Xinjiang Youth Song and Dance Troupe." *Journal of Asian Studies* 67:545–591.

Jameson, Fredric. 1991. *Postmodernism, or, the Cultural Logic of Late Capitalism*. New York: Verso.

———. 1998. "Notes on Globalization as a Philosophical Issue." In *The Cultures of Globalization*, edited by Fredric Jameson and Masao Miyoshi, 54–77. Durham, NC: Duke University Press.

Janelli, Roger. 1993. *Making Capitalism: The Social and Cultural Construction of a South Korean Conglomerate*. With Yim Dawnhee. Stanford, CA: Stanford University Press.

Jao, Tsung-I [Rao, Zongyi]. 1962. "Dunhuang wupu jiaoshi" 敦煌舞譜校釋. *Xianggang daxue xueshenghui jinxi jinian lunwenji* 香港大學學生會金禧紀年論文集. Hong Kong: Xianggang daxue xueshenghui.

———. 1973. "Quzi 'Ding xi fan'—Dunhuang qu shibu zhi yi" 曲子《定西蕃》—《敦煌曲》拾補之一. *Xinshe xuebao* 新社學報 5:1–3.

———. 2022. "Moral Speculation and the Conception of a Sky God." In *Space, Time, Myth, and Morals: A Selection of Jao Tsung-i's Studies on Cosmological Thought in Early China and Beyond*, edited and translated by Joern Peter Grundmann, 220–277. Leiden: Brill.

Jay, Jennifer W. 1997. "Conceptualizing the Frontier in Táng and Song China: A Cultural Perspective." In *East Asian Cultural and Historical Perspectives: Histories and Society, Culture and Literatures*, edited by Steven Tötösy de Zepetnek and Jennifer W. Jay, 61–69. Alberta: University of Alberta.

Jiang, Yuan. 2022. "Unpacking the Belt and Road Initiative: Does Its Public Diplomacy Narratives Match Its Implementation?" *East Asia*, March 14, 2022. https://doi.org/10.1007/s12140-022-09386-1.

Jie, Zhang, and Hu Xiaoming. 2014. "Body Movements and the Creation of Early Chinese Hieroglyphs." *International Journal of the History of Sport* 31 (6): 674–692.

Johnson, Mark. 1987. *The Body in the Mind: The Bodily Basis of Meaning, Reason, and Imagination*. Chicago: University of Chicago Press.

Johnston, Alastair Iain, and Robert S. Ross, eds. 1999. *Engaging China: The Management of an Emerging Power*. London: Routledge.

Jones, Robert A. 2008. "New Directions in 20th Century Buddhist Studies in China: Dunhuang's Mogaoku as Case Study." In *The Intercultural Forum*, 17–26. Louisville: Institute for Intercultural Communication, University of Louisville.

Jones, Stephen. 1996. "Source and Stream: Early Music and Living Traditions in China." *Early Music* 24:374–388.

Kaeppler, Adrienne L. 1967. "The Structure of Tongan Dance." PhD diss., University of Hawai'i.

———. 1971. "Aesthetics of Tongan Dance." *Ethnomusicology* 15 (2): 175–185.

———. 2001. "Dance and the Concept of Style." *Yearbook for Traditional Music* 33:49–63.

Kaeppler, Adrienne L., and Jacob Wainwright Love, eds. 1998. *Australia and the Pacific Islands*. Vol. 9 of *Garland Encyclopedia of World Music*. New York: Garland.

Karp, Ivan, Corinne A. Kratz, Lynn Szwaja, and Tomás Ybarra-Frausto, eds. 2006. *Museum Frictions: Public Cultures / Global Transformations*. Durham, NC: Duke University Press.

Katz, Paul R. 1996. "Enlightened Alchemist or Immoral Immortal? The Growth of Lu Dongbin's Cult in Late Imperial China." In *Unruly Gods: Divinity and Society in China*, edited by Meir Shahar and Robert P. Weller, 70–104. Honolulu: University of Hawai'i Press.

Kern, Martin. 2005. "The *Odes* in Excavated Manuscripts." In *Text and Ritual in Early China*, edited by Martin Kern, 149–190. Seattle: University of Washington Press.

———. 2007. "Beyond the Mao Odes: Shijing Reception in Early Medieval China." *Journal of the American Oriental Society* 127:131–142.

———. 2017. "Language and the Ideology of Kingship in the 'Canon of Yao.'" In *Origins of Chinese Political Philosophy*, edited by Martin Kern and Dirk Meyer, 23–61. Leiden: Brill.

Keulemans, Paize. 2007. "Listening to the Printed Martial Arts Scene: Onomatopoeia and the Qing Dynasty Storyteller's Voice." *Harvard Journal of Asiatic Studies* 67 (1): 51–87.

———. 2010. "Printing the Sound of Cosmopolitan Beijing: Dialect Accents in Nineteenth-Century Martial Arts Fiction." In *From Woodblocks to the Internet: Chinese Publishing and Print Culture in Transition, circa 1800 to 2008*, edited by Cynthia Reed and Christopher A. Reed, 159–184. Boston: Brill.

———. 2020. *Sound Rising from the Paper: Nineteenth-Century Martial Arts Fiction and the Chinese Acoustic Imagination*. Leiden: Brill.

Kielman, Adam. 2022. *Sonic Mobilities: Producing Worlds in Southern China*. Chicago: University of Chicago Press.

Kimiko, Ohtani. 2001. "Dance." In *East Asia: China, Japan, and Korea*. Vol. 7 of *Garland Encyclopedia of World Music*, edited by Robert C. Provine, Yosihiko Tokumaru, and J. Lawrence Witzleben, 59–72. New York: Garland.

Kirshenblatt-Gimblett, Barbara. 1995. "Theorizing Heritage." *Ethnomusicology* 39:367–380.

———. 1998. *Destination Culture: Tourism, Museums, and Heritage*. Berkeley: University of California Press.

———. 2006. *Art from Start to Finish: Jazz, Painting, Writing, and Other Improvisations*. Edited by Howard S. Becker, Robert R. Faulkner, and Barbara Kirshenblatt-Gimblett. Chicago: University of Chicago Press.

Kleingeld, Pauline, and Eric Brown. 2019. "Cosmopolitanism." In *The Stanford Encyclopedia of Philosophy*, edited by Edward N. Zalta. Stanford University, winter 2019 edition. https://plato.stanford.edu/archives/win2019/entries/cosmopolitanism/.

Kneubuhl, John. 1997. *Think of a Garden and Other Plays*. Honolulu: University of Hawai'i Press.

Korsyn, Kevin. 1991. "Towards a New Poetics of Musical Influence." *Music Analysis* 10 (1/2): 3–72.

———. 1999. "Beyond Privileged Contexts: Intertextuality Influence and Dialogue." In *Rethinking Music*, edited by Nicholas Cook and Mark Everist, 55–72. London: Oxford University Press.

Kristeva, Julia. 1980. "Word, Dialogue and Novel." In *Desire in Language: A Semiotic Approach to Literature and Art*, edited by L. S. Roudiez, 64–91. New York: Columbia University Press.

Kuang, Lanlan. 2004. "As Time Unfolds: Understanding and Interpreting the Chinese Folk Song 'Liuyeliu' through Intertextual Processes and Multimedia Representation." Master's thesis, Indiana University.

———. 2012. "Staging the Cosmopolitan Nation: The Re-creation of the 'Dunhuang Bihua Yuewu,' a Multifaceted Music, Dance, and Theatrical Drama from China." PhD diss., Indiana University.

———. 2016a. *Dunhuang bi hua yue wu: "Zhongguo jing guan" zai guo ji yu jing zhong de jian gou, chuan oy uu yiyi* 敦煌壁畫樂舞：「中國景观」在國際語境中的建構、傳播与意義 [Dunhuang bihua yuewu: The formation, transmission, and meaning of "Chinascapes" in the global context]. Beijing: Shehui Kexue Wenxian Chubanshe.

———. 2016b. "Staging the Silk Road Journey Abroad: The Case of Dunhuang Performative Arts." *M/C—A Journal of Media and Culture* 19 (5).

———. 2019. "(Un)Consciousness? Music in the Daoist Context of Nonbeing." In *Music and Consciousness 2: Worlds, Practices, Modalities*, edited by Ruth Herbert, David Ian Clarke, and Eric Clarke, 306–323. Oxford: Oxford University Press.

Kurlantzick, Joshua. 2007a. *Charm Offensive: How China's Soft Power Is Transforming the World*. New Republic Book. New Haven, CT: Yale University Press.

———. 2007b. "China's New Diplomacy and Its Impact on the World." *Brown Journal of World Affairs* 115:221–237.

Kwak, Jun-Hyeok. 2021. "Global Justice without Self-centrism: *Tianxia* in *Dialogue on Mount Uisan*." *Dao* 20 (2): 289–307.

Lakoff, George. 1987. *Woman, Fire, and Dangerous Things: What Categories Reveal about the Mind*. Chicago: University of Chicago Press.

———. 1994. "The Contemporary Theory of Metaphor." In *Metaphor and Thought*, edited by A. Ortony, 202–251. Cambridge: Cambridge University Press.

Lakoff, George, and Mark Johnson. 1980. *Metaphors We Live By*. Chicago: University of Chicago Press.

Lam, Joseph S. C. 1994. "'There Is No Music in Chinese Music History': Five Court Tunes from the Yuan Dynasty (AD 1271–1368)." *Journal of the Royal Musical Association* 119:165–188.

———. 1998. *State Sacrifice and Music in Ming China: Orthodoxy, Creativity and Expressiveness*. New York: State University of New York Press.

———. 2001. "Scholarship and Historical Source Materials: Antiquity through 1911." In *East Asia: China, Japan, and Korea*. Vol. 7 of *Garland Encyclopedia of World Music*, edited by Robert C. Provine, Yosihiko Tokumaru, and J. Lawrence Witzleben, 127–134. New York: Garland.

———. 2012. "Music, Sound, and Site: A Case Study from Southern Song China (1127–1275)." In *New Perspectives on the Research of Chinese Culture*, edited by Cheng Pei-Kai and Ka Wai Fan, 1:99–118. Singapore: Springer Science and Business Media.

———. 2017. *Senses of the City: Perceptions of Hangzhou and Southern Song China, 1127–1279*. Hong Kong: Chinese University of Hong Kong Press.

———. 2022. *Kunqu: A Classical Opera of Twenty-First Century China*. Hong Kong: Hong Kong University Press.

Larson, Steve. 2012. *Musical Forces: Motion, Metaphor, and Meaning in Music*. Bloomington: Indiana University Press.

Lau, Frederick. 2023. "The Ethnographic Selfie—When the Lens Is on Your Own Culture: A Keynote Address." *Asian Music* 54 (2): 77–100.

Lefebvre, Henry. 1991. *The Production of Space*. Oxford: Blackwell.

Legge, James. 1879. *The Sacred Book of China: The Texts of Confucianism*. Oxford: Clarendon.

———. 1976. *The Sacred Books of China: The Texts of Confucianism*. Vol. 4. New York: Gordon.

Levenson, Joseph. 1971. *Revolution and Cosmopolitanism*. Berkeley: University of California Press.

Lévy, Pierre. 1999. *Collective Intelligence: Mankind's Emerging World in Cyberspace*. New York: Plenum Trade.

———. 2002. *Cyberdémocratie: Essai de philosophie politique*. Paris: Odile Jacob.

Lewis, Mark E. 2005. *The Construction of Space in Early China*. New York: State University of New York Press.

———. 2009. *China's Cosmopolitan Empire: The Tang Dynasty*. Cambridge, MA: Harvard University Press.

Li, Dalong. 2001. *Tangchao he bianjiang minzu shizhe wanglai yanjiu* 唐朝和边疆民族使者往来研究 [Interaction with ethnic envoys from the frontiers during the Tang dynasty]. Harbin: Heilongjiang Jiaoyu Chubanshe.

Li, Fang 李昉 et al., comps. 1960. *Taiping Yulan* 太平御覽. Beijing: Zhonghua.

———. 1961. *Taiping Guangji* 太平廣記. Beijing: Zhonghua.

Li, Jing. 2013. "The Making of Ethnic Yunnan on the National Mall: Minority Folksong and Dance Performances, Provincial Identity, and 'The Artifying of Politics' (Zhengzhi Yishuhua)." *Modern China* 39 (1): 69–100.

Li, Minghuan. 2004. "Myths of Creation and the Creation of Myths: Interrogating Chinese Diaspora." *Chinese America: History and Perspectives*, January 1, 1–7.

Li, Waiyee. 2007. *The Readability of the Past in Early Chinese Historiography*. Cambridge, MA: Harvard University Asia Center.

Li, Xiaocong, ed. 2003. *Tangdai diyu jiegou yu yunzuo kongjian* 唐代地域結構與運作空間 [The Tang dynasty's geographic structure and production space]. Shanghai: Shanghai Cishu Chubanshe.

Li, Yongqiao. 1998. *Zhang Daqian lunhua jingcui* 張大千論畫精粹 [The essence of Zhang Daqian's comments on paintings]. Guangzhou: Huachengchubanshe.

Lieberthal, Kenneth. 2007. "How Domestic Forces Shape the PRC's Grand Strategy and International Impact." *Domestic Political Change and Grand Strategy, Strategic Asia* 8:30.

Lin, Hsiao-ting. 2006. *Tibet and Nationalist China's Frontier: Intrigues and Ethnopolitics, 1928–49*. Vancouver: University of British Columbia Press.

Lin, Jing. 2019. "Enlightenment from Body–Spirit Integration: Dunhuang's Buddhist Cultivation Pathways and Educational Applications." In *The Dunhuang Grottoes and Global Education*, 113–131. Cham: Palgrave Macmillan.

Liu, Dongsheng, and Quanyou Yuan, eds. 2008. *Zhongguo yinyue shi tujian* 中國音樂史圖鑑 [Pictorial guide to the history of Chinese music]. Beijing: Renmin Yinyue Chubanshe.

Liu, Xu 劉煦 et al., comps. 1957. *Jiu Tangshu* 舊唐書. Beijing: Zhonghua Shuju.

Liu, Zaisheng. 1995. *Zhongguo gudai yinyueshi jianshu* 中國古代音樂史簡述 [A brief narrative of the history of ancient Chinese music]. Beijing: Renmin Yinyue Chubanshe.

Lomanov, Alexander. 2010. "'Two Grounds on One Stem': Beijing Conference on Contemporary Sinology." *Far Eastern Affairs* 2:120–131.

Love, Jacob Wainwright. 1991. *Sāmoan Variations: Essays on the Nature of Traditional Oral Arts*. New York: Garland.

———. 2003. Review of *Traditionalism and Modernity in the Music and Dance of Oceania: Essays in Honour of Barbara B. Smith*, edited by Helen Reeves Lawrence and Don Niles. *American Anthropologist* 105:437–438.

Low, Setha M., and Denise Lawrence-Zunigais. 2003. *The Anthropology of Space and Place: Locating Culture*. London: Wiley-Blackwell.

Löwy, Michael. 1998. *Fatherland or Mother Earth? Essays on the National Question*. London: Pluto.

Lu, Hanchao. 2002. "Nostalgia for the Future: The Resurgence of a Silenced Culture in China." *Pacific Affairs* 75:169–186.

Lynn, Richard. 1994. *The Classic of Changes: A New Translation of the "I Ching" as Interpreted by Wang Bi*. New York: Columbia University Press.

Ma, De. 2000. *Dunhuang shiku zhishi cidian* 敦煌石窟知識辭典 [A dictionary and guide to Dunhuang Grottoes]. Lanzhou: Gansu Renmin Meishu Chubanshe.

Ma, Jingna, and Cang Wei. 2022. "Similarity of Frescoes to Winter Sports Raises Intrigue." *China Daily*, February 8, 2022. https://govt.chinadaily.com.cn/s/202202/08/WS6201c56 b498e6a12c121e929/similarity-of-frescoes-to-winter-sports-raises-intrigue.html.

Mackerras, Colin. 1989. *Chinese Theater: From Its Origins to the Present Day*. Honolulu: University of Hawai'i Press.

Mahbubani, Kishore. 2022. "What China Threat? How the United States and China Can Avoid War." In *The Asian 21st Century: China and Globalization*, 147–154. Singapore: Springer.

Mair, Victor. 1989. *T'ang Transformation Texts: A Study of the Buddhist Contribution to the Rise of Vernacular Fiction and Drama in China*. Cambridge, MA: Council on East Asian Studies.

———. 1990. "Three Brief Essays Concerning Chinese Tocharistan." *Sino-Platonic Papers* 16:A1–C6.

Mandelbaum, David G. 1966. "Transcendental and Pragmatic Aspects of Religion." *American Anthropologist* 68 (5): 1174–1191.

Marcus, George. 1998. *Ethnography through Thick and Thin*. Princeton, NJ: Princeton University Press.

Martin, Randy. 1995. "Agency and History: The Demands of Dance Ethnography." In *Choreographing History (Unnatural Acts: Theorizing the Performative)*, edited by Susan Foster, 105–118. Bloomington: Indiana University Press.

———. 1998. *Critical Moves: Dance Studies in Theory and Politics*. Durham, NC: Duke University Press.

Masaharu, Arakawa. 2011. "China's View of the World." In *World and Global History: Research and Teaching*, edited by Seija Jalagin, Susanna Tavera, and Andrew Dilley, 59–68. Pisa: Plus-Pisa University Press.

McGiffert, Carola. 2009. *Chinese Soft Power and Its Implications for the United States: Competition and Cooperation in the Developing World*. Report of the CSIS Smart Power Initiative. Washington, DC: Center for Strategic and International Studies.

McGrane, Bernard. 1989. *Beyond Anthropology: Society and the Other*. New York: Columbia University Press.

Melvin, Sheila. 2008. "Tan Dun: Harmonizing Music with Athletics for the Olympics." *New York Times*, August 7, 2008. http://www.nytimes.com/2008/08/07/arts/07iht -tandun.1.15042033.html.

Merleau-Ponty, Maurice. 1962. *Phenomenology of Perception*. London: Routledge Classics Series.

Merriam, Alan P. 1964. *The Anthropology of Music*. Evanston, IL: Northwestern University Press.

Messmer, Matthias. 2012. *Jewish Wayfarers in Modern China: Tragedy and Splendor*. Washington, DC: Lexington Books.

Millward, James A. 1999. "'Coming onto the Map': Western Regions' Geography and Cartographic Nomenclature in the Making of Chinese Empire in Xinjiang." *Late Imperial China* 20:61–98.

Misha, Tadd. 2022. "Global Laozegetics: A Study in Globalized Philosophy." *Journal of the History of Ideas* 83, no. 1 (January): 87–109.

Mitchell, W. J. T. 1994. Introduction to *Landscape and Power*, edited by W. J. T. Mitchell, 1–4. Chicago: University of Chicago Press.

———. 1995. *Picture Theory: Essays on Verbal and Visual Representation*. Chicago: University of Chicago Press.

Mommaas, H. 1996. "The Politics of Culture and World Trade." In *Trading Culture: GATT, European Cultural Policies and the Transatlantic Market*, edited by A. van Hemel, H. Mommaas, and C. Smithuysen, 11–26. Amsterdam: Boekmanstichting.

Moore, J. Kenneth. 2000. "Music and Art of China." In *Heilbrunn Timeline of Art History*. New York: Metropolitan Museum of Art. Last modified September 10, 2011. http:// www.metmuseum.org/toah/hd/mushc/hd_much.htm.

Mullaney, Thomas. 2011. *Coming to Terms with the Nation: Ethnic Classification in Modern China*. Vol. 18. Berkeley: University of California Press.

Myers, Helen. 1993. *Ethnomusicology: Historical and Regional Studies*. New York: W. W. Norton.

Nanzhuo 南卓. 1957. *Jiegulu* 羯鼓錄. Shanghai: Gudian Wenxue Chubanshe.

Nietzsche, Friedrich Wilhelm. 1974. *The Gay Science*. Translated by Walter Kaufmann. New York: Random House.

———. 2001. *The Gay Science: With a Prelude in German Rhymes and an Appendix of Songs.* Edited by Bernard Williams, Josefine Nauckhoff, and Adrian Del Caro. Cambridge Texts in the History of Philosophy. New York: Cambridge University Press.

Nye, Joseph S. 2004a. *Power in the Global Information Age: From Realism to Globalization.* New York: Routledge.

———. 2004b. *Soft Power: The Means to Success in World Politics*. New York: PublicAffairs.

———. 2004c. "Soft Power: The Means to Success in World Politics." Edited transcript, April 13, 2004. Carnegie Council Books for Breakfast. Carnegie Council on Ethics and International Affairs, 2006. http://www.carnegiecouncil.org/resources/transcripts /4466.html.

———. 2004d. "Soft Power and American Foreign Policies." *Political Science Quarterly* 119:255–270.

Nyiri, Pal. 2006. *Scenic Spots, Chinese Tourism, the State, and Cultural Authority*. Seattle: University of Washington Press.

Ortiz, Valérie Malenfer. 1999. *Dreaming the Southern Song Landscape: The Power of Illusion in Chinese Painting*. Vol. 22. Leiden: Brill.

Osborne, Peter, and Stella Sandford. 2003. *Philosophies of Race and Ethnicity*. London: Continuum.

Ou, Jianping. 1988. "Dance Notation System Is Discovered in Ancient Chinese Text." *Dance Magazine*, 5.

Ouyang, Xiu 歐陽修, Song Qi 宋祁et al. 1985. *Xin Tangshu* 新唐書. Beijing: Zhonghua shuju.

Ouyang, Xun 歐陽詢 1965. *Yiwen Leiju* 藝文類聚. Shanghai: Guji.

Owen, Stephen. 2000. "Bi Fa Ji." In *Ways with Words: Writing about Reading Texts from Early China*, edited by Pauline Yu, Peter Bol, Stephen Owen, and Willard Peterson, 213–219. Studies on China 24. Los Angeles: University of California Press.

Packer, Randall, and Ken Jordan, eds. 2001. *Multimedia, from Wagner to Virtual Reality*. New York: Norton.

Pegg, Carole. 2001. *Mongolian Music, Dance and Oral Narrative: Performing Diverse Identities*. Seattle: University of Washington Press.

Pepper, Stephen P. 1948. Review of *Principles of Chinese Painting*, by George Rowley. *Philosophy and Phenomenological Research* 9:329–331.

Peterson, Richard, 1994. "Cultural Studies through the Production Perspective: Progress and Prospects." In *The Sociology of Culture*, edited by D. Crane, 163–190. Cambridge MA: Blackwell.

Petraškevičius, Vladislavas. 2023. "Transformation of Socialist Countries: Market Socialism in China." In *The Paradox of Marxist Economics: Dogmas and Reality*, 273–290. Springer Studies in Alternative Economics. New York: Springer.

Pian, Rulan Chao. 1967. *Song Dynasty Musical Sources and Their Interpretation*. Hong Kong: Chinese University Press.

Picken, Laurence E. R. 1981. *Music from the Táng Court*. Vol. 2. Cambridge: Cambridge University Press.

———. 1988. *Music from the Táng Court*. Vol. 4. Cambridge: Cambridge University Press.

———. 1997. *Music from the Táng Court*. Vol. 6. Cambridge: Cambridge University Press.

———. 2000. *Music from the Táng Court*. Vol. 7. Cambridge: Cambridge University Press.

Picken, Laurence E. R., and Noël J. Nickson, eds. 1981. *Music from the Táng Court*. Vol. 1. Cambridge: Cambridge University Press.

Pivtorak, Yuliya. 2016. "Ukrainian Hopak: From Dance for Entertainment to Martial Art." In *Congress on Research in Dance Conference Proceedings*, 299–305. Cambridge University Press.

Pollatsek, Alexander, Li Hai Tan, and Keith Rayner. 2000. "The Role of Phonological Codes in Integrating Information across Saccadic Eye Movements in Chinese Character Identification." *Journal of Experimental Psychology: Human Perception and Performance* 26 (2): 607.

Por, Shiu Sin. 2023. "'Tian Xia'—China's Concept of International Order." In *China's Development and the Construction of the Community with a Shared Future for Mankind*, edited by L. Wang, 153–160. Research Series on the Chinese Dream and China's Development Path. Singapore: Springer.

Powers, Martin J. 1978. "The Shapes of Power in Han Pictorial Art." PhD diss., University of Michigan.

———. 1991. "Gesture and Character in Early Chinese Art and Criticism." In *Proceedings of the International Symposium on Chinese Painting*, 909–931. Taipei: National Palace Museum.

———. 1995. "Art and History: Exploring the Counterchange Condition." *Art Bulletin* 77:382–387.

———. 1998. "When Is a Landscape Like a Body?" In *Landscape, Culture, and Power*, edited by Yeh Wen Hsin, 1–21. Berkeley, CA: Center for Chinese Studies.

———. 2000. "How to Read a Chinese Painting: Jing Hao's *Bi Fa Ji*." In *Ways with Words: Writing about Reading Texts from Early China*, edited by Pauline Yu, Peter Bol, Stephen Owen, and Willard Peterson, 219–235. Studies on China 24. Los Angeles: University of California Press.

———. 2008. "Landscape Assessment." In *Landscape Theory*, edited by Rachael Z. DeLue and James Elkins, 259–277. New York: Routledge.

Provine, Robert C., Yosihiko Tokumaru, and J. Lawrence Witzleben. 2001. *East Asia: China, Japan, and Korea*. Vol. 7 of *Garland Encyclopedia of World Music*, edited by Robert C. Provine, Yosihiko Tokumaru, and J. Lawrence Witzleben. New York: Garland.

Pulleyblank, Edwin G. 2002. *Central Asia and Non-Chinese Peoples of Ancient China*. Collected Studies. London: Variorum.

Qian, Kun. 2016. *Imperial-Time-Order: Literature, Intellectual History, and China's Road to Empire*. Leiden: Brill.

Ramo, Joshua Cooper. 2004. *The Beijing Consensus*. London: Foreign Policy Centre.

Rao, Nancy Yunhwa. 2020. "The Concept of *Shi*: Chinese Aesthetics and Happy Rain on a Spring Night (2004)." *Music Theory Online* 26 (3). https://mtosmt.org/issues/mto .20.26.3/mto.20.26.3.rao.html.

Rawski, Evelyn S. 2001. "Cultural Interactions in East and Inner Asia." In *East Asia: China, Japan, and Korea*. Vol. 7 of *Garland Encyclopedia of World Music*, edited by Robert C. Provine, Yosihiko Tokumaru, and J. Lawrence Witzleben, 9–37. New York: Garland.

Real, Michael. 1996. *Exploring Media Culture: A Guide*. London: Sage.

Reason, Matthew. 2006. *Documentation, Disappearance and the Representation of Live Performance*. New York: Palgrave Macmillan.

Rees, Helen. 2000. *Echoes of History: Naxi Music in Modern China*. Oxford: Oxford University Press.

———. 2001. "Cultural Policy, Music Scholarship, and Recent Developments." In *East Asia: China, Japan, and Korea*. Vol. 7 of *Garland Encyclopedia of World Music*, edited by Robert C. Provine, Yosihiko Tokumaru, and J. Lawrence Witzleben, 441–446. New York: Garland.

Ren, Bantang. 1962. *Jiao fang ji jianding* 教坊記箋訂. Beijing: Zhonghua Shuju.

Rice, Timothy. 1987. "Toward the Remodeling of Ethnomusicology." *Ethnomusicology* 31 (3): 473–488.

Ricoeur, Paul. 1985. "Narrated Time." *Philosophy Today* 29 (4): 259–272.

Rong, Xinjiang. 2013. *Eighteen Lectures on Dunhuang*. Leiden: Brill.

———. 2020. "A Eurasia Perspective on the Silk Road between Han and Tang Dynasties." In *Studies on the History and Culture along the Continental Silk Road*, edited by X. Li, 1–19. Singapore: Springer.

———. 2022. *The Silk Road and Cultural Exchanges between East and West*. Vol. 14. Leiden: Brill.

Rowley, George. 1947. *Principles of Chinese Painting: With Illustrations from the du Bois Schanck Morris Collection*. Princeton, NJ: Princeton University Press.

Said, Edward W. 2002. "Invention, Memory, and Place." In *Landscape and Power*, edited by W. J. T. Mitchell, 241–259. Chicago: University of Chicago Press.

Samuels, David W., Louise Meintjes, Ana Maria Ochoa, and Thomas Porcello. 2010. "Soundscapes: Toward a Sounded Anthropology." *Annual Review of Anthropology* 39:329–345.

Sanjek, Roger. 1990. *Fieldnotes: The Makings of Anthropology*. Ithaca, NY: Cornell University Press.

Saussy, Haun. 1997. "The Prestige of Writing: *Wen*, Letter, Picture, Image, Ideography." *Sino-Platonic Papers* 75, 1–40.

Schafer, Edward H. 1963. *The Golden Peaches of Samarkand: A Study of T'ang Exotics*. Berkely: University of California Press.

———. 1985. *The Golden Peaches of Samarkand: A Study of T'ang Exotics*. Translated by Wu Yugui. Beijing: China Social Science Press.

Schafer, R. Murray. 1993. *The Soundscape: Our Sonic Environment and the Tuning of the World*. Rochester, VT: Destiny Books.

Schechner, Richard. 1985. *Between Theatre and Anthropology*. Philadelphia: University of Pennsylvania Press.

Schwarcz, Vera. 1989. *The Chinese Enlightenment: Intellectuals and the Legacy of the May Fourth Movement of 1919*. Berkeley: University of California Press.

Seeger, Anthony. 1991. "When Music Makes History." In *Ethnomusicology and Modern Music History*, edited by Stephen Blum, Philip Bohlman, and Daniel Neuman, 23–34. Champaign: University of Illinois Press.

———. 1998. "Music, Dance and Drama: An Anthropological Perspective, Written with Anya Peterson Royce." In *Latin America, Perspectives on a Region*, edited by Jack Hopkins, 226–240. New York: Holmes and Meier.

———. 2008. "Long-Term Field Research in Ethnomusicology in the 21st Century." *Em Pauta* 19 (32/33): 3–20.

Seeger, Charles. 1940. "Folk Music as a Source of Social History." In *The Cultural Approach to History*, edited by Carolyn F. Ware, 316–323. New York: Columbia University Press.

Shay, Anthony. 2002. *Choreographic Politics: State Folk Dance Companies, Representation, and Power*. Middletown, CT: Wesleyan University Press.

Shelemay, Kay Kaufman. 1980. "'Historical Ethnomusicology': Reconstructing Falasha Liturgical History." *Ethnomusicology* 24:233–258.

———. 2001. *Soundscapes: Exploring Music in a Changing World*. New York: Norton.

Shen, Yue 沈約. 1974. *Songshu* 宋書. Beijing: Zhonghua Shuju.

Sheppard, W. Anthony. 2010. "Tan Dun and Zhang Yimou between Film and Opera." *Journal of Musicological Research* 29 (1): 1–33.

Shi, Weixiang. 2002. *Dunhuang lishi yu mogaoku yishu yanjiu* 敦煌歷史與莫高窟藝術研究 [Dunhuang history and research on Mogao Grotto art]. Lanzhou: Gansu Jiaoyu Chubanshe.

Shichor, Yitzhak. 1991. "China and the Role of the United Nations in the Middle East: Revised Policy." *Asian Survey* 31:225–269.

Shigeo Kishibe 岸邊成雄. 1940. "The Origin of the P'i-p'a with Particular Reference to the Five-stringed P'i-p'a Preserved in the Shosoin." *Transactions of the Asiatic Society of Japan*, Second Series, vol. XIX, 259–304.

———. 1954. "The Origin of the K'ung-Hou (Chinese Harp)." *Journal of the Society for Research in Asiatic Music* 14/15:1–51.

———. 1960–1961. *Tōdai ongaku no rekishiteki kenkyū* 唐代音樂の歷史的研究 [Research on Tang dynasty and history]. Tokyo: Tōkyō Daigaku Shuppankai.

Shirk, Susan L. 2007. *China: Fragile Superpower; How China's Internal Politics Could Derail Its Peaceful Rise*. New York: Oxford University Press.

Shu, Yongping, and Zhu Xiaotong. 2018. *Xi jinping guojia pinpai lunshu yanjiu* 習近平國家品牌論述研究 [Research on Xi Jinping's thoughts on national brand]. *Journalism and Communication Review* 71:3–15.

Sima, Guang 司馬光. 1957. *Zizhi tongjian* 資治通鑑. Beijing: Guji.

Sima, Qian 司馬遷 (撰) et al., comps. 1959. *Shiji: Dayuan liezhuan* 史記, 123: 大宛列傳 [Shiji 123: The collective biographies of Dayuan]. Beijing: Zhonghua Shuju.

So, Jenny F., ed. 2000. *Music in the Age of Confucius*. Washington, DC: Freer Gallery of Art and Arthur M. Sackler Gallery.

Spanos, William V. 1990. "Review of *What Was Postmodernism? Modern/Postmodern: A Study in Twentieth-Century Arts and Ideas*, by Silvio Gaggi." *Contemporary Literature* 31:108–115.

Spiro, Audrey G. 1990. *Contemplating the Ancients: Aesthetic and Social Issues in Early Chinese Portraiture*. Berkeley: University of California Press.

Stalling, Jonathan. 2006. Review of *Chinese Aesthetics: The Ordering of Literature, the Arts, and the Universe in the Six Dynasties*, by Zong-qi Cai, and *Chinese Theories of Reading and Writing: A Route to Hermeneutics and Open Poetics*, by Gu Ming Dong. *Chinese Literature: Essays, Articles, Reviews (CLEAR)* 28:197–203.

Stiles, Daniel. 1977. "Ethnoarchaeology: A Discussion of Methods and Applications." *Man* 12 (1): 87–103.

Stockbridge, Sally. 1988. "Music Video: Questions of Performance, Pleasure and Address." *Continuum* 1 (2): 110–121.

Stone, Ruth M., ed. 2002. *The World's Music: General Perspectives and Research Tools*. Vol. 10 of *Garland Encyclopedia of World Music*. New York: Routledge.

———. 2007. *Theory for Ethnomusicology*. New Jersey: Prentice Hall.

Stone, Ruth M., and Verlon L. Stone. 1981. "Event, Feedback, and Analysis: Research Media in the Study of Music Events." *Ethnomusicology* 25:215–225.

Strathern, Andrew, and Pamela J. Stewart. 1998. "Embodiment and Communication: Two Frames for the Analysis of Ritual." *Social Anthropology* 6:237–251.

Sun, Jin. 2004. *On the Theoretical Study of Cultural Hegemony*. Beijing: Shehui Kexue Wenxian Chubanshe.

Sun, Qiuyun. 2001. *Hexin yu bianyuan* 核心與邊緣 [Center and periphery]. Beijing: Renmin Chubanshe.

Szeto, Kin-Yan. 2010. "Calligraphic Kinesthesia in the Dancescape: Lin Hwai-min's Cosmopolitical Consciousness in the Cursive Trilogy." *Dance Chronicle* 33 (3): 414–441.

Teiser, Stephen F., and Franciscus Verellen. 2011. "Buddhism, Daoism, and Chinese Religion." *Cahiers d'Extrême-Asie* 20:1–12.

Thompson, John B. 1996. *The Media and Modernity: A Social Theory of the Media*. Stanford: Stanford University Press.

Thorsten, Marie. 2005. "Silk Road Nostalgia and Imagined Global Community." *Comparative American Studies* 3:302–310.

Thrasher, Alan R. 2000. *Chinese Musical Instruments*. New York: Oxford University Press.

Tian, Qing. 1994. "Recent Trends in Buddhist Music Research in China." Translated and adapted by Tan Hwee San. *British Journal of Ethnomusicology* 3:63–72.

Tien, David W. 2009. "Discursive Resources and Collapsing Polarities: The Religious Thought of Tang Dynasty Scholar-Officials." PhD diss., University of Michigan.

Tu, Weiming. 2001. "The Ecological Turn in New Confucian Humanism: Implications for China and the World." *Daedalus* 130 (4): 243–264.

Tuan, Yi-Fu. 1977. *Space and Place: The Perspective of Experience*. London: Edward Arnold.

———. 1979. "Space and Place: Humanistic Perspective." In *Philosophy in Geography*, edited by Stephen Gale and Gunnar Olsson, 387–427. Dordrecht: Springer.

———. 1991a. "Language and the Making of Place: A Narrative-Descriptive Approach." *Annals of the Association of American Geographers* 81 (4): 684–696.

———. 1991b. "A View of Geography." *Geographical Review* 81 (1): 99–107.

Tuohy, Sue M. C. 2001. "The Sonic Dimensions of Nationalism in Modern China: Musical Representation and Transformation." *Ethnomusicology* 45:107–131.

Turino, Thomas. 2000. *Nationalists, Cosmopolitans, and Popular Music in Zimbabwe*. Chicago: University of Chicago Press.

Wade, Bonnie C. 1998. *Imaging Sound: An Ethnomusicological Study of Music, Art, and Culture in Mughal India*. Chicago: University of Chicago Press.

Wang, Ban, ed. 2017. *Chinese Visions of World Order: Tianxia, Culture, and World Politics*. Durham, NC: Duke University Press.

Wang, Bi 王弼 (等注) et al., annotators. 1976. "Ming xiang" 明象 [Elucidating the image]. In *Zhouyilueli* 周易略例 [General remarks on the Changes of the Zhou]. Taipei: Chengwen.

Wang, Hongyun. 2004. "Tangdai yuewu wenhua chengyin yu yishu xingtai kaoshi" 唐代樂舞成因與藝術形態考釋 [Research on the causes and forms of the Tang dynasty music and dance culture]. 交響: 西安音樂學院學報 *Jiaoxiang: An Academic Journal of Xi'an Conservatory of Music* 23:21–31.

Wang, Ke. 2001. *Minzu yu guojia: Zhongguo duo minzu tongyi guojia sixiang de xipu* 民族與國家: 中國多民族統一國家思想的系譜 [Nation and state: The genealogy of Chinese thought on unified multiethnic country]. Beijing: Zhongguo shehui kexue chubanshe.

Wang, Lizeng. 2003. "Kaihuang yueyi yu Sui chu zhengzhi" 開皇樂議與隋初政治 [The Kaihuang *yueyi* and the politics of early Sui dynasty]. 天津音樂學院學報: 天籟 *Tianlai: An Academic Journal of Tianjing Conservatory of Music* 4:33–36.

Wang, Michelle C. 2018. *Maṇḍalas in the Making*. Leiden, the Netherlands: Brill.

Wang, Ruikun, and Carola Hein. 2022. "From Natural Environment to Artificial System: Chang'an and Its Water System in the Western Han Dynasty." *Frontiers of Architectural Research* 11 (3): 440–452.

Wang, Yushu. 2005. *Selected Poems and Pictures of the Tang Dynasty*. Beijing: China Intercontinental.

Wang, Zhengxu. 2022. "Ideas and Making of the East Asia Pre-modern Minben Meritocratic State." *Global Public Policy and Governance* 2 (2): 252–259.

Warren, Jeff R., and John Reid-Hresko. 2022. "Heidegger on the Slopes and Musical Mountain Biking Multimedia." In *Heidegger and Music*, edited by Casey Rentmeester and Jeff R. Warren, 19–36. Lanham: Rowman and Littlefield.

Wechsler, Howard J. 1985. *Offerings of Jade and Silk: Ritual and Symbol in the Legitimation of the T'ang Dynasty*. New Haven, CT: Yale University Press.

Wei, Shang-Jin. 1995. "The Open-Door Policy and China's Rapid Growth: Evidence from City-Level Data." In *Growth Theories in Light of the East Asian Experience*, edited by Takatoshi Ito and Anne O. Krueger, 73–104. Chicago: University of Chicago Press.

Wei Yuan 魏源. 1984. *Shengwu ji* 聖武記 [Records of military accomplishments of the empire]. Beijing: Zhonghua Book Company, 1984.

Wilcox, Emily. 2019. *Revolutionary Bodies: Chinese Dance and the Socialist Legacy*. Berkeley: University of California Press.

———. 2020. "Diasporic Moves: Sinophone Epistemology in the Choreography of Dai Ailian." In *Corporeal Politics: Dancing East Asia*, edited by Katherine Mezur and Emily Wilcox, 115–134. Ann Arbor: University of Michigan Press.

Wilhelm, Hellmut, ed. 2011. *The I Ching, or Book of Changes*. Vol. 31. Princeton, NJ: Princeton University Press.

Witzleben, J. Lawrence. 1997. "Whose Ethnomusicology? Western Ethnomusicology and the Study of Asian Music." *Ethnomusicology* 41 (2): 220–242.

———. 2001. "China: A Musical Profile." In *East Asia: China, Japan, and Korea*. Vol. 7 of *Garland Encyclopedia of World Music*, edited by Robert C. Provine, Yosihiko Tokumaru, and J. Lawrence Witzleben, 87–94. New York: Garland.

———. 2002. "Music in the Hong Kong Handover Ceremonies: A Community Re-imagines Itself." *Ethnomusicology* 46 (1): 120–133.

———. 2010. "Performing in the Shadows: Learning and Making Music as Ethnomusicological Practice and Theory." *Yearbook for Traditional Music* 42: 135–166.

Wong, Chuen-Fung. 2023. *Even in the Rain: Uyghur Music in Modern China*. Honolulu: University of Hawai'i Press.

Wong, Deborah. 2001. *Sounding the Center: History and Aesthetics in Thai Buddhist Performance*. Chicago: University of Chicago Press.

———. 2006. "Ethnomusicology and Difference." *Ethnomusicology* 50 (2): 259–279.

Wong, Isabel K. F. 1991. "From Reaction to Synthesis: Chinese Musicology in the Twentieth Century." In *Comparative Musicology and Anthropology of Music: Essays on the History of Ethnomusicology*, edited by Bruno Nettl and Philip V. Bohlman, 37–55. Chicago: University of Chicago Press.

Wright, Arthur F., and Denis C. Twitchett, eds. 1973. *Perspectives on the T'ang*. Committee on Studies of Chinese Civilization of the American Council of Learned Societies. New Haven: Yale University Press.

Wu, Ben. 2001. "Archaeology and History of Musical Instruments in China." In *East Asia: China, Japan, and Korea*. Vol. 7 of *Garland Encyclopedia of World Music*, edited by Robert C. Provine, Yosihiko Tokumaru, and J. Larence Witzleben, 105–114. New York: Garland.

Wu, David Y. H. 1990. "Chinese Minority Policy and the Meaning of Minority Culture: The Example of Bai in Yunnan, China." *Human Organization* 49 (1): 1–13.

———. 2004. "Chinese National Dance and the Discourse of *Nationalization* in Chinese Anthropology." In *The Making of Anthropology in East and Southeast Asia*, edited by Shinji Yamashita, Joseph Bosco, and J. S. Eades, 198–207. New York: Berghahn.

Wu, Hung. 1986. "Buddhist Elements in Early Chinese Art (2nd and 3rd Centuries AD)." *Artibus Asiae* 47:263–352.

———. 1992. "What Is Bianxiang? On the Relationship between Dunhuang Art and Dunhuang Literature." *Harvard Journal of Asiatic Studies* 52:111–192.

———. 1996. "The Painted Screen." *Critical Inquiry* 23:37–79.

———. 1997. *The Double Screen: Medium and Representation in Chinese Painting*. Chicago: University of Chicago Press.

———. 2008. "Ji: Traces in Chinese Landscape and Landscape Painting." *Cahiers d'Extrême-Asie* 17:167–192.

Wu, Hung, and Katherine R. Tsiang, eds. 2004. *Body and Face in Chinese Visual Culture*. Cambridge, MA: Harvard University Asia Center.

Wu, Manying, Li Caixiu, and Liu Enbo. 1981. *Dunhuang Wuzi* 敦煌舞姿 [The dance gestures of Dunhuang]. Shanghai: Shanghai Wenyi Chubanshe.

Wu, Xiaoming. 1998. "Philosophy, Philosophia, and Zhe-Xue." *Philosophy East and West* 48:406–452.

Wu, Ye. 2004. "*Con qinqu da hujia xiao hujia shitan Han Tang shiqi beifang shaoshu minzu yindiao*" 从琴曲《大胡笳》《小胡笳》試探漢唐時期北方少數民族音調 [A primary study of the music of northern Chinese ethnic groups during the Han and Tang dynasties from the Qin Repertory Da Huja and Xiao Huja]. *Musicology in China* 1:32–42.

Xiang, Chu. 2019. *Dunhuang geci zongbian kuangbu* 敦煌歌詞總編匡補 [Supplements to the compilation of Dunhuang lyrics]. Hong Kong: Zhonghua shuju.

Xiang, Da. 2009. *Tangdai Changan yu xiyu wenming* 唐代長安與西域文明 [The ancient capital city Chang'an and civilization in the Western Region during Tang dynasty]. Chongqing: Chongqing chubanshe.

Xiang, Yang. 2001. *Shanxi yuehu yanjiu* 山西樂戶研究 [A study of the court musician families in Shanxi Province]. Beijing: Wenwu Chubanshe.

Xie, Wenyu, Wang Zhihe, and George E. Derfer, eds. 2006. *Whitehead and China: Relevance and Relationships (Process Thought)*. New Brunswick, NJ: Ontos.

Xu, Ning, Weiqiang Wang, and Xiwen Qu. 2015. "Recognition of In-Air Handwritten Chinese Character Based on Leap Motion Controller." In *Image and Graphics: 8th International Conference*, ICIG 2015, Tianjin, China, August 13–16, 2015, Proceedings, part 3, pp. 160–168. Cham: Springer International.

Yan, Buke. 2001. *Yueshi yu liguan: chuantong zhengzhi wenhua yu zhengzhi zhidu lunji* 樂師與吏官—傳統政治文化與政治制度論集 [Ritual masters and officials: A collection of discussion on the traditional political culture and political structure]. Beijing: Sanlian Shudian.

Yan, Fuling. 2014. "Zaqu geci 'Shaonian xing' chuangzuo lunxi" 雜曲歌詞《少年行》創作論析 [Composition analysis of "Shaonian xing" zaqu lyric]. *Journal of Hebei Normal University* 37 (5): 5–11.

Yang, Juping. 2009. "Alexander the Great and the Emergence of the Silk Road." *Silk Road* 6 (2): 15–22.

———. 2019. "The Sinicization and Secularization of Some Graeco-Buddhist Gods in China." In *The Global Connections of Gandhāran Art*, edited by Wannaporn Rienjang Peter Stewart, 234–250. Summertown, Oxford: Archaeopress Publishing.

Yang, Lihui, and An Deming. 2008. *Handbook of Chinese Mythology*. Translated by Jessica Anderson Turner. Oxford: Oxford University Press.

Yang, Mu. 1996. "Music Loss among Ethnic Minorities in China: A Comparison of the Li and Hui Peoples." *Asian Music* 27:103–131.

Yang, Xiaoshan. 2003. *Metamorphosis of the Private Sphere: Gardens and Objects as Tang Song Poetry*. Cambridge, MA: Harvard University Press.

Yang, Yinliu. 1981. *Zhongguo Gudai Yinyue Shigao* 中國古代音樂史稿 [Draft of the history of ancient Chinese music]. Beijing: Renmin Yinyue Chubanshe.

Ye, Min. 2020. *The Belt Road and Beyond: State-Mobilized Globalization in China, 1998–2018*. Cambridge: Cambridge University Press.

Ye, Mingchun. 2007. *Zhongguo gudai shenmei guan yanjiu* 中國古代審美研究 [Research on classical Chinese aesthetics]. Beijing: Renmin Yinyue Chubanshe.

Yee, Chiang. 1973. *Chinese Calligraphy: An Introduction to Its Aesthetic and Technique*. Cambridge, MA: Harvard University Press.

Yew Chung Culture Committee, Yew Chung Education Foundation, eds. 2006. *The Analects. A Modern Translation and Contemporary Interpretation*. Hong Kong: Yew Chung Publishing House.

Yip, Poching. 2000. *The Chinese Lexicon: A Comprehensive Survey*. New York: Routledge.

Yong, Heming, and Jing Peng. 2008. *Chinese Lexicography: A History from 1046 BC to AD 1911*. Cambridge: Oxford University Press.

Yu, Fengchun. 2007. "Evolution of Hua-Yi (华夷) and the Building of the Great Unification Thought Frame: A Review on the Relevant Account of 'Historical Records.'" *China's Borderland History and Geography Studies* 17 (2): 21–34.

Yu, Jiyuan. 1998. "Virtue: Confucius and Aristotle." *Philosophy East and West* 48:323–347.

Yu, Ning. 1998. *The Contemporary Theory of Metaphor: A Perspective from Chinese*. Norman: University of Oklahoma Press.

———. 2002. "Body and Emotion: Body Parts in Chinese Expression of Emotion." *Pragmatics & Cognition* 10 (1–2): 341–367.

Yu, Pauline. 1987. *The Reading of Imagery in the Chinese Poetic Tradition*. Princeton, NJ: Princeton University Press.

Yu, Pauline, Peter Bol, Stephen Owen, and Willard Peterson, eds. 2000. *Ways with Words: Writing about Reading Texts from Early China*. Los Angles: University of California Press.

Yu, Sun, and Li Jia. 2021. "On Language Features of Henan Opera." *International Journal of Management and Human* 4 (5): 20–46.

Yu, Yingshi. 1975. "Some Preliminary Observations on the Rise of Ch'ing Confucian Intellectualism." *Tsing Hua Journal of Chinese Studies*, New Series XI.1/2 (December): 105–144.

———. 1976. "Fanzhilun yu zhongguo zhengzhi chuantong: lun Ru, Dao, Fa sanjia zhengzhi sixiang de fenye yu huiliu" 反智論與中國政治傳統: 論儒, 道, 法三家思想的分野與匯流 [Anti-intellectualism and Chinese political tradition: On the convergence and divergence of the political thoughts between Confucianism, Taoism, and Legalism]. In *Lishi yu sixiang* 歷史與思想 [History and thoughts]. Taipei: Lianjing Publisher, 34–40.

———. 1987. *Shi yu zhongguo wenhua: zhongguo zhishi fenzi de gudai chuantong* 士與中國文化·中國知識分子的古代傳統 [Scholar officials and Chinese culture: Ancient traditions of Chinese intellectuals]. Shanghai: Shanghai Renmin Chubanshe.

———. 1997. *Zhongguo zhishi fenzi lun* 中國知識分子論 [On Chinese intellectuals]. Zhengzhou: Henan Renmin Chubanshe.

———. 2000. "'Tiandi bi, xianren yin' de shinian" 「天地閉. 賢人隱」的十年 [A decade during which "the heavenly and the earthly close, the sages hide"]. *Ershiyi shiji* 61: 4–6.

Yung, Bell, Evelyn S. Rawski, and Rubie S. Watson, eds. 1996. *Harmony and Counterpoint: Ritual Music in Chinese Context*. Stanford, CA: Stanford University Press.

Zang, Hui-qian, Zhi-xiang Sun, and Yu-xin Xiang. 2017. "Opera Translation and Globalization of Chinese Local Culture: A Case Study of Wuxi Opera." *Journal of Literature and Art Studies* 7 (8): 1031–1038.

Zbikowski, Lawrence M. 2002. "Music Theory, Multimedia, and the Construction of Meaning [Review of *Analysing Musical Multimedia*, by N. Cook]." *Intégral* 16/17:251–268.

Zhang, Dainian, and Edmund Ryden. 2002. *Key Concepts in Chinese Philosophy*. New Haven, CT: Yale University Press.

Zhang, Longxi. 2005. "History, Poetry, and the Question of Fictionality." *Hsiang Lectures on Chinese Poetry* 3:66–68.

Zhang, Tongsheng. 2014. "Yidong de biansai shi: yi Tang wangchao de biansai yu biansai shi wei zhongxin" 移動的邊塞詩：以唐王朝的邊塞與邊塞詩為中心 [The moving frontier poetries: Focusing on Tang Dynasty frontiers and frontier poetries]. *Journal of Zhejiang Gongshang University* 1:18–25.

Zhao, Quansheng. 1992. "Domestic Factors of Chinese Foreign Policy: From Vertical to Horizontal Authoritarianism." *Annals of the American Academy of Political and Social Science* 519:158–175.

Zhao, Suisheng. 1997. "Chinese Intellectuals' Quest for National Greatness and Nationalistic Writing in the 1990s." *China Quarterly* 152:725–745.

Zhao, Tingyang. 2011. *Tianxia tixi: shijie zhidu zhexue daolun* 天下體系：世界制度哲學導論 [All-under-heaven system: An introduction to the world order philosophy]. Beijing: Renmin Daxue Chubanshe.

———. 2016. *Tianxiade dangdaixing* 天下的當代性 [Modern nature of all-under-heaven system]. Beijing: China CITIC.

———. 2019. *Lishi shanshui quqiao* 歷史山水漁樵 [History, mountain and water, fisherman and woodcutter]. Beijing: Shenghuo Dushu Xinzhi Sanlian Shudian.

———. 2023. "To Be or to Become a Chinese, That Is a Question." *China Review* 23 (2): 13–29.

Zhao, Tingyang, and Joseph E. Harroff. 2021. *All under Heaven: The Tianxia System for a Possible World Order*. Vol. 3. Berkeley: University of California Press.

Zhao, Weiping. 2003. "A Historical Account of Pipa Found along the Silk Route." *Musicology in China* 4:34–48.

Zhao, Xiaohuan. 2022. *Chinese Theatre: An Illustrated History through Nuoxi and Mulianxi*. Vol. 2, *From Storytelling to Story-Acting*. London: Routledge.

Zheng, Ruzhong. 2002. *Dunhuang bihua yuewu yanjiu* 敦煌壁畫樂舞研究 [Research on the music and dance in Dunhuang wall paintings]. Gansu: Gansu Jiaoyu Chubanshe.

Zheng, Su. 2001. "Scholarship and Historical Source Materials: Twentieth Century." In *East Asia: China, Japan, and Korea*. Vol. 7 of *Garland Encyclopedia of World Music*, edited by Robert C. Provine, Yosihiko Tokumaru, and J. Lawrence Witzleben, 135–146. New York: Garland.

Zheng, Zuxiang. 2001. "Rights and Wrongs and Other Related Matters of the *kai huang yue yi* (Discussion in Music during Early Sui Dynasty)." *Musicology in China* 4:105–122.

Zhongguo wudao yishu yanjiu hui 中國舞蹈藝術研究會 and Wudao shi yanjiu zu 舞蹈史研究組, eds. 1958. *Quan Tang shi zhong de yuewu ziliao* 全唐詩中的樂舞資料 [Reference on music and dance from the complete collection of Tang poems]. Beijing: Yinyue Chubanshe.

Zohar, Danah. 2022. *Zero Distance: Management in the Quantum Age*. Singapore: Palgrave Macmillan.

Zucker, Lynne G. 1977. "The Role of Institutionalization in Cultural Persistence." *American Sociological Review* 42:726–743.

Zurcher, Erik. (1959) 1972. *The Buddhist Conquest of China: The Spread and Adaptation of Buddhism in Early Medieval China*. 2 vols. 2nd ed., rev. Leiden: E. J. Brill.

## Recorded Interviews

Dong, Xijiu. Interview by Lanlan Kuang. Video recording. Beijing, October 9, 2008.

———. Interview by Lanlan Kuang. Video recording. Beijing, October 12, 2008.

———. Interview by Lanlan Kuang. Video recording. Beijing, March 17, 2009.

Gao, Jinrong. Interview by Lanlan Kuang. Video recording. Lanzhou, November 26, 2008.

———. Interview by Lanlan Kuang. Video recording. Beijing, December 7, 2008.

———. Interview by Lanlan Kuang. Audio recording. Lanzhou, June 28. 2019.

———. Interview by Lanlan Kuang. Audio recording. Lanzhou, March 26, 2023.

Li, Qi. Interview by Lanlan Kuang. Video recording. Lanzhou, November 26, 2008.

Ma, Shaomin. Interview by Lanlan Kuang. Video recording. Lanzhou, November 24, 2008.

Shi, Min. Interview by Lanlan Kuang. Video recording. Beijing, October 9, 2008.

Wang, Cun. Interview by Lanlan Kuang. Audio recording. Lanzhou, March 23, 2023.

Wang, Qiong. Interview by Lanlan Kuang. Audio recording. Lanzhou, December 4, 2008.

Wang, Xudong. Interview by Lanlan Kuang. Audio recording. Dunhuang, July 30, 2019.

Yang, Chengwei. Interview by Lanlan Kuang. Video recording. Lanzhou, November 24, 2008.

Yang, Qian. Interview by Lanlan Kuang. Audio recording. Changsha, June 12–19, 2023.

Zheng, Binlin. Interview by Lanlan Kuang. Video recording. Lanzhou, November 24, 2008.

## Film, Television, and Other Recorded Media

Kuang, Lanlan, dir. 2012. *Staging the Cosmopolitan Nation: The Re-creation of the Dunhuang Yuewu, a Multicultural Music, Dance, and Theatrical Drama from China*. Produced and directed by Lanlan Kuang. Lanzhou and Beijing. DVD. https://lanlankuangofficial.pub/.

Yang, Qian, dir. *The Local Records of China*. Series 1, episode 366, "The Chapter on Dunhuang, Gansu Province." Aired September 25, 2019, on China Central Television Channel 10. https://tv.cctv.com/2019/10/07/VIDE3q9t8QzHPKmMeda7Pmp3191007.shtml.

# INDEX

Gansu Provincial Radio, Television, and Film Service, 21, 114, 146, 157
Gansu Provincial Vocational School of the Arts, 98, 125, 155
Gao, Jinrong, 14, 19, 44, 51, 73, 91, 94, 97–98, 102–3, 106–12, 116, *117*, 118, 125–27, 129, *130*, 131, 145–46, 155
Gao, Ming, 160
Gao, Shi, 172
Gaozu, Emperor, 84
Gautama Buddha, 54, 72
Geertz, Clifford, 120–21
Gelugpa Buddhism (Tibetan), 13
Germany, 89
Getty Conservation Institute, 14
Global Development Initiative, 27
Gobi Desert, 172
Gould, Richard A., 18
*Grand Dream of Dunhuang, A*, 2–5, 9, 12, 123, 129, 154, 160, 167, 172; in Austria, 5; in France, 5; in Spain, 5
Great Cultural Revolution, 95
*Great Skillful Means Sūtra on the Buddha's Repayment of Kindness*, 5
Great Wall, 67–68
Greco-Buddhist art, 4
Greece, 171; *The Thousand-Handed and Thousand-Eyed Avalokiteśvara* performed in, 5, 123
Greek cultural system, 68
Gu, Mingdong, 34, 46
*guan*, 20, 25n19, 54
*guanfeng* (observing local customs), 20
Guangdong Province (China), 20
Guangxiu, Qing Emperor, 9
Guangzhou (city), 124
Guangzhou Military Song and Dance Group, 131–33, 154
Guiyi Circuit, 54, 171

Hall, Stuart, 31, 89
Han. *See* dynasty
Han and non-Han peoples, 40–41
Han cultural system, 68
hands: in *Dunhuang bihua yuewu*, 109, 126, 154; expressing qi in calligraphy, 116; in

folk dances and classical dramas, 104; in *hu teng* dance, 74; in *hu xuan* dance, 71; in Peking opera, 136
*Han shu* (Ban Gu), 20
Hatten, Robert, 143–44
He, Yanyun, 97, 153
Heidegger, Martin, 8, 23, 65, 99, 121, 139–41; Heideggerian phenomenology, 65
Henan Province, 134
heritage as cultural display, 58–59
hermeneutics, 8, 22, 37, 140, 144
*Heroes of Dunhuang*, 171
Hexi, 67–68; corridor, 19, 28, 54, 96, 171, 176
Hillman, Ben, 60–61
Hilton, James, 60
Hindu thought, 128
*historiopoietes* in ancient Greece, 64–65
history, as a conceptual element in Dunhuang expressive arts, 37
*History of the Han* (Ban Gu), 20
Hong Kong, 117–18, 133, 135, 171
Honors of Kings (MOBA game), 15
*hopak*, 74
Howat, Roy, 144
Hu, Teng Er (dancer), 75
Hua, Guofeng, 96
Huayuan stone chime, 77
Hung, Wu, 44
Hu people, 70
*hu xuan* (dance), 70–73

identity, 30–31, 48, 58, 81, 98, 120, 145; Chinese, 8, 11, 16, 31–32, 146, 152; Chinese musical, 40, 43, 88; ethnic, 62, 88; Korean, 28; national, 152
*If Treasures Could Talk* (documentary), 170
imagery, poetic, 103–4
Imperial Palace, Tokyo, 57
India, 136; influence in China from, 109, 128; Mughal, 17
Indian: dance, 112, 154; cultural system, 68; monks at Dunhuang, 12
Indonesia, 166
instruments. *See* musical instruments
International Council for Ethnomusicology Study Group on Music Archaeology, 17

LANLAN KUANG is Associate Professor in the Department of
Philosophy at the University of Central Florida. She is Chair of the Florida
Folklife Council and Distinguished Fellow of the Center for Ethnic and
Folk Literature and Arts (CEFLA).